D1104561

MURDOCH

MURDOCH

The Decline of an Empire

RICHARD BELFIELD
CHRISTOPHER HIRD
SHARON KELLY

Macdonald

A Macdonald Book

First published in Great Britain in 1991 by
Macdonald & Co (Publishers) Ltd
London & Sydney

The right of Richard Belfield, Christopher Hird and
Sharon Kelly to be identified as authors of this work has
been asserted by them in accordance with the Copyright, Designs
and Patents Act 1988.

A CIP catalogue record for this book
is available from the British Library

ISBN 0 356 20339 5

Photoset in North Wales by
Derek Doyle & Associates, Mold, Clwyd.
Printed and bound in Great Britain by
BPCC Hazell Books, Aylesbury, Bucks.

Macdonald & Co (Publishers) Ltd
165 Great Dover Street
London SE1 4YA
A member of Maxwell Macmillan Publishing Corporation

Contents

Acknowledgements

The origin of this book was the Channel 4 programme *Empire* transmitted on 20 December 1990. We were helped by the various contributions of many people around the world. Some helped with research, others shared their own work on Rupert Murdoch; many gave up their time to share their experiences and opinions, even if they did not always agree with our perspective. Rupert Murdoch was not willing to appear in the television programme but answered questions in writing.

Some of the people who helped us do not wish to be identified, but we would like to thank them and the following: Ella Bahaire, Professor Robert Baxt, Clare Beavan, Eric Beecher, Kym Bergmann, Ron Boland, David Bowman, Shauna Brown, Glen Burge, Paul Chadwick, Frank Crean, John D'Arcy, Adrian Deamer, Peter Dunnett, Daryl Dixon, Roy Evans, David Flux, Mark Fowler, Malcolm Fraser, Vic Giles, Michael Gill, David Gonski, Brian Grey, Bryce Hawley, Anthony Holden, John Howard, David Johnson, Thomas Kiernan, Ed Koch, Glenda Korporaal, James Long, Karen Maley, Tom Margerison, Stephen Martin, Bob McComas, Paul Morris, Neil O'Keefe, John O'Neill, Jane Perry, John Raedel, Lord Romsey, Mike Royko, Colleen Ryan, Chris Schacht, Gary Schieneman, Andrew Schwartzman, Jacquetta Searle-Grey, Ian Sinclair, Max

Suich, Michael Taylor, Roman Tomasic, Dimity Torbett, John Weisman, Jeane White, Peter Wong, Barbara Yuncker.

In particular, we would like to thank Caroline Thomson, who commissioned the original programme for Channel 4, and who was a tower of strength and an invaluable source of sound advice. We would also like to acknowledge the important contributions of Liz Forgan, Michael Grade and John Willis in shaping the final programme and steering it onto the screen. In getting the book into print we express our special thanks to our friend and agent Michael Charters. We would like to thank Jo O'Neill, Barbara Boote and Nann du Sautoy at Macdonalds who ensured that the book was published within a very tight timetable. In addition, many of our colleagues at Fulcrum put up patiently with the demands that the writing of this book made on our time.

Throughout the project lawyers gave their advice and recommendations; they were Mark Lambert, Don Christopher, Jonathan Caplan and Oscar Beuselinck. We would like to stress, however, that any errors are our responsibility.

Finally, we would like to thank Marion Bowman and Ann Howarth for their support, patience and encouragement throughout the writing of this book.

Richard Belfield
Christopher Hird
Sharon Kelly

MURDOCH

Introduction

Rupert Murdoch is probably the most remarkable businessman since the Second World War. He has achieved what none of his peers has managed. He has built a major international media empire and remained totally in control for forty years. But his most remarkable achievement has been to build this empire with other people's money. His company, News Corporation, now has a mountain of debt larger than many Third World countries.

Despite relentless pressure he has never given up the family shareholding in the business. He has argued recently[1] that it is only because of the family stake that he has been able to take the extraordinary risks that have characterised the explosive growth of News Corporation, particularly over the last ten years. Though he is now sixty, Rupert Murdoch has never stopped taking risks. The older he has got, the greater the risks he has taken.

In 1952 Murdoch inherited a small newspaper business from his father. The total assets were less than A$1 million. At that time the Murdoch family controlled 46 per cent of the company. Today the family firm has sales of A$11 billion and assets of over A$26 billion, stretched over four continents. And the Murdoch family, through a series of

1

trusts, still owns 46 per cent of the shares.

Today, News Corporation owns newspapers, magazines, book publishers, record and music cassette production and distribution companies, television stations, a satellite television service, a Hollywood film studio, trucking companies, half an airline, paper manufacturing and distribution companies, an electronic map publishing company and a large livestock farm.[2]

In 1990 News Corporation employed 10,900 full-time workers in the United States, 12,000 in Britain and 15,500 in Australia and the Pacific Basin. In all, News Corporation employs approximately 38,400 people throughout the world, as well as the staff of the airline Ansett, in which it owns a half share. News Corporation currently owns or leases 260 sites covering 5.8 million square feet of building space in the United States, 60 sites covering 4.7 million square feet in Britain, 240 sites covering 6.7 million square feet in Australia, and 130,000 square feet in Hong Kong.[3] News Corporation also owns 31,000 acres of sheep-grazing property in New South Wales and currently owns 110,000 sheep, as well as breeding stud rams and ewes for sale.

Much of News Corporation's growth has been achieved through a series of increasingly audacious takeovers. There is no other business in the world which has grown in this way and remained under the control (and effective ownership) of the person who launched it. In this book we show how he did it.

According to his many supporters, Rupert Murdoch is a hands-on manager who understands every aspect of the newspaper business. They believe he is also a far-sighted visionary able to see into the future and anticipate changes others cannot see. It is this magic touch of management combined with far-sighted vision which has been the foundation of his remarkable success.

Introduction

We paint a rather different picture. There is no doubting Murdoch's newspaper skill and knowledge of the newsprint industry. But the spectacular growth of News Corporation has not been achieved by increasing the circulation of his papers and magazines throughout the world. Murdoch's real skills and those of his close-knit team of managers are more elusive. He and his team have ruthlessly exploited the loopholes of the international tax system. So efficient has this management been that last year News Corporation paid just three pence in the pound, three cents in the dollar, on their world-wide earnings. They have used the weaknesses of accountancy regulations all over the world to create the illusion of profits where there was only an overdraft. News Corporation has ridden the most fashionable financial tricks from greenmailing to junk-bond financing.

Murdoch's great skills as a manager do not consist in giving the public the papers and magazines it wants, as he claims. There have been too many failures along the way for this assertion to be true. His great skill as a manager is that he has always been able to cut costs. His great skill as a businessman is that, until recently, he could always charm his bankers. Even now, though he is operating under the strictest regime from his banks, they will still indulge him. But his greatest skill has been in his lifelong passion for politics.

At school, he loved politics. At Oxford University he was a 'wild-eyed radical'. According to one of his contemporaries, he 'nattered on endlessly about the virtues of the working class and the treachery of the capitalists and the need for revolution'.[4] Now his politics are as far right as they were far left in his student days. The Murdoch mythology has it that, although he is personally right-wing, his main interest is in running a business. Though he has occasionally allowed his papers and magazines to pursue an independent editorial line, he has usually done this with minority titles like the

3

Village Voice. His main titles have rarely strayed far from the right-wing fundamentalism in which he now so passionately believes.

As he has grown older, Murdoch has retained his childhood obsession with politics. As a right-wing ideologue, he cares a great deal about the politics of the papers and television stations he owns and the politics of the people who run them for him. In the case of his newspapers he has consistently interfered with their editorial coverage to guarantee that they reflect his political beliefs. But, more importantly, he has always used his media titles to indulge his real passion for a different sort of politics, the politics of power. He has used his papers to make and break political careers and has welcomed the political and financial dividends that this brings.

With political power has come the chance to exercise his ultimate unique skill – the ability to manipulate regulators and politicians on three continents to ensure that he gets what he wants: both for his business and in the kind of government he wants to support. Murdoch has the reputation of being a businessman who loves competition. Again, we paint a more complex picture of him.

One day in February 1984, Clive Thornton, who had come from the building society sector to run the *Daily Mirror*, was rather surprised to receive an invitation to go and see Rupert Murdoch, the proprietor of the *Sun*, then in the middle of a bitter circulation war with the *Daily Mirror*. Murdoch moved the conversation round to revenues for newspapers and, in particular, price. He asked Thornton what he thought of a price of twenty pence the following year and of an immediate increase of 1p and a further increase later in the year. In other words, price fixing. Thornton turned him down, having been briefed by *Mirror* staff that they had previously agreed with Murdoch that they would both increase their price by a

4

penny – only for Murdoch to rat on the deal and hold the price of the *Sun* down to steal a circulation advantage. Murdoch's instinct was that of a person who knows that a regulated market is to be preferred, so long as you are one of the regulators.

Rupert Murdoch has some remarkable achievements to his name – such as launching a new television network in America in competition with the three existing networks and making his venture succeed. But here as elsewhere Murdoch is more at home in industries where there is no competition or where there is a regulatory framework which controls the competition and which he can manipulate.

Murdoch once said: 'Monopoly is a terrible thing, until you have it.' In the newspaper industry he has sought to gain control of as much of it as possible. He has proposed price-fixing deals. He has made big profits from monopoly airline operation in Australia, profits which disappeared with the arrival of competition.

During the 1980s Murdoch conceived a grand strategy of creating the world's largest international media combine, which would operate like a one-stop shop – a department store – for the world's major advertisers. This proved impossible, principally because the world's great advertisers and their agencies were not really interested. Murdoch slowly abandoned the grand strategy and replaced it with a global plan, which was to be either a major or the dominant player in every market where News Corporation operates. He became much more opportunist, buying other companies as they became available. The main criterion for purchase seems to have been whether they added to his political clout. In the last few years he has sold off nearly all his consumer magazines throughout the world to help meet the bills of his fledgling American network television station, Fox, and his satellite television operation Sky.

No matter what companies he has bought or where he has operated, the management style has not changed. One of the key features of the Murdoch corporate culture is the relentless hatred of bureaucracy and excessive layers of management. Deals are concluded in weeks rather than months. Decisions are made quickly, often after a short conversation on the phone or in the corridor when he is on the way to do something else, rather than in the formal setting of a boardroom.

Murdoch has never had fancy offices or the kind of architect-designed major headquarters building so much beloved by many similar-sized corporations. His personal management style is that of an ascetic, rejecting flamboyance and corporate expense. Many who know him speak of his extraordinary charm. Journalists who worked for him at *The Times* privately talked of the Don Giovanni syndrome. One of them told us:

> It's like a woman with a womaniser who thinks she will be the woman to turn this man. That's what all of Murdoch's editors think. They know the stories of carnage in the past, but they each have such wonderful encounters with him in the beginning. They believe, I'll be the one to turn this man around, find the idealist within him. The problem is that it isn't there.

Underneath the charm he is ruthless, hiring and firing more editors than any other proprietor in the history of journalism. For a man who has spent his life in journalism he has a remarkable contempt for reporters. Rupert Murdoch's journalism is that of the sub-editor, the rewrite artist, who can shape and deliver reality for others. The philosophy is can-do, will-do. He loves sub-editors, particularly English ones, who can work up a story, write a nerve-jangling headline, put some juice into it. The *Sun* has been as close to the Murdoch ideal of any paper he has ever owned, with its huge headlines like 'GOTCHA!', when the Argentinian cruiser, the *Belgrano*, was sunk with the loss of 368 lives, 'FREDDIE STARR ATE MY HAMSTER' or more recently 'NEW BALLS PLEASE' for a story about two Wimbledon officials having an affair.

From his earliest days in Australia, his papers have been characterised by loud headlines, bold typeface, underlined text, particularly in editorials, and crossword-puzzle layout. Before Murdoch took over the *Sunday Times*, the journalists defined a good story as one that someone, somewhere, does not want you to read. This approach is incomprehensible to Murdoch. His journalism is about pap, dressed up as sensationalism. For forty years UFOs have landed in the pages of Murdoch's papers, astrologers have made millions of predictions and city streets have been terrorised by the type of people who do not read a respectable family newspaper like the one Rupert Murdoch has just sold them.

Murdoch is stretched now over four continents. He cannot read every headline or check every story before it goes to press. Instead, he lays down a template which his editors follow. If they hear nothing from him, they can assume their performance is acceptable. But he likes to keep them guessing by ringing them at all times of day or night or turning up and asking them why they ran a particular story six weeks earlier.

To carry the torch around the world, he has created a managerial class on four continents who share his approach to life and to business. Those who do not want to go along with his way of doing things tend to leave, often quickly. From his first days building his empire back in Australia in the 1950s, he has always been an enthusiastic firer, particularly of editors. Those who stay and succeed are Murdoch's people through and through.

But who are Murdoch's people and what are they like? News Corporation's 1987 Annual Report gives an extraordinary insight into the Murdoch corporate mentality. The board of directors for that year were all male and had an average age of fifty-eight. But the body of the Report contains profiles of key personnel, all of whom are much younger. The average age for the women is thirty-one, for the men it is just over thirty. This is what they say. Murdoch corporate woman says:

First you rip off the competition. Then you develop your own style. It doesn't take brilliance, just a keenness to work hard and the ability to steer clear of negative things.

We have become very aggressive in any area likely to generate business. Our domination of the marketplace is very exciting and we intend to build on this. The big challenge is to maintain the pace and the excitement.

I'm a pretty good fixer-upper. I'm pretty good at making something out of nothing. Keep watching, we're going to get even better. You work long hours here, but it's eminently worth it. I have to be thinking ahead all the time. This was a chance I had to take. We leave the feminist movement alone because, while I am all for equality, the movement is alienating.

The Murdoch corporate man says:

The days of throwing masses of reporters at a good story are gone. Change is inevitable. We can't ignore it. We have to take the challenge. Sometimes luck places you in the fast lane. We have to figure out where it leads. Excellence is there to be found. It just needs to be recognised. We'll buck the trend. It is a chance to be unconventional.

Introduction

It's the sort of job where you have to make quick decisions and live with them. It's so dynamic that from day to day we never know what is around the corner. I think it intimidated the real experts, but I got the hang of it within a year. All you needed was a bit of confidence. Waste factor down, performance factor up. The result of low overheads and good management. This is the perfect job. I wouldn't be anywhere else in the world. It seemed enough that hard work would pay off.

These quotations are not from one woman and one man but from a large number of them, run together. They produce just one voice – that of Rupert Murdoch.

For both the men and the women there are not enough hours in the day. Personal time is always 'snatched' and all the more valuable for it. For these people problems do not exist, only challenges. In this Murdoch world anyone can turn their hand to anything. Expertise or carefully acquired skills will always be defeated by the enthusiastic amateur.

They are a superhuman bunch. The men all play sport: windsurfing, cricket, tennis, karate, racketball, softball, squash, golf or racing Noddy cars. They work all the hours God sends and still have time to be good and loving fathers. What spare time they do have is spent with their children at the funfair, on the beach or romping in the pool. The women combine dynamic careers with full marriages. They are fit, doing Tai-Chi in the morning, forty push-ups at night, swimming, playing tennis and squash. They are more cultural than the go-getting Murdoch male. They play the flute, collect antiques, learn Greek, fashion marble and alabaster sculptures and read books. The exception is the then *News of the World* editor, Wendy Henry, who is photographed comforting a small mountain of bagels outside Ridley's Bakery and Delicatessen. Interestingly, none of the women are photographed cooking, though two of the male executives are shown to be dynamic chefs. There are no blacks on the Murdoch team of 1987.

Murdoch's ability to create an international managerial class in a common image has been critically important in establishing a common culture within News Corporation. One of the most remarkable features of the company is the way in which Murdoch has been able to stamp his identity on nearly all the company's products and its management style, despite its enormous size.

Murdoch is careful in the people he chooses – those who can be relied on to share his ideas, to second-guess him when necessary and to pick up the significance of the comments he makes. He is also speedy in removing those who do not fit this system. As one former Australian editor said: 'I think he regards the people that work for him as fairly dispensable. If they are working and loyal to him and toe the line, that's fine, but if it's not working then there is always another editor in another building he can recruit.'[5] Those who do fit in are frequently moved around the News Corporation organisation – spreading the Murdoch values but, at the same time, preventing them from becoming indispensable to the organisation. In this way Murdoch has created an organisational apparatus in which, although he doesn't make every decision, he can be sure that he is influencing all important decisions.

All those who work for or have worked for Murdoch recount how on his visits he will flick over the content of the papers and magazines, providing a stream of comments on their layout, content, marketing plans, sales – all liberally laced with his own political opinions. In this way executives are left in no doubt about what is expected of them. These individual visits are reinforced by conferences in which people from throughout News Corporation are brought together. One editor recalls the regular annual session at

Aspen, Colorado, attended in 1988 by about fifty senior executives and columnists from papers throughout the world. There were two or three days of discussion on politics and economics with presentations from former American President Richard Nixon, British politician David Owen and American neo-conservative Norman Podhoretz. In addition to talks from marketing people on how to increase circulation, there was a specially cut film, including clips from John Wayne movies, selling the message that the *Sun* newspaper always got its man. Recalling the atmosphere, one participant said: 'It was like a cult but one that I hadn't signed up for'.[6]

A similar meeting had been held in February 1987 just after the Herald and Weekly Times takeover, when thirty-seven of Murdoch's Australian editorial executives were put up at a hotel on the Australian Gold Coast. One of those there later recalled: 'It was like I imagined the Moonies behaved. Each of us had to reaffirm the Murdoch ethos: the kind of newspapers *he* wants, *he* gets and *he* controls.'[7]

Meetings like this are not unusual in a large organisation and are held with the intention of creating a common set of values within the firm. But in the case of News Corporation such meetings are not held to encourage the dissenting voice but to lay down the political line; they are not held to create a common culture, but to impose Murdoch's own. In many respects the system has succeeded in doing what Murdoch wanted it to do, but such an approach encourages the production of newspapers and magazines to a formula; as News Corporation has expanded, this approach has come under strain. The formulae which work in the tabloid press in the United Kingdom do not work in the American magazine market; formulae which work in national newspaper markets do not work in metropolitan markets. Many of News Corporation's failures have been the result of trying to import unsuitable formulae to new markets. As we show in the last chapter of this book, it is one of the ironies of News Corporation's current condition that the area of business doing best is the one over which Murdoch himself has hardly any influence or control.

This has not been an easy book to write. There are already five biographies of Murdoch and he gets a walk-on part in many other books. We have drawn on this body of work and added a great deal of our own research from documents and conversations with those who have worked with him. We have aimed to provide a profile of Murdoch's business, his methods and his money. In ordering the material, anyone who tackles the life and times of Rupert Murdoch and his empire has to decide whether to tell the story chronologically or thematically. Murdoch himself once said, 'My past consists of a series of interlocking wars,'[8] and the chief difficulty is making sense of this interlocking pattern. Operating across four continents, it is not always easy to see the connections between what Murdoch is doing in Britain, America, Australia and Hong Kong. We have found that the best way to see the pattern is to follow a roughly chronological approach.

In many ways the 1980s was Murdoch's decade. The extraordinary growth of his empire was intimately bound up with the two western politicians who made the greatest impact – Ronald Reagan and Margaret Thatcher. But as their glamour and appeal faded quickly at the end of the decade, so did the Murdoch mystique. Like many of his contemporaries, he financed his development today with money to be repaid tomorrow. His legacy is that of the 1980s, a mountain of debt. His borrowings currently stand at US$8.2 billion, roughly $20 for every man, woman and child in the United States, Britain and Australia.

Much of this book deals with the events of the 1980s, parts of the Murdoch story never told before. But we start with an overview of Murdoch's development during the 1950s and

60s, when he built his Australian base and learned the management skills which he was to put to such effective use elsewhere in the world.

Throughout the Murdoch story there is one recurrent theme. He is a gambler – whether it is betting on whether a coin lands head or tails with miners at Broken Hill, betting on the international currency markets or staking the company on the belief that a particular idea will pay off.

There has been no overall grand strategy, but he does think ahead. He is a gambler, but he is not illogical. To the immense irritation of the experts who write management textbooks, Murdoch breaks the rules: he does not stick to what he knows, he does not develop the business gradually. He simply indulges his 'great ideas', some of which have been highly successful, while others have failed. These have included the belief in a major market for pan-European advertising, the fully integrated international media company, the move out of print into electronic media and the crying need for a new tabloid paper in Britain. His problem as a businessman is that he believes too much in these ideas. The *Sun* succeeds – so *only* the *Sun* can succeed, and his other tabloids are made to the same formula. Satellite television will come – so Sky *must* succeed.

As a former colleague of his said: 'If there's one person you don't want to be taken in by the mystique of Rupert Murdoch, it's Rupert Murdoch. If he has a fault, it is hubris.' It is this presumption that he can always take on and defeat the system that has sustained him for the last forty years. Whether it will now carry him through News Corporation's current financial crisis or lead to his downfall is too close to call – just the sort of odds he has played all his life.

As his lifelong friend and fellow board member, Richard Searby, is fond of saying: 'Fundamentally Rupert's a fidget.'

1

Chronology

When Rupert Murdoch was just seventeen he started his first magazine at Geelong Grammar School in Australia. *If Revived* was a literary journal which gave an opportunity to everyone 'to air their opinions, so long as they are well expressed'. He produced two issues in the year, winning the N.B. de Lancey Forth Prize for Tree Knowledge.[1] But his father, Sir Keith Murdoch, a newspaper proprietor, wanted him to become a real journalist and fixed him up with some work as a cadet reporter on the *Herald*, covering the courts, where he learnt that nothing is as good as a cheap spicy court case. The copy only needs a journalist with a pad and pencil and the story can keep readers enthralled for days.

Before he went off to Oxford University he did a short stint on the *Birmingham Gazette*. There is a story about Rupert Murdoch as a student which illustrates more than many others the character of the man. During a vacation from Oxford University he went on a motoring holiday in France,

15

with a friend, in a car his parents had given him. Wherever they went he chose the restaurant to eat and the place to stay. When his companion complained, Murdoch told him that it was his car and he would therefore make the decisions.

In 1949 Rupert Murdoch's father took a minority holding in News Limited, a small newspaper business which published a daily paper, the Adelaide *News*. Three years later he died and Rupert Murdoch inherited what was left of his father's empire. Although Sir Keith was chairman of Herald and Weekly Times Limited, he only had a small percentage of the shares, which had to be sold to pay death duties. In his will Sir Keith wrote: 'I desire that my said son Keith Rupert Murdoch should have the great opportunity of spending a useful, altruistic and full life in newspaper and broadcasting activities and ultimately occupying a position of high responsibility in that field . . . ' It was a heavy burden to lay on a young man having a lot of fun on the other side of the world.

Sir Keith had built up the Herald group from nothing. He owed his rise to his friendship with politicians, many of whom were in debt to him. Rupert Murdoch learnt two lessons from his father: one, never lose control of the company you are building; two, let politicians fear your power, and call in the favours when necessary.

In 1953, at the age of twenty-two, after a short stint on the *Daily Express*, Rupert Murdoch returned to Australia to take over the family firm, News Limited. Murdoch had dominion over the Adelaide *News*; the *Sunday Mail; Radio Call*, a little weekly listings paper; and a paper in Broken Hill called the *Barrier Miner*: not a bad start. While Murdoch's power expanded, the Adelaide *News* editor's contracted. For nearly forty years now, Murdoch has not changed his management style. Though News Corporation is now the largest family-controlled media business in the world, it is still his car and he still decides where they go and what they eat.

From the start, one paper was never going to be enough for Murdoch. He immediately began to buy other papers. Between 1954 and 1956 he bought *Sunday Times* in Perth and *New Ideas* magazine in Melbourne. In the mid-1950s Murdoch showed his expansive tendencies when he offered A$14 million for the Adelaide *Advertiser*. It was a large sum of money, particularly as he did not have it. His bid was rejected with contempt by the owners. But Murdoch had shown his colours. Despite his plans for expansion he did have time to get married in March 1956 to Patricia Booker.

He loved newspapers. He had a natural flair for layout and writing snappy headlines. Throughout his working life he has always been drawn to others with the same skill. But though his first love is newspapers, he was fascinated by the coming of television, even though he could not influence the content in the same sort of way.

In 1958 Southern Television Corporation Limited, which was 60 per cent owned by News Limited, was granted one of the two commercial TV licences in Adelaide, NWS-9, and started transmission in September the following year. (In 1967 News bought the remaining shares in Southern.)

By February 1960 he was already fed up with small-town life in Adelaide and decided to move to Sydney, where he bought Cumberland Newspapers Limited, after John Fairfax and Sons Limited turned down the deal. Cumberland owned twenty-four suburban papers. Murdoch was also fed up with his unhappy marriage, and it ended with his move to Sydney.

Despite Fairfax's animosity towards Murdoch, three months later its managing director, Rupert Henderson, sold him Mirror Newspapers Limited in Sydney, which published the *Daily Mirror* and the *Sunday Mirror*. Murdoch was starting from a position of real weakness. The *Daily*

Mirror, which was in competition with Fairfax's other paper the *Sun*, was losing the circulation war. But Murdoch did what he has done to most newspapers since – he took it down market. Murdoch's *Mirror* quickly became a viable and dangerous competitor to Fairfax's *Sun*. The *Mirror* was a crucial landmark in Murdoch's rise. It put him in the big time and established him as a major newspaper publisher. There was good news for Murdoch on the romantic front as well. Soon after buying the *Mirror* he met Anna Torv, a trainee reporter. They began to see a lot of each other.

Murdoch also bought two smutty down-market weeklies, both of which were called *Truth* and were printed in Brisbane and Melbourne. Their content was hard for his mother, Dame Elizabeth, to stomach. He promised her that he would sell them as soon as possible. Counting the two *Truth*s in with his other operations in Sydney, Perth and Adelaide, Murdoch now had printing capacity in every Australian state.

In 1963 Murdoch was still keen to expand his television interests. He tried to get the Sydney Channel Ten-10 television station but was vetoed by the Prime Minister, Robert Menzies, in favour of Ansett Transport Industries. This was one of the last occasions when a politician would try to stop one of Murdoch's acquisitions.

But Murdoch was not deterred. His motto was: where there's a rule, there's a way round it. He set up camp just outside the Sydney metropolitan area where he took an interest in the Wollongong WIN4 TV licence. The station was within the range of Sydney TV viewers. Having a shrewd idea of what the viewers wanted to see, he also bought 2,500 hours of current popular American programming before Fairfax or Packer could bid for it. It was a huge gamble but it paid off. The expansion continued and Murdoch bought 25 per cent of Packer's Channel 9 television station in Sydney.

As an established newspaper proprietor, Murdoch began

to flex his muscles in the rough and tumble of Australian daily politics. Murdoch's *Daily Mirror* supported the Labour leader Arthur Calwell against the Liberal Robert Menzies in the November 1963 election. Murdoch made a substantial cash contribution to the Labour Party's funds. As always, he was well aware of the value of social contact – Calwell was a regular guest at lunches with Murdoch and his senior journalists.[2]

In 1963 News Limited made its first million Australian dollars. But Murdoch was ambitious and Australia was never going to offer enough. His first foray out of Australia was in 1964, but he only went across the Tasman Sea to New Zealand where he bought 25 per cent of Wellington Publishing Company, New Zealand – publishers of the newspaper *Dominion*.

1964 was a big year for Rupert Murdoch. In July he started Australia's first national paper, *The Australian*. Murdoch had spotted a big hole in the market. Australian newspapers delivered a rich diet of strong local news *The Australian* concentrated on national news and federal politics. It had to encompass the different attitudes of readers in Sydney and Melbourne. There were problems establishing the editorial pitch for the back pages too. Melbourne football has different rules from those in Sydney. At first it was published in the capital, Canberra, but there were often difficulties sending it to other metropolitan cities. Former employees tell stories of Murdoch going to the airport in his pyjamas and using all his powers of persuasion and undeniable charm to convince the pilots to take off in the fog. Murdoch described himself at this time as 'the independent proprietor'.

In 1966 he bought his 6,000-acre Australian home 'Cavan'. John McEwen, the Deputy Prime Minister, helped him to find it. 'Cavan' would quickly become the setting for meeting politicians as well as carving up the Australian media.

Murdoch married Anna Torv in 1967 in Sydney, where he had also moved *The Australian*. Many commentators believe

19

that the years of Adrian Deamer's editorship from 1968 to 1971 were the paper's best. But Murdoch did not like the way many of the stories were aimed at 'bleeding heart liberals', so he sacked Deamer. The paper wholeheartedly supported the Labour Party in the 1972 election, and then viciously attacked the same party three years later in the 1975 election. The journalists who worked on *The Australian* thought the paper so biased they went on strike. Murdoch 'considers it a personal monument. He's right: his loves, hates and manoeuvres are spelt out there as nowhere else.'[3]

Back in 1968 Murdoch arrived in Britain. A phone call from an old friend, Lord Catto, the head of the merchant bank Morgan Grenfell, told him that the Carr family, who controlled *News of the World*, were falling out. The paper and the company could be for sale. The *News of the World* was a perfect fit for Murdoch. Its mixture of scandal and sanctimonious humbug was a formula which he knew only too well. It was also Europe's largest-selling scandal sheet. Better still, the company was badly run but rich in assets. Under the guidance of Lord Catto and with the help of the *News of the World*'s own bank, Hambros, Murdoch helped the incumbent members of the Carr family fight off a bid from Robert Maxwell. The deal was vintage Rupert Murdoch. Buying his *News of the World* shares involved taking on a great deal of debt. And once he had made it profitable, he used the cash flow to take on more debt and continue his world-wide expansion.

Back home in Australia, he needed to call in some political favours to get the deal through. Murdoch could not afford to pay for the whole of his stake in *News of the World* so he swapped some of his Australian assets for shares in *News of the World*. This could have presented him with a serious problem with Australian regulators. The Australian Treasurer, William McMahon, favoured a nationalist policy and might not take kindly to a British company owning Australian assets. Besides, McMahon was not favourably disposed towards Murdoch as he had used *The Australian* to stop McMahon becoming Liberal leader and prime minister earlier in the year. But luckily for Murdoch he had a more powerful friend, the politician who beat McMahon in the election – John Gorton. Gorton gave Murdoch the nod. The deal could go through.

Having promised to be the Carr family's saviour he quickly outmanoeuvred Sir William Carr, pushing him into a position of complete powerlessness. Then, with less than 50 per cent of the *News of the World*'s shares, Murdoch took control of the company and ran it as his own. He sold off parts of the business, paid out big dividends to help shore up his Australian company and looked around for something else to buy. He soon found it.

At the end of 1969 Murdoch bought the *Sun* for £800,000. The sellers, International Publishing Corporation (IPC), had made several attempts to revamp the old *Daily Herald*, a traditional Labour Party-supporting paper. These had all been costly failures. Murdoch was keen to get a daily paper which would keep his *News of the World* presses busy during the week. He also had a vision. He saw the main British tabloid paper, the *Daily Mirror*, as too 'preachy'. He believed there was room for a paper which didn't take itself too seriously, didn't talk down to the readers. The style was to be 'breezy, not sleazy'.

He found an experienced popular newspaper editor, Larry Lamb, who shared this vision, and a large number of experienced sub-editors from the old *Daily Herald* who were excited about the idea of putting their skills to work. The new *Sun* rose. Murdoch spent an unprecedented £1.2 million on advertising the paper, and it was an immediate success. Within the first year sales rose from 650,000 to just over one and a half million. By 1971 they were over two million. At first the *Sun*, being an anti-establishment paper, supported the Labour Party, but this support soon evaporated. The *Sun* quickly achieved notoriety and changed the course of British journalism. In November 1970 it introduced pictures of topless women. And as the 1970s progressed, the *Sun*'s politics veered quickly to the right, as it became a fanatical supporter of Margaret Thatcher. Any semblance of objective news reporting was junked. Between them the *News of the World* and the *Sun* became the cash cows for the whole of the News Corporation empire – generating the money to pay the interest on the loans Murdoch kept raising to finance his world-wide expansion into other forms of media.

Murdoch's next expansion in Britain was in 1971, when he bought a large stake in London Weekend Television (LWT), the commercial television company. He immediately involved himself with programming, although this was against the rules of the Independent Broadcasting Authority which prevented newspaper owners playing a formal executive role in television – in other words, programme planning. But Murdoch has always followed the motto that rules are there to be broken. His friends say he did a good job there, bringing in programmes like *On The Buses* and *Upstairs Downstairs*.

In June 1972 Murdoch was back in Australia and building up his empire by adding to it the Sydney *Daily Telegraph* and *Sunday Telegraph*. This reduced the ownership of the Australian news media from four empires to three. Murdoch's papers in the capital cities now accounted for 28 per cent of the metropolitan readership. He was also investing in his political future. Murdoch's quality paper, *The Australian*, backed the favourite, the Labour leader Gough Whitlam, in the December 1972 general election, establishing Murdoch's policy of backing winners.

Murdoch's move to Britain in 1969 – though financially rewarding – had been only a stop-over before his intended destination. He really wanted to go to America, which he had been visiting regularly since the 1950s. In 1973 he made the move and at the end of the year he bought three newspapers in San Antonio, Texas. His world-wide empire now encompassed eighty newspapers, eleven magazines, television and radio stations, printing, paper and shipping companies.

The next year he started the *National Star* in competition with the notorious but well-established *National Enquirer*. Initially the tabloid weekly magazine was not a success. It could not compete against the well-established *National Enquirer*, and 'National' was later dropped from the title. The *Star* was a brassy tabloid which served up the usual Murdoch diet of recipes, gossip and horoscopes, wrapped up in a sensationalist layout. It took several years to establish itself, but by the late 1970s it was a great success. He sold it in 1987 for US$400 million.

During the 1970s – partly as a result of his experience with the British print unions, partly as he grew to love America – Murdoch's own politics became more right-wing. He admired the American President, Richard Nixon, and was horrified by the (eventually successful) campaign to force his resignation. He believed that Nixon's departure would be a disaster for the western alliance in its battle against communism, and would lead to a resurgence of socialism and welfarism in America.[4]

Back home, his move to the right was confirmed. His papers campaigned against the Australian Labour Prime Minister, Gough Whitlam, in 1975. *The Australian* was so biased that its journalists went out on strike and demonstrators burnt Murdoch's papers in the street. A Labour MP later asked: 'Is this country to continue to be run with governments being made and broken, and men being

23

made and broken, by snide, slick innuendoes of a lying perjuring pimp – Rupert Murdoch?'[5]

Two years later he had another journalists' protest on his hands – and for the same reason. At the end of 1976 Murdoch had bought the politically liberal but money-losing *New York Post*. It was his eighty-fourth newspaper acquisition. He used his tabloid formula and immediately pushed the paper down market. This increased the circulation but lost the advertisers. Like their counterparts on *The Australian*, the journalists complained about the paper's powerful political endorsement of Ed Koch, the right-wing Democrat candidate for mayor of New York. The endorsement was successful. Koch, who began the contest as a rank outsider, won. He has remained grateful and loyal to his 'friend' Rupert ever since.

Later that year Murdoch's friend Clay Felker asked him to help him out financially by buying into the company that owned *Village Voice, New West* and *New York* magazines. Murdoch helped him by buying the magazines out from under him. It was a typical Murdoch manoeuvre. (Murdoch has always found it impossible to share power with any of the partners he has had in his joint ventures. Typical of these relationships going sour was the successful joint venture with the French magazine *Elle* in the 1980s. It came to an end in 1988 partly because the French co-owners found Murdoch's unconventional management style, such as not turning up to board meetings, frustrating. The one exception is the airline Ansett, which he owns jointly with the transport group Thomas Nationwide Transport, now known as TNT.)

Murdoch didn't interfere with the American magazines that Felker brought to him even when the *Village Voice* made a thinly veiled suggestion that the *New York Post* was getting a reduction on its South Street building because of supporting Ed Koch.[6] This is often quoted as an example of Murdoch allowing his journalists to express themselves. But in reality *Village Voice* was a tiny paper which appealed to people whom Murdoch did not care about. It had little political clout so he ignored it.

Murdoch got his first experience of the film industry in 1978 when he teamed up with Australian film producer Robert Stigwood to make *Gallipoli*, a film about the Australian Army in the First World War. Murdoch was drawn to the film because his father, Sir Keith, had made his name as a journalist writing about the awful conditions the soldiers faced. The film was a great success, but when it was shown in New York in 1981 there was a faint hissing sound when Murdoch's name came up on the credits.[7]

Murdoch still wanted to expand his television interests. In early 1979 he bought United Telecasters Sydney Limited which owned the Sydney Channel Ten-10 (the licence he'd been refused in 1963). He sold his share in London Weekend Television to pay for the acquisition. The Australian Labour Party, which was still bitter about the 1975 election, and other interest groups tried to prevent him getting approval for the licence from the Australian Broadcasting Tribunal. Like many other politicians and interest groups before and after, they did not succeed in stopping the relentless expansion of the Rupert Murdoch world-wide media empire.

Almost immediately after this victory Murdoch started buying shares in Ansett Transport Industries, which now owned the Channel Ten (ATV-10) television station in Melbourne. Eventually he bought half the company. Sir Peter Abeles's company TNT owned the other half. Murdoch's total disregard for the rules governing television licences brought a two-year investigation, from which he emerged triumphant. The rules were changed. So closely did the new rules fit his needs that they were immediately dubbed 'the Murdoch amendments'.

By now Murdoch's achievements were considerable. From a small paper in Adelaide he had built a media empire in three continents. Annual sales were about A$1 billion. But it was the 1980s that were to be the Murdoch decade. Sales grew more than tenfold to A$11 billion in 1991 as he bought up newspapers, book publishers, magazines, television stations and film companies across the globe.

One of the first moves of the decade was to form News Corporation as the new holding company and get control of the whole of his burgeoning UK offshoot, News International. Ever since the takeover of the News of the World organisation he had owned just under 50 per cent of the British subsidiary, though he ran it as his own personal company.

Politically, the decade started as it was to go on, with a controversy. His support for Carter got him into trouble with the Senate Banking Committee in May 1980. Murdoch had supported Carter in the *New York Post* and had had lunch with him at the White House. On that same day he had received a loan from the Eximport Bank at a favourable rate. The Senate Banking Committee looked into allegations that Carter had done a deal with Murdoch. They found nothing. We have spoken to a former colleague of Murdoch's who met Murdoch just after the Carter meeting. He asked Murdoch how the meeting had gone. 'Very good', Murdoch told him, 'but he's going to get a hell of a shock when I support Reagan.'

Murdoch's adulatory support of Thatcher in the *Sun* was rewarded in January 1981 when his takeover of *The Times* and *Sunday Times* was not referred to the Monopolies and Mergers Commission. He was required, however, to guarantee editorial freedom and the security of the editor. Murdoch agreed but privately said the promises were not worth the paper they were written on. He constantly interfered in the editorial process, and after a year Harry Evans, the editor of *The Times*, was forced to resign.

But Murdoch's type of journalism was appreciated by the American Jewish Congress in New York, which named him 'Communications Man of the Year' in April 1982. The Congress's President was Howard Squadron – Murdoch's lawyer.

However, many American journalists didn't feel the same. In August 1982 when Murdoch attempted to take over the Buffalo *Courier Express* its journalists decided they would rather see the newspaper fold than Murdoch as proprietor.[8] The Queen, in Britain, was also not impressed. She had taken legal action against the *Sun* following certain stories on the Royal family, the first time she had ever done so against a newspaper.[9]

He had also begun his expansion into book publishing. In May 1981 News Corporation bought Australia's publishing house Angus and Robertson. It also tried to extend it to Britain by making a hostile takeover bid for William Collins. Although this failed, Murdoch kept a substantial shareholding and in 1989 was able to gain complete control and merge the company with the American publisher Harper and Row, which he had bought in 1987.

In 1982 Murdoch started the *Daily Sun* in Brisbane. It was the first new metropolitan paper for nearly twenty years. In America he bought the *Herald-American*, later called the *Boston Herald*.

Murdoch wanted to buy more newspapers in America, where his 'big idea' was to create a national chain of papers. In March 1983, to the dismay of the paper's journalists, he bought the *Chicago Sun-Times*. He sent in his heavy boys from England and Australia to shake it up and once again took an essentially up-market paper down market. Neither this nor the 'great idea' worked. For all his skill in the tabloid market, Murdoch didn't have the magic touch elsewhere. As ex-*Sun-Times* columnist Mike Royko wrote: 'No self-respecting fish would be seen dead wrapped in a Murdoch newspaper.'

But by 1983 the Murdoch grand design was beginning to emerge. Murdoch was convinced that, in future, his empire would not survive if it continued to be based on paper. The future was based on the silicon chip. So he had to continue his expansion into television, particularly satellite. By now Murdoch was hooked on satellites. His world view was the same as his satellite's – neither recognised national boundaries. He launched a satellite venture in the United States but cancelled it within months because there was no market for the product. He lost A$20 million on the project. But what he lost on this he regained on the financial markets.

He made a US$40 million profit, almost a third of News Corporation's total profits that year, when he 'greenmailed' film studio Warner's. This was a favourite device of corporate raiders in the 1980s, who bought large stakes in companies and then made the company's life intolerable. In desperation the company then bought the shares off them to get some peace. Murdoch started buying Warner Brothers shares at the end of 1983. Warner's fought hard to stay out of his clutches. They took him to court, where much of their defence focused on the personality and behaviour of Murdoch himself. In March 1984 he gave up the battle and Warner's bought his shares. Before the battle he had paid an average US$24 a share. Warner's bought them off him at US$31 a share and also paid his legal costs of US$8 million.[10]

In August that year he made another handsome profit from a similar exercise. He bought shares in the forest products company St Regis Corporation. They also stopped him, but he again made a large profit of US$37 million on the shares he had accumulated.[11]

With the cash from the Warner deal and the increasingly healthy profits from his British newspapers, Murdoch went on the takeover warpath in America. In November 1984 News Corporation paid US$350 million to buy the business publications division of the privately owned Ziff-Davis publishing company. This acquisition was made through News America Publishing and was his first venture into trade publications in America.

By 1984 Murdoch's personal wealth was estimated to be US$240 million, making him the wealthiest person in Australia. His empire now stretched over three continents and he controlled assets valued at US$1.5 billion. Within the next five years it would grow to nine times this size.

Though he had failed to take over Warner's, Murdoch still wanted a Hollywood film studio. He paid US$250 million in March 1985 for a 50 per cent stake in 20th Century-Fox. He bought the stake from Denver oil man Marvin Davis. Again, he was not happy sharing power with a partner. He bought the other half of Davis's stake later in the year. But this was also the start of another 'great idea' – to start a new national television service in America. He spent a further US$2 billion buying Metromedia, which owned seven of the biggest US TV stations. These stations would form the basis of a mini-network, which would transmit during the highly profitable prime-time slots.

But now Murdoch ran foul of the American rules on television station ownership, which forbade foreign owner-ship. To satisfy these regulations he became an American citizen in September 1985. His assiduous courting of Reaganite politicians paid off when the Federal Communications Commission (FCC), the government agency which regulated commercial television, waived the rules on cross-ownership of television stations and newspapers in one area. In an unparalled decision Murdoch was given two years to get rid of the papers he owned in New York and Chicago, where he now owned television stations. The TV station in Boston was put in the hands of a trust whilst he looked for a buyer for either this or the *Boston Herald*. Murdoch's gamble was that within the two-year period the law would be changed so that cross-ownership would be allowed. This was a gamble that went wrong.

Although Murdoch had spent his time in America courting politicians he had also attacked a fair few. One he probably wishes he hadn't was Senator Edward Kennedy. Kennedy was just the sort of politician Murdoch detested. He was a well-connected very rich liberal who came from an established family. Murdoch's Boston paper constantly attacked Kennedy on his home ground of Massachusetts. Kennedy got his revenge in 1987. He tried to bring in a new law at the end of 1987 which would prevent the FCC from giving temporary waivers of the cross-ownership rules. This was clearly aimed at Murdoch and a Federal judge overruled it, but the effect of the political row was that the existing FCC ban on *permanent* waivers was enshrined in law. Murdoch had to sell his New York paper and his Boston TV station. The Chicago paper had gone in 1986.

At the end of 1985 Murdoch was strapped for cash because of the $2.6 billion he had borrowed for the Fox/Metromedia deal. His empire had doubled in size in two years. His British papers were crucial to finance the deal, but even their profits didn't cover the interest bill of over A$200 million a year. His solution was to cut the UK newspapers' costs. He moved over to new technology and a new headquarters in Wapping. The printers went on strike in January 1986. The strike lasted a year but Murdoch won.

He wasn't too busy with the strike to help his friends in the Conservative Party over the Westland affair. Thatcher and the Trade Secretary, Leon Brittan, wanted the British helicopter company to be rescued by the American company Sikorsky – Murdoch was a non-executive director of its parent company. Michael Heseltine, the Defence Secretary, supported a European consortium. While the political wranglings, leaked letters and dirty tricks went on in Whitehall, Murdoch helped his old friend Mrs Thatcher. TNT, the company which had just signed a lucrative contract for the distribution of all his British newspapers, and which was the joint owner with News Corporation of Ansett Airlines, secretly bought a crucial shareholding in Westland and supported the Thatcher position.

At the end of the year he expanded in Hong Kong, buying the *South China Morning Post*. He used a spectacular tax dodge which gave him a huge tax break, surprising even Hong Kong's highly imaginative tax lawyers.

In February 1987 Murdoch took over Australia's largest media group, the Herald and Weekly Times Limited (HWT), making him the world's largest newspaper publisher. Throughout the battle for HWT he was helped enormously by the Labour Government and the regulators. He now controlled over 60 per cent of Australia's newspapers.

Murdoch bought another British paper in July 1987, the loss-making *Today*, for £38 million. Once again it wasn't referred to the Monopolies Commission. In Britain Murdoch now owned three dailies and two Sundays and controlled 35 per cent of national newspaper circulation. By now he had gone beyond the legendary press barons who came before him – he was the single most powerful media lord on earth. But still this was not enough. In 1988 he embarked on what he has called 'an expansionary lunge'.

He started modestly enough in February by selling the *New York Post* for just over $37 million. The paper had lost an estimated $150 million in the eleven years he had owned it. But then in August he paid $3 billion for Triangle Publications, in the most expensive magazine deal ever. News Corporation was already $4 billion in debt. In expanding his empire to such dimensions Murdoch has increased the company's present debt to US$8.2 billion from US$237 million in 1983. But Murdoch liked the Triangle deal so much he bought options in News Corporation shares while he was putting the deal together.

But, although Murdoch was putting together billion dollar deals, some parts of his empire were soon in serious financial trouble. He had made the twin mistakes of many of the entrepreneurs of the 1980s. He had borrowed heavily and believed that the world economy would keep growing. As the 1980s came to a close, growth ground to a halt, the banks lost their enthusiasm for lending money and the weaknesses in News Corporation's business became only too obvious. The empire started to crumble.

The Fox idea had not yet started to work. By the end of December 1988 it had run up a pre-tax loss of $80 million and the UK satellite TV venture, Sky, had lost almost $74 million since 1983.

But Murdoch was undaunted. In 1989 he succeeded in his bid for William Collins, which he merged with Harper and Row, bought in 1987. He spent a further A$600 million buying two other book publishers to merge with the new group. However, the first signs of financial strain now started to appear. An ambitious plan in March 1989 to raise a further A$5 billion to spend in the media industry had to be abandoned in the autumn as investors had grown tired of the Murdoch mystique. News Corporation only managed to meet its bankers' controls on its borrowings by a skilful piece of financial engineering. In November 1990 the cash drain caused by Sky forced Murdoch to merge the TV station with its rival BSB – again, the regulators watched helplessly as the deal was waved through.

Chronology

By the spring of 1990 News Corporation knew that the days of growth by borrowing were over. At the end of the summer it had to go to its bankers and ask for help. For three months the company fought for survival. By the end of January 1991 it had secured an agreement which gives it three years to sort itself out. However, the terms are extremely tough and not everything is going according to plan. Assets are proving harder to sell than expected. The world is still in a deep recession. It is a remarkable turn round for a business which for the last twenty years has been so powerful that it could call the tune for politicians on three continents.

2

Manipulation:
Murdoch Learns his Trade

In 1947 a young left-wing politician, Frank Crean, was invited to a debate at Geelong Grammar School, an expensive private school for the children of the Australian middle class. The motion was that the waterside workers' union, which was refusing to load ships to the East Indies, were dictating the Labour Party's foreign policy. Crean, who was arguing against this motion, arrived at the school to find that the student supporting his position was a radical 16-year-old called Rupert Murdoch.

When, three years later, Murdoch went to Oxford University, his radicalism was undimmed. He joined the Oxford Labour club, had a bust of Lenin in his rooms and was known as 'Red Rupert'. Not that this prevented him going on a motoring tour of Europe – an expensive activity for a student in those days – or staying at the Savoy Hotel whilst working in his holidays for the *Daily Express*. Murdoch also

34

learned that rules and regulations were not there to limit his activities. They were there to be challenged and broken when necessary. He planned to stand for the post of treasurer of the Oxford University Labour Party but broke the rules on canvassing and was barred.[1] It was one of the few times in his life that he broke the rules and did not get away with it.

Today Murdoch's politics are a collection of the conventional reactionary responses of the super rich. He claims he is against the death penalty, but said to Tom Kiernan: 'Electrocution is a waste of good electricity. The real answer is to kill them before they have a chance to kill others.' He sees capital punishment as a solution to the violence and lack of discipline stalking the streets. He sees the welfare state as weakening the national fibre. He is strongly against increasing taxation. Kiernan quotes Murdoch talking of 'the way the energy and prosperity of industrious white America was being drained by the tremendous black problem.'[2] One ex-editor said: 'I regard him as worldly wise but deep down he's a redneck who has extremely paranoid social values.' The 1980s was his decade. He welcomed Thatcherism in Britain, Reaganomics in America and Hawke's deregulated markets in Australia.

In the 1970s, as his empire expanded across the globe, Murdoch's politics moved rapidly to the right. Throughout this decade, he became skilled not only in breaking the rules but in political power-broking. Politicians around the world believed that he had power over their electoral futures and many went out of their way to help him get what he wanted. By 1980 'Red Rupert' had vanished without trace.

'Murdoch liked to see himself as a king-maker,' explains one ex-editor. 'There was always a queue of politicians outside his office door. He would be like a schoolmaster, shut the door and give them instructions. He liked the image, he would say, "What can I do, bloody Hawke's trying to get me again." ' The present Australian Prime Minister, Bob Hawke, has occasionally sought Murdoch's advice. Once Hawke visited Murdoch to tell him that he had decided to 'unload' his predecessor, Bill Hayden. Hawke wanted to get Murdoch's agreement and check that his papers would support him.[3]

But what Murdoch likes more is his business and anything and anyone who helps News Corporation. He doesn't only support right-wing ideologues and their leaders. He supports winners who are going to support his business interests.

Murdoch likes men and women of action. In 1982 he visited Israel shortly after the invasion of Lebanon. Frank Giles, editor of the *Sunday Times*, asked him his opinion of Ariel Sharon. Murdoch replied: 'He's a man of action.' But, Giles asked, suppose the action is wrong or misguided? 'That's not the point,' argued Murdoch. 'He gets things done.'[4] This explains his disappointment with Thatcher when she opposed the Reagan invasion of Grenada. Murdoch told an Australian paper that Thatcher had 'gone out of her mind', 'run out of puff' and was not 'listening to friends'.[5]

Back in 1960 Murdoch had learnt the powerful lesson that if you want to be in with the rich and powerful, you do not offend them. At this time, in Australia, the Adelaide *News* had been campaigning against the conviction of Rupert Max Stuart, an Aborigine who had been convicted of murder. Murdoch had written many of the editorials criticising the judges. A court action was brought against the paper for defamation and seditious libel. Both Murdoch and the paper's editor, Rohan Rivett (who was to be the first editor, but by no means the last, that Murdoch sacked), were called to give evidence. Murdoch refused to answer a long list of questions. Although News Limited was acquitted, Murdoch had upset some powerful people. It was the last time he was personally involved in a campaign to correct an injustice which offended the establishment.

Throughout the 1960s he assiduously courted politicians, making the contacts which would oil the wheels of government for him. As the contacts grew, so did his confidence. In January 1968, when Britain and the United States were being seduced by the emerging flower power movement, Rupert Murdoch was getting involved in some serious power-broking. In January, just three days before the vote for the leadership of the Australian Liberal Party, he decided to get involved. His quality daily, *The Australian* published a report headed 'Why McEwen vetoes McMahon: Foreign Agent is the Man between the Leaders'. Murdoch did not like William McMahon, one of the potential Liberal leaders, while McEwen, the temporary Prime Minister, was a friend of his. *The Australian* report said that McEwen objected to McMahon's 'close association with an agent of foreign interests'. This 'foreign agent' was a former Murdoch editor, Maxwell Newton, who worked as a consultant for, among others, the Japan Export Trade Organisation. In his writings Newton had been critical of McEwen's protectionist policies which McMahon also opposed. The climate of suspicion created by the report, and others in Murdoch papers over the next few days, made it impossible for McMahon to stand for the leadership of the Liberal Party. Instead John Gorton became the leader and subsequently Prime Minister.[6] Murdoch developed a close friendship with Gorton which proved useful in his takeover of the *News of the World* in Britain in 1969.

Murdoch had proposed that he transfer some of his Australian assets to London to get control of the *News of the World*, though the company would retain a majority of British shareholders. Murdoch was worried that the Treasurer, William McMahon, whom he had campaigned against the previous year, and the Government, which was unhappy about the overseas corporations taking control of key Australian assets, would put obstacles in his way. But Gorton, the new Prime Minister, whose rise had been aided by Murdoch, sent reassuring signals. Murdoch regarded Gorton as a 'great Australian'.[7]

Over in Britain, the establishment was giving him a rough ride. They patronised him and excluded him. Murdoch was hurt, and resented the snobbery of the British establishment. This warped snobbery was to help him in the battle for the *News of the World*. The then chairman, Sir William Carr, was a venomous racist who preferred to sell to the Anglo-Saxon Murdoch, rather than the 'foreigner', Robert Maxwell. After Murdoch had bought the *Sun* and the *News of the World* he let loose with some of his rage against the establishment. In the 1970 general election the *Sun* supported Harold Wilson. Many of the *Sun*'s sub-editors came, after all, from the old Labour-supporting paper, the *Daily Herald*. In June 1970 Murdoch devoted two columns of the *Sun*'s front page and half the second page to explain 'why it must be Labour'.[8] Labour lost, but Murdoch continued to have lunch with Wilson to discuss politics.

Commercial television in Britain was closely regulated and imposed strict limitations on the activities of newspaper owners. In the early 1970s LWT was in financial crisis. LWT's managing director, Tom Margerison, encouraged Murdoch to buy into it in 1970. Even though British television regulations prevented newspaper proprietors from controlling television programmes, Murdoch sat on the executive committee anyway. When Margerison resisted, Murdoch sacked him. Murdoch declared that in future he would chair the executive committee, meaning he would select the programmes. After complaints from heads of other programme contractors, the Independent Broadcasting

Authority, which licenses commercial television, made three demands. One of these was that 'the next managing director's name would not be Rupert Murdoch'.[9] Murdoch agreed to an executive chairman. As his politics still tended to Labour, he approved John Freeman. Freeman had been editor of the leftish weekly magazine *New Statesman* and had been appointed by Harold Wilson as High Commissioner in India.

Despite his chummy chats with Harold Wilson, Murdoch's sympathies with left-wing causes had gradually diminished throughout the 1960s. By 1971 he had had enough of his paper *The Australian* covering 'bleeding heart issues'. The paper was against Australia's involvement in the Vietnam War and against the proposed South African Springbok rugby tour. Murdoch also did not see the point of having stories on the plight of the Aborigines, as they did not buy his papers. One of the many stories that have appeared to explain why he supported a Jewish candidate for mayor in New York against an Italian reported him saying that there were more Jews than Italians in the city.

In 1972 Murdoch expanded his Australian newspaper empire by buying the Sydney *Daily Telegraph* and *Sunday Telegraph* from Sir Frank Packer. The sale reduced the Australian news media from four empires to three. As soon as the deal was finalised Murdoch informed the Prime Minister, William McMahon (who had been eventually elected Liberal leader despite Murdoch's earlier campaign against him in 1968), and the leader of the Labour Party, Gough Whitlam, of the sale. He telephoned McMahon and said: 'I can promise, Prime Minister, that we will be as fair to you as you deserve.' Packer, who was listening, said: 'If you do that, you'll murder him.'[10]

The election later that year gave Murdoch a chance. Rather than support the Liberal McMahon – whose politics were likely to coincide with his own views – Murdoch decided to back Whitlam, the Labour leader. It was not because he agreed with his policies but because he thought he would win. *The Australian* wasted no time in throwing itself into the fray. After Murdoch had gone on a cruise round Sydney Harbour with Whitlam, *The Australian* described Labour's promises as 'exciting' and a 'radical alternative to the Australia which exists today.'[11]

Murdoch was concerned that Whitlam lacked credibility with the business community. He thought that it would help Whitlam's standing if he announced that he would appoint Dr H. C. Coombs, the former governor of the Reserve Bank, as his personal economic advisor on taking office. After long talks between Whitlam, Murdoch and the Labour Party, Whitlam made the announcement. It was the main news story in *The Australian*. But *The Australian* had a low readership and Murdoch knew it would not change the results by a single seat in the election. His *Mirror*, however, had a much larger circulation. The paper did not advocate a position on the election until nine days before the poll, when Murdoch himself wrote an unsigned column called 'Mirror Election Viewpoint' supporting Labour.[12]

Murdoch supported the Labour Party financially as well, donating nearly $75,000 to its advertising outlay. He also helped design the adverts for the final week of the campaign on the floor of his office and worked closely with Labour's two key strategists Mick Young and Eric Walsh.[13]

What was to be considered news was decided by Murdoch and the Labour Party. When Eric Walsh gave a press statement to the news editor of the *Daily Mirror*, the editor asked: 'What's new about that?' Walsh replied: 'As far as you're concerned, mate, what's new is that it's Rupert's idea.'[14]

McMahon sent an envoy – the future Prime Minister

Malcolm Fraser – to see Murdoch in the hope that Murdoch would give a more sympathetic ear to the Liberal Government's policies. He did not.

Not all on the left were happy with Murdoch's support. Ironically, one of the people who was to become Murdoch's best present political mate, current Prime Minister Bob Hawke, was one of the most critical. As President of the Australian Council of Trade Unions he said to Whitlam: 'You're going to regret the day you got into bed with Rupert'.[15]

Although Murdoch was still supporting the Labour Party in Australia, his politics had started to change with his move to America in 1973, where he first of all struck up a friendship with Richard Nixon. He had wasted no time in courting the right politicians in America. This became obvious to the *Sun*'s designer, Vic Giles, when he was helping Murdoch on the *National Star*, a weekly tabloid magazine Murdoch launched in February 1974.

> I was handling a piece about Richard Nixon, this was when he was President. Rupert said that he didn't like the headline, I replied that it was the words used in the copy. He shouted to his secretary, 'Dot, get Nixon on the phone.' The phone rang and he said, 'Dick, Rupert Murdoch here, I've got this piece here about you and it says this, this and this ... ' He turned to me and said: 'You're wrong, Dickie says it's this way. See you next week, Dick.' The man had only been in the States for a couple of months and already he knew everybody. He was talking to Carter and LBJ as if they were his bosom friends.[16]

Murdoch was very concerned in the summer of 1974 when the attack on Richard Nixon gathered strength. Murdoch believed that if Nixon was hounded out it would be a disaster

41

for the western alliance which relied on America in the battle against communism. His departure would lead to a resurgence of socialism and welfarism which would lead to national bankruptcy.[17]

At the same time as Nixon's resignation in 1974, editors on *The Australian* and Sydney *Mirror* say he ordered those papers to begin their anti-Whitlam smear campaign. One journalist said: 'It was like Rupert was getting revenge for Nixon, his new hero in America. One could just imagine him declaring: "If the lefties in America can strike down a conservative like Nixon, I'll show the world what a conservative can do to a lefty leader here." '[18] Also, Murdoch's support of the Labour Party had not paid dividends. In March 1974 the Government refused permission for a Murdoch company and its American partner to develop a profitable bauxite mineral project on environmental and foreign investment grounds.

Murdoch started his campaign against Whitlam early in 1975. He took a personal hand in it during several visits to Australia, spurring his editors on to dish the dirt on Whitlam.[19] Murdoch installed a new editor, Leslie Hollings, at *The Australian*, who took a much more active role than the previous editor in deciding what political stories would be printed. But Hollings's role was usurped more and more by the editor-in-chief, Bruce Rothwell, who slavishly followed the Murdoch line, and some journalists believe went even further in attacking Whitlam than Murdoch would have done.[20] Most of the Australian press were critical of Whitlam and his Government, but Murdoch's papers were the most stridently hostile and vitriolic.

The 'loans affair incident' was to become the staple diet of the Murdoch press in the early months of 1975. By 1975 the Australian economy was a shambles. Trying to stop the decline, the Labour Government had embarked on a secret search for loans from Arab sources early that year. They had done this through a dubious broker called Tirath Khemlani. They wanted to raise A$2 billion, but Khemlani failed and the scheme was officially abandoned.[21] But the story was not abandoned by *The Australian*, which resurrected it again and again in the crisis that was to come.

Murdoch's papers had a field day when, on 15 October 1975, Malcolm Fraser, who had become Opposition leader earlier in the year, announced 'the deferral of supply'. This meant the Senate stopped the Bills providing legislative authority for the Government's annual expenditure. Murdoch had known about this possibility for months. His source was impeccable. Sir John Kerr, the governor-general, had already spoken to Murdoch about the role he should play if the problem arose.[22]

Murdoch's papers were soon to tell Kerr what he should do. The day after supply was stopped *The Australian* headed its editorial: 'No more Petty Tricks – Let the People Decide'. Two days later its main front-page story announced: 'Governor-General will act soon, says Fraser'. *The Australian* stood by Fraser's decision to stop supply and published articles urging Kerr to sack Whitlam. Over the next eight days Fraser created an atmosphere of crisis. The story hardly developed but his continually repeated remarks were given full exposure in *The Australian*.

After nearly two weeks of this reporting, over seventy journalists from *The Australian* wrote to Murdoch expressing their concern about the paper's reporting:

The Australian has become a laughing stock. Reporters who were once greeted with respect when they mentioned *The Australian* have had to face derisive harangues before they can get down to the job at hand. It is not so much the policy itself but the blind, biased,

43

tunnel-visioned, ad hoc, logically-confused and relent-less way in which so many people are now conceiving it to be carried out, both in the editorial and news columns.[23]

They argued that they could not be loyal to a 'propaganda sheet' and it was impossible to be loyal to the traditions of journalism if they accepted the deliberate slanting of headlines, the seemingly blatant imbalance of news presentation and political censorship.[24] Murdoch had not bothered to answer the letter when Kerr dismissed Whitlam on 11 November 1975.

The journalists eventually went on strike and were joined by demonstrators who burnt Murdoch's papers in the street. *The Australian* went on regardless, ignoring the furore Kerr's actions had caused, and stated that the economy was 'the real debate'.[25]

Malcolm Fraser became Prime Minister on 13 December. Fraser, who had been ignored by Murdoch three years earlier, was now so pleased with *The Australian* that he asked the editor to become his speechwriter.[26] But eight years later, even though his Government had persistently helped Murdoch, he too was discarded as Murdoch switched his political allegiances to Bob Hawke.

In a television interview after Whitlam's dismissal, Murdoch denied that his papers were biased or that he sought the downfall of the Labour Government. He claimed that he had not influenced his papers' content in any way even though he was concerned at what would happen to Australia if Whitlam was re-elected because 'we are having imposed on us a European-style type of socialism which has caused ruin and misery in other countries for all to see.'[27] Despite Whitlam's dismissal, Murdoch had not finished exposing the Labour Party. In February 1976 he received a phone call from someone he did not know – Henry John Fischer. Those who did know Fischer knew him to be an extreme right-winger, and a commentator on the intelligence world later described him as an envoy for the Australian Secret Intelligence Service.[28] Fischer would only speak to Murdoch. Murdoch, although running a world-wide empire and employing thousands of journalists, listened to the story himself. Fischer claimed that he had been hired by the Labour Party to raise money from Arab sources for their advertising campaign. He said that he had met with some Iraqis and Whitlam had met two of them personally to discuss the matter. After Fischer had spoken to him, Murdoch still had the time to take personal control over the story, checking the facts and writing the copy. The by-line when the first instalment appeared in the *Daily Telegraph* and *The Australian* was 'a special correspondent'.[29]

After the Iraqi affair Murdoch was quoted in his paper *The Australian*, in response to the claim that he sought the downfall of the Labour Party and the public disgrace of Whitlam, as saying: 'Nothing could be further from the truth. We have always worked for the maintenance of two strong democratic alternative parties.'[30] This statement is hard to believe when looking at Murdoch's record. His only support is for the party which endorses him and his company, and frequently he allows his papers to make hysterical attacks on their opponents.

Whitlam believed the main reason for Murdoch's relentless attack on his Government was the refusal of the bauxite concession and his turning down of Murdoch's proposition that he should become High Commissioner in London.[31] (Murdoch has denied that he seriously requested the post.)[32] But Whitlam also believes that Murdoch was not as powerful as he liked people to think. Whitlam does not believe that Murdoch got him elected or dismissed. He believes that Murdoch backed him in 1972 as he backed Fraser in 1975, in order to take credit for the victory.[33] But Fraser recognises the help Murdoch gave: 'Over time newspapers can influence voting, newspapers are one of the things that influence people.'[34]

The battle Murdoch had fought with the journalists over biased political coverage now moved to New York. By 1977 his continual editorial interference at the *New York Post* caused that paper's journalists also to protest. Murdoch used the previously liberal paper, which he had bought in November 1976, to support the right-wing democrat outsider, Ed Koch, for New York mayor.

Barbara Yuncker, who was a Newspaper Guild official at the *New York Post*, described the paper as 'a broadsheet for Koch. Pictures of Koch were on Page One, of Koch with Beth Myerson, to stop rumours that he was gay, and news stories were confused with promoting Koch.'[35] Murdoch understood something about New York. As Yuncker explains it is a city which has centres of power; Murdoch became a power-broker. There is an invisible government of people who talk to each other and Murdoch became one of these. Koch himself is happy to admit how helpful Murdoch's support was to him: 'Without it I would not have been elected.'

'Murdoch felt it was right to use news columns for propaganda. We had a protest over the Koch stories which everyone on the editorial staff joined because we felt that it damaged the newspaper's reputation,' says Yuncker. Complaints were met with little response. 'Murdoch summoned me into the office – he never raises his voice, he's very controlled and withering. He told me that when I paid for the paper's debts I could say what went into the paper.'

Murdoch confirmed this on American television when he told Barbara Walters that his reply to the journalists had been: 'I said that I'm losing ten million dollars on this newspaper and I'm entitled to support who I like.'

Of course, he wasn't losing any money – the company he controlled was. But it was also a remark which showed the gulf between Murdoch's world view and that of the liberal establishment. He believed that money could buy anything and only what was paid for had any value. They believed that newspapers were partly public property: they brought with them a broader responsibility than the requirement to make money for their owners. It is a divide which will always separate Murdoch and his acolytes from the large section of those on whom he relies to produce his products.

Murdoch's constant presence in America became a problem when, in 1979, he briefly returned to Australia to buy United Telecasters Sydney Limited which owned the city's Ten-10 television station. The acquisition made commercial sense: United had made over A$4 million post-tax profit in 1977–78. Murdoch ultimately paid A$36 million for the company, which at nine times post-tax profits seemed cheap.[36] But there was a snag.

Murdoch had to go before the Australian Broadcasting Tribunal (ABT) to have the transfer of the licence approved. There were two major arguments against his takeover. First, an unexplored part of the Australian Broadcasting and Television Act (B & TV Act) said that a company was not eligible to hold a TV licence if a person who was 'not a resident of Australia' controlled 15 per cent of that company. Clearly, Murdoch controlled 15 per cent and was not a resident of Australia. When he took the stand he argued forcefully for his Australianness: 'Who in this room can say that I am not a good Australian or a patriotic one? Who else chooses to be battered and bruised ten months of the year in being an Australian when it would be easier not to be one?'[37]

Murdoch won the argument despite the letter of the law – though his residency was to come back and haunt him in later cases. Secondly, the Tribunal ignored the arguments against Murdoch that control of a Sydney channel by News Limited would not be in the public interest because of the way Murdoch's papers had been used in the past, especially during the 1975 election. The transfer of the licence was approved.[38]

The decision ignored the question of whether Murdoch was in breach of the rule which did not allow any one 'legal person' to hold more than 5 per cent of the shares in more than two licences. Murdoch having added United to his other channels in Adelaide and Woollongong was in breach of the law. Knowing this, Murdoch had sold his Woollongong station. The transfer of the licence was awaiting the approval of the ABT. But Murdoch had bought the Sydney Channel 'unconditionally', in other words, he owned it whether the ABT approved or not. This meant that for a while he owned more than 5 per cent in three channels.

The ABT's silence on the issue gave Murdoch the green light for future unconditional purchases – a signal to storm the citadel.[39] The storming began in September 1979 when he decided to buy the network partner to his Sydney channel, the Melbourne Channel Ten (ATV-10) owned by Ansett Transport Industries. Murdoch's battle to take control of Melbourne would take two years. It is a story of contempt for the law, illegal shareholdings and lies. Murdoch's basic dilemma was that he needed the approval of the ABT before buying over 5 per cent, and the B & TV Act only allowed a company to own two licences.

He got around the law in several ways. First, when he bought shares in Ansett during September 1979 he bought just under 5 per cent. He kept it purposely at this level, as he later admitted, to avoid ABT approval. But Murdoch would need more shares if he was ever to stand a chance of getting control of the station. He decided to get some help from his

48

British merchant banking friends, Morgan Grenfell and Hambros. The chairman of Morgan Grenfell, Lord Catto, was a close friend of Murdoch's and had helped him take control of *News of the World*; Hambros had also been involved with the deal and has been used by Murdoch ever since. In October, after a dinner between some of the banks' directors and Murdoch,[40] Morgan Grenfell and Hambros bought just under 5 per cent between them.

Murdoch has said that he was approached by senior executives of Morgan Grenfell who asked if they could help, and he had replied: 'Yes, why don't you buy some shares?'[41] Despite their willingness to help their long-time client Murdoch, they approached News Corporation's finance director, Merv Rich, to ask if they could be protected if they lost money on their investment in Ansett. Rich readily agreed and a put option was arranged on 12 October 1979. A put option gives the holder the right to sell the shares at a predetermined price some time in the future – to 'put' the shares on someone else. In this case a News International subsidiary, Ordinto, was required to repurchase the Ansett shares from Morgan Grenfell if it wanted to sell. Morgan Grenfell was indemnified against any losses. There was also a similar agreement with Hambros who were to be paid an additional fee of ½ a per cent of the total purchase price.

Murdoch knew he had little chance of getting control of the Melbourne channel at first because there were others interested in taking a larger share of Ansett and possibly taking it over. TNT, under the aegis of Sir Peter Abeles, and the Bell group controlled by Robert Holmes à Court, were both trying to increase their stake. But Murdoch wanted a place at the negotiating table. He believed he could get control from the ultimate victor. 'I thought that to get an interest in these would give me a very useful bargaining lever to persuade whoever was the eventual winner to sell me

49

(News) ATV-10.'[42] And he did just that. He was worried that if all the big shareholders started bidding for the Ansett shares there might be a wild auction. To stop this he set up a meeting at his ranch, Cavan, on the weekend of 27 and 28 October, between himself, Sir Peter Abeles and Robert Holmes à Court. The outcome of this conversation between Australia's business heavyweights was in Murdoch's favour: a firm promise of ATV-10.

The problem they all had was that back in August Sir Reginald Ansett, the chairman of Ansett, had set up a deal to frustrate any bid. He had done a deal with the oil company Ampol Petroleum. Ansett bought 20 per cent of Ampol, Ampol bought 20 per cent of Ansett. Any bidder for Ansett would now have to deal with Ampol as well.

Murdoch, Sir Peter and Holmes à Court agreed that Holmes à Court would acquire both Murdoch's and Sir Peter's Ansett shareholding at a price of $2.50 per share to be paid half in cash straight away and the balance in twelve months' time. It was also proposed to make a similar offer to Ampol. At the meeting it was also agreed that Ansett would buy the operating assets of the Bell group to fund the purchases. Once in control, Holmes à Court would offer the Melbourne channel to Murdoch and the Brisbane channel to Ampol.

A barrister who was later involved in challenging Murdoch's right to have the Melbourne licence said: 'The most extraordinary thing was the meeting at Cavan. It was like a giant game of monopoly, you can have Ansett if I can have Channel Ten, and you can have this if I get that.'[43]

Murdoch wanted to look after his pin-stripe friends Morgan Grenfell and Hambros. He told Holmes à Court: 'You will have to make the same offer to these people who are friends of mine, who are here to support me, and I cannot get out without them having the same chance, the same opportunity.'[44]

Sir Reginald felt he could handle Holmes à Court, and at least it got Murdoch and Sir Peter, neither of whom did he like or trust, off his back. On 30 October Sir Reginald and Ampol agreed to the deal in principle. Thinking the scheme was going to go through, News sold its Adelaide station NWS-9. Murdoch knew that although the ABT had studiously ignored the fact that he had broken the law before, it would make life a lot simpler if he sold the station before getting the one in Melbourne. The channel was sold on 16 November for A$19 million. Once again Murdoch's banking friends helped: Hambros supplied the buyers with finance. But unfortunately for Murdoch things didn't go according to plan.

By 20 November the valuation of the Bell Group assets had been dragging on for nearly three weeks. Sir Reginald thought that he could carry on, now he had seen Murdoch and Abeles off the share register. Then on 29 November the deal between Holmes à Court and Sir Reginald fell through. Holmes à Court immediately called Murdoch who offered the same price that he was going to receive from the shares (A$2.50). Sir Reginald repeatedly telephoned Holmes à Court to ask him to change his mind. But it was too late. Holmes à Court sold his 15 per cent stake to Murdoch for A$27 million, making an A$11 million profit.

The sale was unconditional, in other words, whether the ABT approved or not. Murdoch's right-hand man in the deals, Martin Cooper, a lawyer with a close knowledge of television law, tried to make it conditional but was told by Murdoch that Holmes à Court would not agree: 'and in fact he insisted on interest on his money from the minute that I hung up on the telephone'.[45]

Murdoch had made the agreement while playing tennis at a friend's, and in his usual style he wasted no time in making the necessary arrangements. Murdoch rang up Cooper with

51

the news that he had bought the shares and told him to fix the deal up. Murdoch then telephoned Rich, the finance director, and told him to find the money.[46]

Even though Murdoch had already done the deal to buy the Ansett shares, at a board meeting the day after his agreement with Holmes à Court Murdoch simply reported that News International had decided to make a significant investment in Ansett and would be purchasing shares on the market up to a total of 15 per cent and 'Mr Holmes à Court had since held discussions with News and had offered to sell his interest in Ansett.'[47] Luckily for Murdoch, although predictable considering his power over News's board, the directors approved the purchase he had already made.

The announcement to the Stock Exchange about the purchase and the intention to acquire a further 4 million shares in Ansett said: 'The acquisition of Bell Air Charter [the company that held Holmes à Court's Ansett shares] is subject to the approval of the Australian Broadcasting Tribunal.'[48] Once again Murdoch was implying that there was not a definite agreement with Holmes à Court.

Murdoch telephoned the chairman of the ABT, Bruce Gyngell, to confirm his plans about purchasing the Ansett shares from Holmes à Court's company. Murdoch discussed the need for ABT approval after he bought the shares and had 50 per cent of Ansett. There was no mention that he had already bought Holmes à Court's shares unconditionally.

The Ansett board smelt a rat. They also met on 30 November. They believed Murdoch had broken the B & TV Act. Until the matter was resolved they considered not registering News's shares. On 5 December the company wrote to both the ABT and the Attorney-General, arguing that Murdoch had broken the law by buying shares in Ansett without having the approval of the ABT for the Melbourne station Ansett owned.

Murdoch went on buying shares regardless and so did his future partner in half of Ansett, TNT. On 12 December Murdoch bought Ampol's 20 per cent stake for nearly A$35 million and Sir Reginald, having received no replies to his letters, gave in gracefully and sold the Ansett family holding to Murdoch. The next day Murdoch was named as chief executive and on 14 December announced he had 50 per cent of Ansett.

TNT made an offer for all Ansett shares, but Murdoch refused. They compromised with TNT buying the rest of the outstanding shares and both becoming joint partners of Ansett. The half equity in Ansett had cost News between A$90 and A$100 million: a considerable price for a channel that Murdoch had previously described as a loser.

The next day's papers reported Murdoch as saying after his appointment that Sir Reginald would remain chairman in a 'non-executive' capacity. Any decision to relinquish this position would be entirely up to Sir Reginald. The non-executive chairman seemed confused by this title but it did not worry him: 'If he doesn't want to consult me then I will be damned surprised.'[49] Looking at Murdoch's track record he should have been surprised if Murdoch *had* wanted to consult him. Sir Reginald finally resigned on 14 February 1980.

Murdoch gave the impression that everything was above board: 'What we're doing is entirely within the law and we'll be going forward to the tribunal to make all the necessary applications,' he said. 'We've informed them of all our moves step by step . . . they know exactly where we stand.'[50]

But the ABT did not know where Murdoch stood or that he was still in breach of the law. Murdoch and his lawyers knew that he had more than a 5 per cent interest in more than two stations. By taking over Ansett Murdoch had acquired not only the Melbourne station but also the Brisbane channel TVQ.

In February, Ampol, which had first refusal on the station

from the original deal with Holmes à Court, agreed to pay
$17 million for it. But there was a snag: News, through
Ansett, owned 10 per cent of Ampol and therefore would
own 10 per cent of the Brisbane licence after Ampol bought
it. Ampol realised that it would only be able to buy two-thirds
of the station, so it found a buyer for the other third. Their
partner broadcasting station 2SM Pty Ltd (2SM) was only a
small company, so Ampol agreed to make them an
interest-free loan and guarantee a minimum dividend. Just
days before the ABT hearing into the Melbourne licence,
Hambros bought 6 million Ampol shares to lessen News's
interest in the Brisbane channel.

The hearing began on 1 April 1980. The Australian
Labour Party which had objected to Murdoch's ownership of
the Sydney channel once more objected. But this time they
made sure they were properly represented, by Alistair
Nicholson as senior counsel and Stuart Morris as his junior.
The thrust of their argument was that there had been
breaches of the Act. Nicholson, not having been party to the
wheeling and dealing that had gone on, wanted to discover
the facts in cross-examination. The chairman, Bruce
Gyngell, ruled that cross-examination would be limited to
thirty minutes, refused to investigate breaches and demanded
an apology for the suggestion that News Limited had acted
unlawfully.

Nicholson argued that when News bought the Ansett
shares it had simultaneously owned at least three prescribed
interests in television stations, thereby breaking the law, and
had not sought ABT approval. All this was very embarrassing
for the ABT. Murdoch had pulled exactly the same stunt in
buying the Sydney channel, and the ABT and its chairman
Bruce Gyngell had ignored the breach. Nicholson's
insistence on it as a central issue drew attention to the ABT
and Gyngell's failings.

Nicholson and Gyngell constantly clashed over procedures. The final straw for Nicholson was when he was required to request more time to question Murdoch. Nicholson felt it was impossible to proceed with their argument under these conditions. He and his junior picked up their papers and walked out in protest. Unfortunately for Murdoch they appealed to the High Court of Australia, which instructed the ABT to carry out a full investigation and stated that breaches of the Act were a fit subject for its enquiries. Gyngell, whose chairmanship was coming to an end, stood down and appeared as a witness at the new ABT hearing to explain his previous behaviour.

Murdoch's lawyers had now to accept that breaches of the Act arising from share purchases were relevant. They denied they had occurred but if they had, they had been approved by the ABT. The details of the Ansett acquisition were laid out, and Abeles and Holmes were called as witnesses, and told their stories of the Cavan 'summit'. Murdoch himself testified for three days.

On 6 June all the evidence had been heard. The pleas were completed. The Australian Broadcasting Tribunal adjourned to make its decision. But early in July the whole issue surfaced again. The application for three Brisbane commercial licences came up for renewal. Stuart Morris, Nicholson's junior, intervened to demand that the ownership of the former Ansett Brisbane channel should be investigated. He argued that if News still had a 'prescribed' interest through Ampol, then the licence should not be renewed. The case turned up some incredible material.[51]

The ABT avoided the issue of non-renewal but agreed to Morris's demand for an investigation by reopening the hearing into the Melbourne licence. What Morris was looking for was some sort of 'warehousing' arrangement. The ABT subpoenaed Ampol documents. One memo caused a sensation. Ted Harris, Ampol's chief executive and a close friend of Murdoch's, had written to his board saying that while the company would buy 66.5 per cent of the Brisbane licence, the remainder would be held 'under appropriate warehousing arrangements'. Warehousing is a term used to cover secret share-buying arrangements where one party buys shares secretly for another and stores them, 'warehouses' them, until they are required. But Harris's defence was that 'warehousing' meant to him an opportunity to repurchase stock, subject to certain terms and conditions.[52]

Morris's claim that the warehousing agreement meant that 2SM's holding in the Brisbane channel continued to be under Ampol's control, so News Limited's indirect interest still exceeded the legal limit. The ABT once again adjourned indefinitely.

As a result News was in danger of being denied ATV-10 in Melbourne. To prevent this happening, News sent ABT a telex saying that neither it nor Ansett had been aware of the arrangements between Ampol and 2SM. However, if the ABT found that News held a prescribed interest in Brisbane, News would reduce its holding in Ampol to below 10 per cent. If this was not satisfactory further hearings should take place.[53]

Further hearings began on 15 August. Murdoch's lawyers called Martin Cooper, Murdoch's 'fixer', to describe his part in the negotiations between Ansett and Ampol. Cooper said that he had only negotiated with Ampol's legal officer. He added that he had not become aware of any arrangement between Ampol and 2SM until much later. However, Cooper was then shown two sheets of handwriting which he agreed were his. They appeared to be drafts of the sale agreements between Ansett and Ampol and between Ansett and 2SM. He was shown another piece of notepaper, again written in

56

his own handwriting. One item on the page said 'Warehousing'.[54] Unlike Harris, Cooper had no idea what he meant by the word, although he thought it might apply to a warehouse building.

On 26 September approval for transfer of the Melbourne licence was refused in a public decision. The detailed decisions released later argued that there had been breaches of the Act through unconditional purchases. However, the ABT said that if these breaches had been the only considerations for refusing approval it would have exercised its discretion in favour of News. But it gave two other grounds for refusing. 'The concentration of media interests by the News Group resulting from the common ownership will have an adverse effect on the freedom of choice of the other members of the network, and is not in the public interest.'[55] But despite the ABT ruling Murdoch held on to the Melbourne station. Under the law if the ABT wanted to order News Limited to sell the Melbourne station it had to issue the order within six months of the acquisition. Because of the length of the proceedings, time had run out; no order could be made.

The ABT couldn't make Murdoch sell the station, but he couldn't own it either under their ruling. Murdoch went to the Administrative Appeals Tribunal (AAT) to appeal against the ABT decision. The AAT had been set up to test decisions made by administrators like the ABT. Murdoch and those who opposed him could present old and new evidence. The AAT hearings began in April 1981 and took three times as long as the ABT's, with Murdoch spending nearly seven days on the witness stand.[56]

Mr Justice Morling dismissed the question of past contraventions of the Act by News Limited. In his opinion, they did not warrant the refusal of a licence. Morling also decided that common ownership of channels within a network was not, as the ABT argued, against the public interest. He approved the holding of News in the Melbourne channel, overturning the ABT's decision.[57]

While the courts had been deliberating, Murdoch's political friends had been at work on his behalf. Malcolm Fraser's government had changed the law so that in future TV buyers could do exactly what Murdoch had done. In June 1981 the Government took advantage of its Senate majority to pass amendments to the B & TV Act. They so favoured Murdoch that they became known as the 'Murdoch Amendments'. The amendments made citizenship, not residency, the test. Companies could now seek the approval of the ABT after they had bought the channel. If a company had prescribed interests in more than two stations the company had six months to bring the interests down to two. Finally it removed ABT's power to decide what was in the public interest.

Both Fraser and Ian Sinclair, the minister for Communications at the time, deny that the amendments were in any way a favour to Murdoch or, more importantly, that the Government was influenced by him or his papers in any way. They argue that the Act was too complicated and the amendments were obviously needed to clarify the Act.[58] It is especially hard to accept their view as there is evidence that Murdoch's close associates talked to politicians when the Bill was going through.

Richard Searby had been at school with Murdoch and had become a director of News Limited in May 1980 and chairman in April 1981. He had also worked as a consultant to the Government. He was a close personal friend of Malcolm Fraser's. Searby had hosted Fraser's fiftieth birthday party, with Rupert Murdoch as one of the honoured guests.

Searby had also talked to Fraser about the draft amendments to the Broadcasting & Television Act. When asked, he said that he had not passed on the substance of these discussions to Murdoch. But Searby also talked to Ian Sinclair, the minister for Communications, who believed that Searby was acting for News Limited. Searby insists that he did not talk to Murdoch about the discussions he had had with the Government.[59]

But it was not only Searby who offered his thoughts to Fraser. On the night before the August 1981 Budget Murdoch attended a dinner where he was seated one remove from Fraser. During the meal the conversation turned to the Middle East and the American request for an Australian component in the Suez peace-keeping force, over which the Cabinet had been hesitating. As they rose at the end of the dinner, Murdoch seized Fraser's upper arm and exclaimed for all to hear: 'Show a bit of muscle, Malcolm, show a bit of muscle.'[60]

Whether in reaction to this long-ago comment or for more altruistic motives, Fraser is now adamant that Australian media owners should be citizens of that country:

> There are international implications if a media proprietor is not a citizen. Suppose Australia was having a major argument with the US Administration, for example over export controls and Australia was in a bad trade position. If the Australian Government decided to stand up for Australia a foreign proprietor could find it more convenient to be hard on the Government because he is an American citizen. The fact that this situation could arise should be sufficient reason not to test it.[61]

3

The Times

During the 1970s Rupert Murdoch was known in Britain as the 'Dirty Digger', a nickname he hated. He was the country's most prominent gutter publisher. The *News of the World* was Britain's foremost scandal sheet. Its regular diet of the secret sex lives of vicars, minor public figures and the occasional Government minister made it the best-selling Sunday paper in the world. The *Sun*'s bright and breezy style had transformed British tabloid journalism. But it was the introduction of topless women on Page Three in November 1970 which made Murdoch's name. As always with any new Murdoch venture there had been no shortage of humbug. The first Page Three picture carried a warning for its critics: 'From time to time some self-appointed critic stamps his tiny foot and declares that the *Sun* is obsessed with sex. It is not the *Sun*, but the critics who are obsessed. The *Sun*, like most of its readers, likes pretty girls.'[1]

By 1978 the *Sun* overtook the *Daily Mirror* to become Britain's best-selling paper, with daily sales of just under 4 million. The *Sun* redefined the gutter for British papers. Its main competitor, the *Daily Mirror*, continuously moved down market to compete, but throughout the 1970s and 80s steadily lost circulation to the *Sun*.

Not surprisingly, Murdoch was asked, throughout the 1970s, whether he would also like to breathe life into *The Times*. It was usually asked with a slight *frisson*, just in case the 'Dirty Digger' should answer 'yes'. Instead Murdoch, to the relief of the many who asked, always answered 'No'. Privately he had discussed it numerous times with his friend, Gerald Long, the chief executive of Reuters.[2] But despite any private ambitions he might have nursed, even as late as November 1979 he declared: 'To buy *The Times* would be a highly irresponsible thing to do for your shareholders.'[3] Despite his denials, he bought it.

After the purchases of the *Sun* and *News of the World* it was the smartest deal of his career since leaving Australia more than ten years before. It was to transform News Corporation's fortunes, though few saw it at the time. This was not so surprising. *The Times* was in a mess. It was plagued by weak management, aggressive unions and poor circulation. None of this put Murdoch off. For him, already the owner of the down-market and highly popular *News of the World* and the *Sun*, buying *The Times*, traditionally regarded as the most prestigious paper in Britain, was quite a coup. The purchase made him the dominant voice in the British press, owning titles which accounted for just under 35 per cent of Britain's national newspaper circulation. As a press baron ownership of *The Times* opened doors into British society which had been denied to him since the early 1970s when the *News of the World* had dredged up the Christine Keeler scandal and horrified the British establishment. It turned him from being a cheerleader for right-wing views to being a serious power-broker in British national politics.

The deal was similar to the highly successful purchases of the *Sun* and the *News of the World*. He paid a small amount for a poor company which could be turned round and made highly profitable. While all these deals were essentially long shots, his risk was limited by the comparatively low prices he paid. The high-priced deals which grabbed the headlines would not come until later in the 1980s when he began to gamble the cash flow from his British newspapers on increasingly expensive acquisitions in the United States.

But *The Times*' takeover differed from the *News of the World* and the *Sun* takeover in one crucial regard. The brash young Antipodean taking advice from an avuncular merchant banker had gone. The manipulator of politicians had replaced him. Whereas Murdoch's takeover of the mass circulation papers had caused hardly any political ripples, taking over Times Newspapers thrust Murdoch to the centre of the political stage. But he was well able to apply the lessons learnt in America and Australia over the last ten years.

The background to Murdoch's takeover was not auspicious. By the late 1970s *The Times* was beginning to lose its prestige as the noticeboard of the British establishment. It was also losing vast amounts of money. A Canadian, Lord Thomson, had bought the paper in 1966. He was thrilled with the purchase, writing in his autobiography: 'This deal was the greatest thing I have ever done. It was the summit of a lifetime's work'. He promised the Monopolies Commission that he would meet the losses of the daily from the profits of its sister paper the *Sunday Times* and, when necessary, from other companies in the Thomson group. He also guaranteed the editorial independence of the paper.

But by mid-1978 the romance had soured. Lord Thomson had died and his son Kenneth had had enough and wanted to sell. The losses of *The Times* were so great that the Thomson parent company was having to subsidise the paper. When Murdoch started printing the *Sun* during the week on the *News of the World*'s presses, he had managed to cut the workforce by a quarter, but he was alone among Fleet Street proprietors in securing these kind of advances. Most British newspapers still used ancient technology and employed many more people than were necessary. Both the management and the unions had been notoriously conservative in embracing change. By the late 1970s something had to give. Papers like *The Times* were losing money but could be made profitable by the introduction of new technology, which allowed direct input by journalists. Unfortunately for the industry, neither side had any skill or experience at managing the change in working practices that this demanded.

In April 1978 'Duke' Hussey, the chief executive of Times Newspapers, began to talk to the trade unions. He hoped that he would be able to persuade them to accept some new American technology. The talks soon collapsed over what appeared to be a small but significant feature of the new system. This small feature would rip Fleet Street apart and lead directly to Murdoch making his dramatic move to Wapping.

The Times Newspapers management wanted to introduce new technology. This new system would allow advertising employees to take down classified advertisements by putting them directly into the system through electronic keyboards. They would therefore be setting part of the paper. The National Graphical Association (NGA), which represented the typesetters, rejected this proposal and called for 'double key-stroking': 'double' being the operative word. They wanted to maintain the traditional divide. Copy could be typed by others on the paper, including journalists, but it had to be retyped by NGA members. In the days of hot metal presses this made sense, but the new computer-based technology meant that copy only needed to be 'single-keyed', i.e. it could be typed and set straight into the system. And that meant that the NGA members would be out of a job and the future of the union thrown into jeopardy.[4]

Double key-stroking quickly became the central issue. Neither side could agree. In an unprecedented move the management decided to close down Times Newspapers' operations on 30 November 1978. No papers were published, but journalists – who had agreed to the introduction of new technology – continued to be paid. The closure lasted for the best part of the year. It cost the Thomson group several times the subsidy it had already pumped in to cover the losses of the previous six years. On top of this, the company lost the dispute. When the paper reappeared a year later in November 1979, Thomson had to concede on the main issue as the NGA had already established the double key-stroking principle at three other national newspapers.

The Times Newspapers' closure was the biggest financial disaster Fleet Street had ever seen. The company lost £39 million and the experience remained scorched in the memory of all the proprietors, including Murdoch. They were determined to break the power of the unions, one day. After a year's closure the *Sunday Times* came back to a better circulation figure than before the dispute, but the circulation of *The Times* had dropped. Its future was now in the balance.[5]

Murdoch was in much better shape and well placed to bid for *The Times*. Earlier in 1980 he had completed a reorganisation of News International – his UK company – which enabled him to unlock the full value of News of the World Organisation which he had taken over in 1969, and which now had considerable resources. Murdoch's close involvement in the day-to-day running of News International – as News of the World Organisation was renamed – and his personal domination of the company often distracted attention from the fact that he did not, in fact, own. When News Corporation, the company in which the Murdoch family owned 46 per cent of shares, took control of News of the World in 1969 the Murdochs ended up with only 49 per cent. The balance of the shares was owned by various financial institutions and odd members of the Carr family.

This was a perfect example of the Murdoch technique of using Other People's Money to expand his empire. He was in unchallenged control of News International, but that meant that for 51 per cent of his time he was working to make others rich. This was not a condition which came naturally to him, and the more successful News International became the more it rankled. By 1979 News International was making annual profits of around £30 million, four times as much as the profits of News Corporation. Half of his American operation, which included several papers and magazines, was also owned by News International. It was only a matter of time before Murdoch did something about it. That time was the spring of 1980.

Murdoch proposed to the holders of the 51 per cent of the shares in News International that they should exchange them for a new type of Special Dividend Shares (SDSs), the dividend of which would be related to the dividend paid by News Corporation in Australia. If anyone didn't want the SDSs, then News Corporation was willing to buy half of the issue.

From the point of view of the outside holders of the News International shares this was a rotten deal. They currently owned a half share in a highly profitable company which was rich in assets in Britain, the United States and Australia. In return they were being offered in effect a much smaller share in an Australian company, which included many businesses in which they were not remotely interested. If they accepted the cash offer they knew that in the end the money would only come from the News International coffers, which they were about to hand over completely to Murdoch. Some shareholders objected, but most saw that in practice Murdoch had them in a corner. If they didn't go along with the plan he could freeze them in News International. If he chose to use his domination of the company not to pay dividends, then their News International shares would quickly become valueless. Murdoch got his way, and with 100 per cent of the News International ordinary shares, access to the company's substantial funds.[6]

At the end of June 1980 News International had cash and stock market investments of £35 million, compared with total bank loans of only £11.5 million. Murdoch was ready and able to bid for Times Newspapers.

The picture at Times Newspapers could not have been sorrier. The pre-tax loss of Times Newspapers was £13.9 million, with little prospect of any improvement in the near future. Relations between management and unions continued to be bloody. Times Newspapers had been back in business for less than a year before it was hit again by industrial action. This time it was the normally docile *Times* journalists who went on strike, for the first time in their history, in August 1980.

The following month, Murdoch met Kenneth Thomson in the Concorde departure lounge in New York. Thomson was tired of the uphill struggle. There was only one thing on his mind: the problems of British trade unions. 'We only talked for a few minutes,' Murdoch said. 'And the conversation was pretty general – all about what a mess England was in and how dreadful the unions were.' Murdoch had the first sniff of a deal. 'I sensed he was getting sick of it and wanted out.'[7]

Murdoch kept a watchful eye on developments. Early the next month, October 1980, there was another dispute. This time it was the *Sunday Times*, which lost a million copies. Since Lord Thomson had bought *The Times* in 1967 he and his son had sunk £70 million into the two papers and now Kenneth was looking at a pre-tax loss of £15 million for the year. For Thomson this latest industrial action was the last straw. He decided that it was impossible to get co-operation from the unions. He wanted to sell.

Later that month Murdoch was again travelling on Concorde. This time he met Sir Denis Hamilton, the chairman of Reuters and Times Newspapers. Both he and Murdoch were travelling to a Reuters board meeting in Bahrain. In the course of the flight they chatted about the problems at Grays Inn Road, the headquarters of Times Newspapers. What Hamilton knew, and Murdoch did not, was that the decision to sell had already been made.

Hamilton played his cards close to his chest: 'I had to be pretty Delphic in everything I said. There were five or six other Reuters directors on the plane, all chairmen and chief executives of Fleet Street newspapers.'[8] The sale was announced on 22 October and handled by the merchant bank, S.G. Warburg, which drew up a prospectus for interested parties. A time fuse was fixed to the deal. The final date for the bids was New Year's Eve. If there was no sale, Thomson would close the papers in March, cut their losses and write off their investment.

Though Murdoch had sensed Thomson's wish to sell, he claims he did not react immediately when the sale was announced. 'My first thought was that I had no chance and it was a month before I woke up.'[9] Murdoch spent much of November in America and it was not until the end of the month, on Thanksgiving weekend, that he finally decided to go for *The Times*. (Thanksgiving seems to have acquired a mythological significance for Murdoch and takeovers. Exactly six years later he would decide to mount a bid for the Herald and Weekly Times Group of newspapers in Australia on Thanksgiving weekend – see Chapter 5).

With his News International money still burning a hole in his pocket, and with just over three weeks to go before the deadline Murdoch rang Gordon Brunton, the chairman of Thomson British Holdings, on 8 December, and told him he was interested in bidding for Times Newspapers. S.G. Warburg hurried around to Murdoch and he signed a pledge of confidentiality to receive the 'information memorandum' on the papers' prospects.

As soon as he saw Warburg's figures, Murdoch was sceptical. For several days he telephoned senior Thomson executives with detailed questions about every aspect of the business.[10] He quickly reached the conclusion that despite all its problems, he was in with a serious chance of turning it round. For Murdoch, Times Newspapers had two major attractions, one short-term and one long-term. The short-term attraction was the *Sunday Times*, which was potentially extremely profitable. The long-term attraction was that, maybe, there was a concealed jewel in the company which few had noticed – its shares in Reuters. He went into overdrive. On 10 December he asked Gerald Long, then chief executive of the news agency Reuters, whether he would be managing director of Times Newspapers. 'After a full three second pause',[11] Long accepted.

The choice of Long was, in itself, interesting. At the beginning of the 1980s for most people Reuters was the name at the bottom of some foreign stories in newspapers. It was a famous news agency which reported from abroad. This was also the view of many of the newspaper proprietors who owned the company. For complex historical reasons Reuters was effectively run as a trust. It paid no dividends to the newspapers who owned it and they showed little interest in its affairs.

68

However, beneath the surface things were changing. Largely under the influence of Long, a dour but competent manager, Reuters had moved into selling on-line financial information to business. This had quickly turned into a highly profitable operation with enormous potential. Long was one of the first people to realise that there was a problem brewing. He knew that once it became clear that Reuters was not a non-profit-making news agency but a valuable commercial business, even the dozy Fleet Street proprietors would notice. He felt a deep attachment to Reuters as an institution and to the trust which protected it from interference. He favoured selling off the valuable financial services business in some way so that the Fleet Street papers could continue to subsidise the news-gathering operation. He discussed this at several meetings with an old friend of his, a merchant banker from Lazards, Ian Fraser. They always agreed that there was no prospect of selling off the company because of the trust agreement.

Murdoch had been a board member of Reuters since 1980 and was impressed by Long and his conviction that, whatever Fleet Street editors claimed, you could run a news operation to a budget. He was Murdoch's type of manager. Murdoch was also one of the first Reuters directors to spot the potential in the company. Although it was only a year later, in November 1981, that he told fellow newspaper magnate Victor Matthews 'this Reuters business is very useful, going to make us a lot of money',[12] he probably saw something of the potential in 1980. With Times Newspapers owning 40 per cent of Reuters and with their board completely unaware of its value, it was a hidden asset in the business.

But the immediate key to the deal was the *Sunday Times*. Unlike *The Times*, the *Sunday Times* had been a commercial success story since Lord Thomson had bought it back in 1959. Its circulation had increased from 900,000 to 1.5

million in the late 1960s and remained near this figure throughout the 1970s. The healthy cash flow and the high circulation figures excited Murdoch.

Some journalists had nicknamed News International 'Shoestring International' and Murdoch clearly believed that he could cut costs in his traditional manner. The *Sunday Times* would then become highly profitable, and he planned to use the profits from the *Sunday Times* to outweigh the reduced losses on *The Times*, until he could make that paper profitable as well. But apart from its profitability, the *Sunday Times* was everything he disliked in a newspaper. It was preachy, cerebral and liberal. It was compassionate and caring. It campaigned and would not give in. Throughout the 1970s it fought a long and expensive legal battle to win the right to publish the results of a massive investigation into the manufacture, clearance and sale of the drug Thalidomide. The drug had been cleared and prescribed by doctors to pregnant women with horrific results. Hundreds of children were born with deformities. The pictures of Thalidomide children were to haunt a generation of newspaper readers round the world.

Though he did not like the editorial of the *Sunday Times*, that did not matter – for the moment. Murdoch knew that he could do something about that later. More importantly he guessed that if he bought both papers he had a chance of success. He would become the largest employer on Fleet Street. This made him much more vulnerable to industrial action, but it also gave him the power ultimately to defeat the unions.

In addition, the political climate in Britain was changing. In 1979 his favourite politician – Margaret Thatcher – had been swept to power. One of her major priorities was to eliminate the power of the trade unions. Although her Government had had an uncertain start in some areas of policy, changes in trade union law were quickly on the statute book. For an enthusiastic supporter like Murdoch it increased the odds of success when the battle with the unions came – as it was to do in 1986.

By December 1980 all the pieces of the jigsaw were beginning to fit into place. Though it was losing money, the purchase of *The Times* gave him something money could not buy – real power and influence. During the bid his mother, Dame Elizabeth, was asked by a television interviewer why her son wanted *The Times*. Her reply was instructive:

> I'm really sure it's not a thirst for power or thirst for money – least of all the money – but I think he just loves the challenge to his capacity and so far he's proved it to be a very big one. So I just hope he does get *The Times*, that Britain will perhaps learn to know that he's a pretty good chap.[13]

With two days to go before the deadline 'the pretty good chap' put in a bid: a derisory £1 million, with the *Sunday Times* building thrown in (worth at least £8 million) and the redundant management paid off by the sellers (which would cost Thomson £1 million plus).[14] Murdoch admitted that his original bid was cheeky. 'It was just to get my foot in the door,' he said. The offer was rejected, but he was told that he had until 12 February to iron out difficulties, including terms with the unions. In other words, negotiations were to continue.

Because they are such a powerful influence in society, newspapers are rarely sold like other companies. Everyone wants their say: the government of the day, the people who write for the paper and the people who print it. The purchase of Times Newspapers was no exception. Murdoch had to square all three groups. It was to call on all his ingenuity, charm and cunning.

On the day the sale was announced, William Rees-Mogg, editor of *The Times*, had announced his intention to form a syndicate including journalists and other staff to buy the paper. Harold Evans, editor of the *Sunday Times*, agreed that it would be better to separate the two papers and mounted a bid for his paper. Although their respective bids were rejected, they created an atmosphere in which the continued editorial independence and journalistic integrity guaranteed by the previous owners became an important consideration. But Murdoch's past behaviour of making promises and then breaking them was notorious. As Harry Evans observed, 'Murdoch issued promises as prudently as the Weimar Republic issued marks'.

Although the negotiations were still at a relatively early stage, Murdoch was already in the driving seat because of a fundamental weakness in the Thomson negotiating position. Thomson wanted a clean sale and that meant – if possible – selling both titles to the same bidder. By New Year's Eve, Brunton could not conceal that News International was the only single bidder for the entire package and therefore hot favourite to secure the deal. The deadline had been set for 12 February. If both sides failed to agree by then, it did not leave enough time for a second bid and both papers would shut down in March.[15] Like two people on a tandem they had to stay on together or both fall off. They had to come to a deal.

The crunch came at Stratford Place, the Thomson headquarters, on the evening of 21 January 1981. Murdoch was interrogated by the vetting committee, which was made up of the editor-in-chief of Times Newspapers, Sir Denis Hamilton, three national directors, Lords Dacre, Green and Roll, and the editors of both papers, Harold Evans and William Rees-Mogg. He put on a good show and finally agreed to their terms. After midnight the deal was finally made, despite near breakdown when Murdoch demanded

72

that Thomson guarantee in writing not only that the company's assets were worth £17.9 million but that current losses would not exceed £14.5 million.

Murdoch had one further stumbling block. The legal requirements had changed since he bought the *Sun*. Now, an owner of a paper with a circulation above 500,000 who wanted to buy another paper had to be examined first by the Monopolies Commission. There was only one way to avoid the Monopolies Commission. The Secretary of State for Trade did not need to refer the bid to the Commission if he was satisfied that the paper to be bought would otherwise go out of business. At Times Newspapers, the situation was unclear. *The Times* might be in peril of extinction but it was less easy to argue this for the *Sunday Times*.[16]

To overcome the threat of a reference to the Monopolies Commission, Warburg supplied figures to the government showing that the *Sunday Times* had lost £600,000 in the first eleven months of 1980.[17] On 27 January John Biffen, the then Secretary of State for Trade, concluded that neither *The Times* nor the *Sunday Times* was economic as a going concern as a separate newspaper and therefore the papers could be transferred to Murdoch without referral to the Monopolies Commission. But this arrangement was subject to a number of conditions.

As part of the bargain, Murdoch had to make a series of binding guarantees to safeguard the position of the independent national directors and to preserve editorial independence. The national directors would appoint and remove editors. But most important, the papers would be free from political bias and sectional interest, regardless of Murdoch's politics or other commercial interests. These promises were enshrined as a condition of his purchase.

But journalists who worked for the *Sunday Times* were prepared to take Biffen to court over his decision. Their central argument was that the figures Biffen had used were misleading. They argued that the *Sunday Times* had made a profit at least in the past three months and profits would be made in the future. Central to their case was the conclusion of a leading partner of a well-known City firm of liquidators, Cork Gully, who said: 'If I were the receiver of Times Newspapers Ltd and decided to close down the *Sunday Times* . . . I should expect a claim against me for negligence'.[18]

The journalists proposed legal action to force a reference. Thirty-six hours before the court hearing, Murdoch offered the journalists a deal: halt the court action in exchange for further guarantees on editorial independence plus the appointment of two working journalists to the newspaper's main board. After a long and heated debate they agreed.[19] Murdoch's leverage was that if they did not accept him as owner, the papers might close and none of them would have jobs.

Yet again, Murdoch had demonstrated his brilliance in waltzing past the regulators. The key to his fancy footwork was that he was not dancing alone. He was supported by an old ally, the Prime Minister Margaret Thatcher, who felt she 'owed a real debt of gratitude'. At one stage during the battle for Times Newspapers, a member of the staff consortium trying to buy the *Sunday Times* rang an old friend working as an adviser to Thatcher at 10 Downing Street. Playing on the Government's apparent commitment to competition, he urged a halt to the Murdoch takeover. He was told to stop wasting his time. 'You don't realise, she likes the guy.'[20] When the takeover came to be discussed by a Cabinet committee, Thatcher chaired the meeting. Murdoch was, in effect, being rewarded for his papers' years of loyal support. In the words of *The Times'* editor, Charles Douglas-Home, Murdoch was seen as one of 'the main powers behind the Thatcher throne'. In 1984 he said:

Rupert and Mrs Thatcher consult regularly on every important matter of policy, especially as they relate to his economic and political interests. Around here he's often jokingly referred to as 'Mr Prime Minister', except that it's no longer all that much of a joke. In many respects he *is* the phantom Prime Minister of the country.[21]

There is no doubt that Murdoch's ownership was in both his and Thatcher's interests. Thatcher and Murdoch had been political allies throughout the late 1970s. Before she became Prime Minister, Mrs Thatcher used to attend *Sun* editorial meetings. These confirmed her radical right-wing populist zeal and gave her a platform for her views. The *Sun* campaigned for her throughout the 1979 election. She knighted the editor of the *Sun* who helped her so much, Larry Lamb. Vic Giles, who designed the *Sun* for Rupert Murdoch, watched it happen:

Once the country got a very strong leader, like Margaret Thatcher, who opened up the path for Rupert Murdoch to develop his new type of newspapers, he couldn't believe his good fortune. I mean he's been noted for changing governments in the past and having certain influence on governments. I think that at last he'd come home. Thatcher was his girl.[22]

As soon as he got hold of Times Newspapers, Murdoch was determined to avoid the mistakes of the previous owners. He immediately negotiated a tough deal with the unions. They agreed to a loss of 563 jobs (15 per cent of the workforce), a three-month wage freeze and the phased introduction of modern photo-composition technology. Crucially the unions agreed to a disputes procedure so that production would continue while a dispute was resolved.

Despite this agreement there was a walk-out in June 1981 and another in September by the NGA. Murdoch responded by closing the papers for three days. He told the unions that every time there was a walk-out by any of them he would respond by closing the paper.[23]

The key problem, though, for his two new papers was that their circulations were still depressed from the year-long dispute fifteen months before. The *Guardian* had gained 90,000, the *Daily Telegraph* had retained 160,000 and even the *Financial Times* had put on 5,000. *The Times*, in contrast, was still off 50,000 at 276,000. Murdoch moved Harry Evans, in his words 'one of the world's great editors', across to *The Times* in March 1981. Evans redesigned the paper. It was made clearer and easier to read. As a nice touch, Evans restored the Royal crest to the masthead on the first page. Evans continued to re-establish the notion that *The Times* was the paper the royals read. On the day before the royal wedding of Prince Charles and Lady Diana Spencer, *The Times* included a free four-colour magazine and sold out its press run of 500,000 copies. The following morning a full colour photograph of the royal couple was wrapped around the paper, which sold 400,000 copies. The increased revenue from these stunts was not enough to cover costs, but Murdoch was thrilled, because they had reintroduced the paper 'to thousands of readers who had not seen it for some time'.[24]

As part of the cutbacks *The Times* had no promotion budget, but Evans was having a dynamic impact on the market, pushing the circulation up from 276,000 to 300,000. Advertising was down because of the recession and Murdoch expected *The Times* to run up losses for some years to come.

Though he was delighted with the improvements Evans had made to the product and to the increased circulation, Murdoch could not stand his politics; and he hated it because, for once, his room for manoeuvre was limited. As part of the takeover deal he had had to give formal undertakings to John Biffen on the vexed question of editorial independence. This quickly created a great deal of friction. Murdoch was a Thatcherite monetarist. Evans was not. 'Hell, I'll go to prison if I speak a word to you,' Murdoch said to Harry Evans, the day after the Commons debate.[25] As soon as he took over, it was a 'risk' he was prepared to take. He began systematically to break the formal promises he had made to the directors of Times Newspapers and to the Government. For Evans 'passing from Thomson to Murdoch was a transition from light to dark'.[26]

Murdoch could not stop interfering. In 1982 he said to Fred Emery, home editor of *The Times*: 'I give instructions to my editors all round the world, why shouldn't I in London?' When Emery reminded him of his undertakings to Biffen on editorial independence, Murdoch retorted: 'They're not worth the paper they're printed on.'[27]

But it was not only Fred Emery who began to feel the full force of Murdoch's interference. According to Frank Giles, then the editor of the *Sunday Times*, Murdoch 'came and went in his peripatetic way, making a point when he was in London on a Saturday of dropping into my office in the evening about the time the first copies of the paper came off the presses and were delivered to me'.[28]

For journalists who have worked for Murdoch anywhere in the world the style was instantly recognisable. Jabbing his fingers at articles he disapproved of, he would say: 'What do you want to print rubbish like that for?' or accusing correspondents of being a 'Commie', especially when the reporting was on Reaganite policies in Central America. Because these gibes were often so extreme, Frank Giles was never sure whether they were meant seriously or were just said to get a reaction. But often Murdoch's gibes would provoke slanging matches.[29] Increasingly during Frank Giles's editorship Murdoch used to regard the *Sunday Times* as 'a nasty, left-wing radical organ, staffed for the most part by a bunch of left-wing layabouts.'[30]

One story which brought down the Murdoch fury was Evans's invitation to the latest Nobel-Prize-winning economist to write a piece about Thatcherist economics. The piece was less than adulatory of his heroine, Mrs Thatcher, and Murdoch berated Evans, asking him why he printed this 'shit'. When Evans pointed out that he was a Nobel-Prize-winning economist, Murdoch dismissed this, saying he was anti-Thatcher. The row lasted all the way from *The Times* building to Evans's home where they were both going for dinner that evening.

By now Murdoch's personal politics were so deeply rooted in right-wing fundamentalism that even centrist politics were suspect. Supporting the newly emergent Social Democrats in Britain was a serious crime. 'Murdoch's wish that *The Times* should be valiant for Thatcher in Britain and stalwart for Reagan in the United States had been obvious from the start of my editorship. It gradually developed into warfare only with the rise of the Social Democratic Party.'[31] This policy of supporting Reagan was soon to become familiar to journalists on the other side of the Atlantic. After he bought the *Chicago Sun-Times* in 1983, the journalists were told that they could not criticise Reagan directly. If there had to be criticism then it had to be directed at his aides, but Reagan himself had to be blameless.[32]

Back in England, *The Times*'s journalists soon discovered that, as Hugo Young observed, Murdoch did not believe in neutrality. 'Indeed, rather like politicians themselves, he had difficulty comprehending it. As far as he was concerned, journalistic detachment was a mask for anti-Thatcherism. If we were not for the Government, we were quite plainly against it.'[33]

Others who worked for Murdoch at Times Newspapers were upset by the Murdoch style of management. Philip Knightley, the prize-winning former *Sunday Times* journalist, said: '[Murdoch] journalists are not meant to have opinions. They're not meant to have emotions and they're not meant to have ideas. They're meant to report as objectively as he demands, what he feels is his view of the world.'[34]

Murdoch became increasingly frustrated that he could not control Harry Evans. Worse still, he could not get rid of him because of the binding pledges he had given in 1981. He turned to an old friend for help: Mrs Thatcher. Murdoch proposed an extraordinary deal to the Prime Minister. He asked her if Evans could be offered some grand post to take him away from *The Times*. Mrs Thatcher, intrigued by Murdoch's ploy, asked the chairman of the Conservative Party, Cecil Parkinson, if Evans could be offered some prominent position in a Government-controlled quango. Parkinson was unable to help – even though Murdoch was one of the Government's most powerful supporters. Murdoch's position was that Evans was not a good daily newspaper editor, but his central point was that Evans was not a Tory. 'And that is what matters from our point of view,' Parkinson told a colleague.[35] It was precisely what mattered to Murdoch as well, but for once he did not get his own way.

His fertile mind worked on other solutions to get rid of the troublesome Evans. The new ploy was much more within the conventions of Fleet Street's traditional 'stab in the back' style of management. Murdoch, exploiting the disquiet within the paper, slowly denied Evans the editorial freedom he had guaranteed him in his promises to Parliament and fomented disaffection through Evans's deputy, Charles Douglas-Home.[36]

Rumours began to circulate Fleet Street that Evans was going to be fired. Murdoch denied it, making a full vote of confidence in him. But this was as valuable as the traditional vote of confidence given to a football manager by the chairman of the board. Shortly after, as Evans returned from his father's funeral, Murdoch called him upstairs and demanded his resignation. After eight days of heavy pressure from the Murdoch camp, Evans gave in. He moved to New York, where ironically he is now Murdoch's publisher at Random House, which had commissioned Murdoch to write his autobiography before Evans's arrival. Murdoch was paid a reported $1 million advance, which prompted a joke: Why didn't Murdoch sell his book rights to his own publisher, HarperCollins? *Because they could not afford the advance.* Evans was replaced by Douglas-Home. Murdoch could not resist a dig at Evans in his annual report to shareholders, the following year. He told them that morale on *The Times* had been improved and 'the newspaper is once again speaking with the authority which gave it its traditional authority in Great Britain'.[37]

When he was first interviewed by the independent directors they were impressed by his quiet reassuring manner. During the battle for control of *The Times* he was asked by Tom Kiernan whether he intended to live up to the promises he had just made. Murdoch told him:

> One thing you must understand, Tom. You tell these bloody politicians whatever they want to hear, and once the deal is done you don't worry about it. They're not going to chase after you later if they suddenly decide what you said was not what they wanted to hear. Otherwise they're made to look bad, and they can't abide that. So they just stick their heads up their asses and wait for the blow to pass.

Quite.

4

Wapping

In the years since Harry Evans was effectively sacked as Editor, *The Times* has never recovered its position in British society as the authentic voice of the British establishment. Its views no longer carry any special weight in government circles and its influence is limited. It is doubtful whether it has ever really recovered from the 'Hitler Diaries' fiasco, which turned the previously staid *Times* into the laughing stock of newspapers and magazines round the world. On Saturday 23 April 1983 *The Times* devoted its front page to the most dramatic story of the decade – the diaries of Adolf Hitler. These diaries were a crude forgery. They destroyed *The Times*'s traditional standing as a journal of record.[1]

For once, Murdoch had no one to blame but himself. The 'diaries' were offered to him after they had been bought by *Stern* magazine. He was tremendously excited and personally took charge of the negotiations. The Hitler diaries seemed to prove that his grand strategy of building an internationally integrated media company was viable. *Stern* was only offering the British rights, but Murdoch's vision was wider than that. He also wanted to run them in his American papers, the *Boston Herald* and the *New York Post*. *The Australian* could pick up the Australian rights.

His Channel Ten-10 television station in Sydney could make the movie. And nothing was going to stop him. Philip Knightley heard a rumour of the impending purchase of the Hitler diaries. He remembered an earlier scam when the *Sunday Times* had ended up buying the 'Mussolini diaries' in 1968, which had turned out to be embarrassing forgeries. Knightley sent a memo to the *Sunday Times* editor, Frank Giles, to be forwarded to Murdoch, warning him of the dangers. It was too late. Murdoch had already done the deal, paying US$1.2 million for the English language serialisation rights. Under great pressure from him, the diaries were authenticated by the English historian Hugh Trevor-Roper (later Lord Dacre), who was also one of the Times Newspapers' independent directors.

The diaries were quickly proved to be an amateur forgery. But Murdoch and his aides seemed unconcerned. When Bruce Rothwell, one of his henchmen at News Corporation, was dispatched to Germany to try and check the diaries' authenticity, his only concern had been to secure their publication.[2] The day the diaries were conclusively proved to be a fake, Murdoch said: 'I always had open reservations about the diaries . . . In any case I haven't lost any money yet.' In the end News Corporation made money on the deal. Under the contract, News International got all its money back if the diaries were not genuine. For the *Sunday Times* it was good financial news. It kept 20,000 of the new readers it had gained as a result of its 'scoop', which it had now acquired for free. Referring to the controversy the 'diaries' had aroused, not to mention the mockery, Murdoch said: 'It made some great Fleet Street rat-packery bang-bangery.' *Times* journalists were told not to be overly concerned about the damage to the credibility of the *Times* papers: 'After all, we are in the entertainment business,'[3] he told them.

But since then the credibility of Times Newspapers has been continually undermined by one issue above all: broadcasting. Since 1985 the Times papers, in concert with the *Sun* and the *News of the World*, have maintained a relentless attack on the BBC. A major line of attack has been the cost of the licence fee. To put this in perspective, the current BBC licence is £77, for which the BBC provides 15,943 hours of television and 235,140 hours of radio. This is virtually the same cost as a year's supply of the *Sun*. Murdoch's papers, including *The Times*, have been excited cheerleaders, supporting and promoting his satellite television company, Sky. Typical of *The Times* coverage was an interview, in February 1989, with Andrew Neil, the executive chairman of Sky and also the editor of *The Times*'s sister paper, the *Sunday Times*. He was lobbed a series of easy questions like, 'What are your plans for the Arts Channel?' which allowed him to promote Murdoch's satellite service. He was not asked any rigorous questions, like why so few people could actually watch the exciting range of programmes on offer because there were no dishes available in the shops. Since then the plugging of Sky has got a little bit more subtle. *The Times*'s, reporting the 1991 Budget speech by Norman Lamont, the Chancellor of the Exchequer, carried a photograph taken off a television screen with the Sky News logo clearly visible in the bottom corner.

Apart from promoting his other media interests in their editorial columns, the main function of Murdoch's British newspapers has been financial. Since the early 1980s they have been a crucial source of cash to meet the interest payments on the debt he had taken on to expand News Corporation, particularly in the United States.

By 1985 his British papers were profitable, but not profitable enough. By 1985 he had turned Times Newspapers round from a regular loss-maker to a profitable organisation, making pre-tax profits of just under £7 million for the year. He had cut the wage bill and cut the number of workers. He had even managed to introduce some new technology. In 1982 *The Times* became the first broadsheet paper to be printed entirely by photo-composition. Though the management had got a grip on industrial relations, the profit margin of News International stayed stubbornly around 8 per cent. Murdoch knew from his ownership of papers in Australia and the United States that his production in Britain was antiquated.

Murdoch had already committed himself to satellite television in Europe and wanted to expand more into television, particularly in the United States. But before he could commit himself to any more expansion in the United States he needed a stronger cash flow from his British businesses to excite his bankers. If he was going to continue his expansion into electronic media, he had to do something about it – and quickly.

Back in 1975 Murdoch had already started to make tentative plans for the future printing of his British newspapers. The machinery in Bouverie Street, where he printed the *Sun* and the *News of the World*, was run down, and printing in Manchester was going to come to an end. He bought 13 acres at Wapping in East London's docklands. According to his former chief executive, Bert Hardy: 'We looked at sites in King's Cross but the middle-class Camden socialists were messing us around because of who Murdoch was, so we went to the working-class socialists at Tower Hamlets who were happy to have Murdoch.' But Murdoch himself was not so enthusiastic – he thought the new plant was a white elephant.[4] Even when building work began in

1978 Murdoch was still not sure. 'After doing the deal Murdoch blew hot and cold about Wapping. He knew we needed a new plant', remembers Bert Hardy. 'He would say, spend more money on it and make it into a monument for my family. And then the next minute he would cut back the costs and size.'

By 1981 Murdoch expected the work at Wapping to be completed within two years. He boasted that Wapping was to be 'one of the most advanced printing centres in Europe'. The budget at this stage was £40 million on the building and another £30 million for plant. Murdoch talked of printing the *Sun* and the *News of the World* at Wapping, but knew he had no agreement from the unions to move from his existing site in Bouverie Street.

But time was running out. Back in 1982 the losses at Times Newspapers were threatening the whole of the Murdoch empire – profits from all his UK newspapers, including the cash cows of the *News of the World* and the *Sun*, had disappeared. In the year to June 1982 his British papers lost £5 million, compared with a profit of over £20 million the year before. Planning for a closure of Times Newspapers, he transferred the valuable titles to another part of News International. This was a clear breach of the undertaking given to the British Government, and it had to be reversed when it was discovered.

News Corporation was clearly at the crossroads. On the one hand it was riding the wave of technological innovation by expanding into satellite television in the United States and Europe. On the other, the British newspaper business, which used to be the profit powerhouse of the group, was operating with antiquated technology and industrial relations to match. Negotiations for staffing the Wapping plant continued throughout 1983 and 1984. At the end of 1983 events outside London took a dramatic turn. Eddie Shah, a former television floor manager, had built a very successful free sheet empire in the north-west. Shah used union labour but fell out with their union, the NGA, and decided to produce his papers with non-union workers. For the NGA, which had successfully negotiated agreements with other regional newspaper groups over the issue of direct input, this became a test case.

It quickly escalated into a major industrial dispute in which Shah was presented as the plucky entrepreneur fighting the backward unions. Amongst his most vociferous supporters was the *Sunday Times*, edited by the Murdoch-appointed right-wing ideologue Andrew Neil. Neil and Shah spoke frequently on the phone and Shah produced his newspaper, the *Stockport Messenger*, without union labour, despite the massive demonstrations and violence outside his plant.

But it was not until the following February that the two met at the Savoy Hotel in London. Shah told Neil that he was thinking about launching a national paper. Neil supported the idea, arguing that new technology meant it was possible, and the new labour laws brought in by the Thatcher Government made it achievable. Neil's view was that only an outsider like Shah could do it. On the plane back home, Shah began to crystallise his plan for a new daily paper called *Today*, and within a month was talking to his bankers about the idea.

While Shah was busy raising the money for his new venture, News International management proudly showed a video to the Bouverie Street Fathers (the trade union officials at their Fleet Street plant) of what they called 'our super new printing plant'. The unions were unimpressed with this vision of their electronic future. By March the talks were breaking down. By October Shah's accountants had drawn up the business plan for *Today*. If it could be done in Stockport, why not Fleet Street? Murdoch started to plot. He needed to bypass the NGA.

By now a sea change had taken place in the attitudes of the print unions. The Warrington dispute had badly shaken their national leadership. The leaders of the two main unions – Tony Dubbins at the NGA and Brenda Dean at SOGAT (the Society of Graphical and Allied Trades) – were no fans of their Fleet Street branches. They had negotiated agreements over new technology in the regional papers and knew that change was needed in Fleet Street. The Warrington dispute had shown the Fleet Street branches just how much the traditional power of the unions had been eroded by the new changes in union law.

In addition, in the middle of 1984 there had been a change of management at the *Daily Mirror*. The old owners, Reed International, had brought in a new chairman, Clive Thornton. Coming from a background in the building society sector Thornton was untouched by the traditions of Fleet Street. He secured a wide-ranging agreement with the *Mirror* unions to reduce staffing and introduce new technology. No sooner had this been done than Reed International changed tack and sold the company to Robert Maxwell, the publishing baron who had previously fought Murdoch for control of the News of the World Organisation. So by the end of 1984 it was clear that at last negotiation was possible with the Fleet Street print unions. Murdoch's mind, however, was racing ahead of this. He realised that it was possible to produce his papers without any sort of agreement at all with the unions. Whilst his managers maintained an appearance of interest in negotiating in London, more serious talks were taking place on the other side of the Atlantic.

An American computer firm, ATEX, had installed 300 direct input systems throughout the world. In early February 1985 two of Murdoch's American executives approached ATEX. They wanted to sign a contract for the installation of a direct input system in Britain, but the contract had an unusual condition: all the work had to be done outside Britain, in terms of great secrecy. The next week, on 10 February 1985, Murdoch called a meeting at his New York apartment. Several of his key British executives were flown in on Concorde the day before. Present were Bruce Matthews, News International's managing director, and Charlie Wilson, the deputy editor of *The Times*, who had been one of the Murdoch team sent in to sort out the *Chicago Sun-Times*, and whose American experience had turned him into a fan of new technology. Matthews and Wilson were crucial to the success of what Murdoch had in mind. They were the executives who would have to drive it through. Ken Taylor, the technical director of News Group Newspapers, was the man who would have to make it all work. Also present were Christopher Pole-Carew, his colleague Stan Dzuiba and Geoffrey Richards, a lawyer from Farrers and Co.[5]

Pole-Carew, a former director of the Nottingham Evening Post, was now a consultant helping companies install direct inputting. He was tough. His advice to Portsmouth and Sunderland Newspaper Group in 1979 had been succinct: 'We told the unions that when the first brick went through the window of the home of a loyal member of staff we would retaliate with a petrol bomb through the window of a union official's home.'[6]

Murdoch outlined his plan, his 'dash for freedom' to Wapping. They also discussed starting a new paper, the *Post*, with computer input by the journalists, but this was unlikely to be anything other than a diversion. The following week Eddie Shah signed the final document for the equity funding of *Today* and the first of the American ATEX executives flew in to London. The next month, March 1985, the American computer team arrived in London. Murdoch was now looking at a complete front-end system for the editorial and advertising departments of the *Sun, News of the World, The*

Times and *Sunday Times*. The proposed *London Post* was not even discussed.[7]

The same month the first of the computers were moved to a disused warehouse in Woolwich, south London, where a shadow system was built. By the beginning of May they ran the first tests. At the end of May 1985 the computer system was secretly shipped to Wapping. Nothing leaked out. Murdoch's team had installed the largest computer typesetting system in the world, without anyone in Fleet Street being any the wiser. The Wapping plant was almost ready. Wapping could now produce both the *Sun* and the *News of the World* from the plate-making stage onwards.

The move to Wapping gave Murdoch two big problems: production and distribution. He guessed, in the end correctly, that enough journalists would go to Wapping to guarantee the production of the papers. The *Sun*, which was the main money-spinner, was basically a subs' paper, and required a surprisingly small number of people to produce it. The new printing technology, though not state of the art, was advanced enough not to require skilled labour. Distribution was a headache, as this had always given the unions their stranglehold over the proprietors in the past. But with four papers, News Corporation was big enough to organise its own distribution. In March, News International approached TNT, a company with which Murdoch had close connections – they jointly owned the major Australian airline Ansett. TNT were asked to draw up plans to distribute all four newspapers by road. The plan was called 'Project 800' and classified 'Top Secret' within News International.

It was a gamble, but Murdoch had reduced the odds dramatically. The prize glittered. If he succeeded, News International's papers would be profitable in a way none of them had ever been before. And there was no turning back.

He had already committed his new profits before News International had earned them. In March 1985, just after the 'dash for freedom' was conceived, Murdoch agreed to buy the American Metromedia television stations from John Kluge. These six stations would form the basis of a new television network, Fox, to challenge the majors.

Although Murdoch needed clearance from the FCC he was confident he would get it. (See Chapter 5 on Fox). This was a huge gamble for him. It would impose a massive burden on News Corporation's cash flow. The improved profits he expected from Wapping were crucial to his planned expansion in America.

The talks with the British print unions continued. Like Murdoch, they too were watching events in the United States with great interest. But the unions completely misread the situation. They believed that he would not take them on because of the Fox venture. What they did not realise was that it was precisely because of the Fox purchase that he had no alternative. He had bet the company on Wapping and there was no turning back. He had to take them on and he had to succeed. If he failed, then his move into American television would also fail and the whole News Corporation empire would be in danger.

As Murdoch became more confident in the technology he began to apply the pressure. In March he had announced that he was going to publish a new paper, the *London Post*, which would be published from Wapping – though by now it was hardly being discussed with the people from ATEX. By September Murdoch knew that Wapping could produce all his UK newspapers and he could walk away from 'the snake pit' of Fleet Street's traditional industrial relations. He gave the unions a deadline of three months to reach an agreement on manning the new paper.

According to one of Murdoch's senior executives: 'There

was no plot about putting up Wapping and getting rid of the unions. But quite rightly we weren't going to let the old practices continue.' However, by the end of 1985 the strategy was to move to Wapping whether the unions liked it or not. Once there, they would have to accept the new working conditions. It was the traditional Murdoch negotiating position of 'you either stay on my terms or you leave'.

At the end of 1985 – two weeks before the deadline ran out – News International announced that the Wapping plant was ready for the launch of the *Post* and the plant was also ready to meet the 'urgent requirements of the News group's other newspapers'.[8] Murdoch continued to apply the pressure. Five days before the meeting with the unions a section of the *Sunday Times* was printed there without union agreements.

The final meeting between News International and the print unions opened on Thursday 23 January 1986 at the Park Lane Hotel, Piccadilly. There was a rich irony to the venue. By coincidence it was run by Clive Carr, one of the former owners of the *News of the World*. Murdoch's whole attitude was that it was too late. He said: 'The horse has bolted at Wapping.' He shocked the unions by telling them that the plant at Wapping was not on the agenda. He said that he intended to print the *London Post* there and that was that. Murdoch had been in London for nearly two weeks before this meeting. He had reserved a total of four weeks for the British operation. This was an unheard-of amount of time for him to spend in one country. It shows how confident he was that he would get the deal he wanted.

The unions bent over backwards to try and get an agreement. It was too late. Brenda Dean from SOGAT, who represented Fleet Street's clerical and ancillary workers, effectively surrendered the power of the Fleet Street chapels. She outlined a plan worked out with the other unions that conceded management's right to manage, agreed to binding arbitration on any dispute, gave flexibility between unions, prohibited wildcat strikes and promised ballots before strikes. None of the General Secretaries there that day was sure they could even sell the deal to their own members. But it was the union's olive branch. To their utter amazement Murdoch dismissed it: 'If this had come three months ago, the answer might have been "yes".'[9]

Tony Dubbins, from the typesetters' union NGA, was furious. The NGA had already conceded more to Murdoch than any other Fleet Street proprietor. They agreed to accept the principle of direct computerised typesetting by journalists on the *London Post*, although it would be a threat to the NGA's very existence. Dubbins was amazed and baffled that News International had dismissed their offer, which to them was the ultimate sacrifice.

In the final meeting Murdoch seemed off-hand and more abrupt than anyone had ever seen him. Then suddenly he delivered a bombshell. 'It's too late for Tower Hamlets,' he said. 'Grays Inn Road and Bouverie Street will have reduced manning. We will employ some hundreds of your members.' He would not specify the numbers or even say whether this was negotiable.[10] The remaining 5,000 workers would be made redundant and would receive the minimum allowable under the Redundancy Payments Act: one week's pay of up to £156 between the ages of 21 and 40 for each year worked and one and a half week's pay for each year worked for those over 40. No existing worker would be offered work at Wapping.

Murdoch told the unions that they were five years too late for Wapping. If they had gone to him with their offer even two years before, he told them, there would have been a deal. 'I told you in September, I am not prepared to let time stand still.'[11] He was now offering five-year legally binding contracts and wanted total flexibility of staff, who would be chosen by the company, and he also wanted mobility between his plants. 'I want to print newspapers,'[12] he told them.

Brenda Dean went on to say that they could now negotiate with the company for agreements which would cover all his plants. To which he answered: 'Three years ago, yes. Now, no.'[13]

After an adjournment Murdoch came back in the room for the last time and told them that there would be no union recognition for their members at Wapping.

At the press conference after the meeting, Brenda Dean, from the mainly clerical workers' union SOGAT, said: 'I rather got the feeling that the company did not want a settlement.' Tony Dubbins from the typesetters' union, the NGA, was shocked at Murdoch's audacity: 'We had given him an olive branch and he'd broken it in two and beat us around the head with it.'[14]

For Rupert Murdoch, it was one of the most exhilarating days of his life.

In his confidential advice to the Portsmouth and Sunderland Newspaper Group back in January 1979, Christopher Pole-Carew, Murdoch's consultant on Wapping, told them: 'Choose the right time for a strike. Summer provides good picketing weather and also holiday time. This, from your point of view, is not a good time for a strike. Probably the best time is January or February'. The advice from Geoffrey Richards, his lawyer, was along the same lines. Shortly before the meeting at the Park Lane Hotel, Richards wrote to Bruce Matthews, News International's Managing Director, with a copy to Rupert Murdoch, as they were now 'much nearer the date of a possible explosion'. His advice was to the point. 'Since the very first day I was involved ... I have advised that, if a moment came when it was necessary to dispense with the workforces at TNL and NGN, the cheapest way of doing so would be to dismiss employees while participating in a strike or other industrial action.'[15] The point was that under the law anyone on strike could be dismissed instantly and lose any redundancy payments to which they might otherwise have been entitled.

As negotiations looked doomed, the three print unions, SOGAT, the NGA and the AEU (Amalgamated Engineering Union), decided to hold ballots on industrial action. Under the new laws there had to be a valid reason for the strike. As 'negotiations', no matter how feeble, were still taking place, it was hard to justify. The unions held ballots and all produced majorities in favour of strike action. On 24 January 1986, the day after the final meeting with Murdoch, workers from all three unions went on strike. As they left the building they were handed a letter which said: 'You have shown that you are not willing to perform your contract of employment. In these circumstances, we accept this repudiation by you of your contract of employment and hereby dismiss you without effect.' News International saved millions on the reduncancy payments the company would otherwise have had to pay. The *London Post* was never mentioned again.

Murdoch spent the first two weeks at Wapping sleeping on a camp bed, doing every sort of job including helping to load paper, and keeping up people's spirits. Then he left for America, where he had to get his new national TV network under way.

News International's move to Wapping cost around £70 million. The company had been expecting trouble. Wapping was a fortress, ringed with razor wire in huge coils, fenced with steel and constantly scanned by the shifting eyes of closed-circuit cameras. It was built to be picket-proof. It needed to be. Under the legislation no more than six pickets were allowed at each gate. But demonstrators turned up in their thousands. Injuries were frequent and on one occasion the police resorted to a cavalry charge to clear the area outside the plant. In the first ten months of the dispute the average number of police used was over 1,000 a day. Overtime payments alone came to £4.6 million.

In the 1970s a move to Wapping would have been unthinkable because of the power of the trade unions. But the Thatcher Government, constantly prompted and encouraged by the Murdoch papers, had brought in tough new legislation in 1980 and 1982. This severely limited the powers of trade unions to deal with a situation like Wapping. The legislation was so tightly written that it is doubtful that, even if Murdoch had been on the other side, he could have found a way round. The new laws meant that picketing was only legal if it took place at the place of work. Secondary picketing, which had been such a powerful weapon for the unions in the 1970s, was now illegal. This meant that the print unions could not picket News International's suppliers to prevent delivery. If they did, then News International could take legal action against the union. Eddie Shah had already successfully used this law against the NGA at Warrington and the NGA had been heavily fined, losing a substantial portion of its assets. News International continually used the courts against the print unions, which suffered heavy fines and further sequestration of their assets.

Anna Murdoch says of Wapping: 'Managements were weak and the unions so strong that someone had to do something. I thought that the move to Wapping was historic. After Rupert committed himself to it, he was probably more relaxed than anyone else. He has revitalised newspapers.'[16] But it was not just British newspapers that were revitalised.

In fact, British newspapers have not been revitalised. Two new national newspapers have appeared but both were conceived before Murdoch established himself in Wapping. *Today* was started by Eddie Shah, the father of the electronic revolution, and the *Independent* was inspired by his example.

What *has* been revitalised is Murdoch's finances.

The move had a dramatic effect on News International's profit and loss account. It cut the News International wage bill by £45 million. In 1985, before the move, News International made £39.1 million on sales of £423 million in Britain. But two years later, when the dust had settled, the pre-tax profit was £98.3 million on sales of £502 million. In 1988 the pre-tax profit was greater still: £165 million on sales of £586 million, and in 1989 it was £161 million on sales of £680 million. In 1990 it was £142 million on sales of £675 million. The Wapping gamble had succeeded spectacularly and gave Murdoch the stake money he needed to bet on establishing the fourth network station in the United States and later to continue his takeover trail in Australia and America. But there was a price to pay.

Murdoch and his aides have always claimed publicly that he was not against unions, just for modern methods of working. But he granted no union recognition in the Wapping plant and has scrapped even minimal consultation. And in his anxiety to get into Wapping he failed to spot just how outdated his plant really was. His advisor, Christopher Pole-Carew, warned him that his printing machines were 'antiquated'.[17] Despite his reputation for being a brilliant newspaper man who is at one with the technology, Murdoch has not much time for such details. One former executive remembers his comment about one printing machine: 'the same price as an aeroplane and not as much fun'. But at Wapping this was a costly error. Scrapping old machines cost him £75 million between 1988 and 1990. And their replacement burdened him with debt just when he could least afford it.

Wapping had only been possible because of the new tough anti-union laws brought in by the Thatcher Government. While the pickets were battering at the gates, one

Government Minister got through the demonstrators to lend his support. Norman Tebbit, a minister in Mrs Thatcher's Government and one of the architects of the anti-labour laws, was taken round by the *Sun*'s editor, Kelvin Mackenzie. At the end of the thirst-making tour Tebbit was offered a drink. Unfortunately Wapping was dry and the best Mackenzie could manage was a glass of lemonade. Tebbit replied: 'You must be fucking joking!'[18] He later accepted Murdoch's offer of a job and became a presenter on Sky Television.

Though some members were not so keen on the Wapping hospitality, the Conservative Party was very much in favour of Murdoch and supported the move to Wapping. As always, he was only too happy to return a favour to a friend in need, especially when they were as powerful as Margaret Thatcher, who had got herself into quite a mess with the Westland affair.

In 1985 Sikorsky, a subsidiary of the American company United Technologies, had proposed a rescue plan for Britain's only helicopter company, Westland. Murdoch had recently got his American citizenship and was a non-executive director of United Technologies. This plan was supported by the Westland board, Mrs Thatcher and the Secretary of State for Trade, Leon Brittan. Westland had huge debts and needed a major financial reconstruction to survive.

The complexity of the plan meant that the board needed a 75 per cent majority approval by the shareholders. Normally this would have gone through without a hitch, but there was another bidder. Known as the European consortium, it was led by helicopter man Alan Bristow, and supported by helicopter companies from France, Germany and Italy together with two British firms, British Aerospace (BAe) and the General Electric Company (GEC). It was also supported by the Secretary of State for Defence, Michael Heseltine.

The battle quickly split into two camps: the Thatcher/ American camp and the Heseltine/European camp.

Although in public she advocated evenhandedness, in Cabinet Mrs Thatcher argued that nothing and nobody should be allowed to undermine the American bid. She tried to silence Heseltine in Cabinet but failed. At the height of the battle Heseltine wrote a letter which provoked the *Sun* to take sides. Its headline, aimed at Heseltine, was: 'You Liar'. Before the battle was over both Heseltine and Brittan resigned, and for an afternoon the Government looked to be in serious trouble.

But this was not the only help Murdoch gave Thatcher. In the end it was the shareholders who had to decide. Just before the final crucial meeting six shareholders from Switzerland, Panama and Australia bought shares in Westland and voted for the American bid. On 24 January 1986, the day before printing officially began at Wapping, the London brokers Rowe and Pitman got a call from Australia asking them to buy 2.6 million Westland shares. This was a crucial number as it was just under the 5 per cent limit at which shareholdings need to be declared to the Stock Exchange. The shares were booked in the name of Actraint No. 34 Pty of Canberra. This was a cover for TNT, the company which had just signed a £1-million-a-week contract with Murdoch to handle the distribution of all News International's papers out of Wapping. TNT was also the half-owner with News Corporation of the Australian airline company, Ansett.

One senior Westland figure, at least, was not surprised by TNT's sudden interest in the helicopter company's affairs. 'Rupert undoubtedly knew what was going on and he may have thought he could help out.'[19] Despite a parliamentary investigation, a concert party between the six mystery shareholders who bought 20 per cent of Westland's shares was never proved. Once again Murdoch had slipped the net.

The Government supported Murdoch throughout the early days of Wapping. Without the changes in industrial law which the Conservative Government had introduced, Wapping would not have been possible. Murdoch had reciprocated its generosity by ensuring that Mrs Thatcher had the easiest ride any Prime Minister had received from the British press for twenty years. The uncritical support of News International's papers, particularly the *Sun*, had helped the Conservative Party win two general elections. It meant that there was no love lost between Murdoch and the Opposition Labour Party. In 1986 the Labour Party threatened that a future Labour Government would ban foreign ownership of the press. As always, Murdoch was one step ahead of even those regulators who hoped to be in power in the future. He was asked how that would place him. No problem, said Murdoch. It would not worry him at all. 'My children own all the shares and they were born in England. Mr Kinnock doesn't know that,' he chuckled. 'He hasn't checked that one out yet.'[20]

5

Fox

In 1985 Murdoch launched his attack on the American television market. This was a major strategic move into new territory for News Corporation. It was inspired by the grand strategy of creating a world-wide media empire which gripped him throughout the 1980s. Like many of his other deals it depended on him exploiting the opportunities presented by a highly regulated world. Like his other ventures it was to be very costly. It was also a huge gamble. As he assesses his future in the 1990s he still does not know whether it has been successful.

Though he was seen in the early 1980s as an inky-fingered newspaperman, Murdoch was no stranger to television. He'd been involved with television stations in Australia since 1958 and he had been an active shareholder in Britain's London Weekend Television in the early 1970s. His roots in American television went back a long way too. On an early trip to the United States Murdoch met Leonard Goldenson, the head of the American Broadcasting Corporation (ABC) which at that time was establishing itself as a rival to the two already established television networks, CBS and NBC. Goldenson and Murdoch immediately took to each other. Both were outsiders knocking at the door and easily identified with each other's struggle. Goldenson was sufficiently impressed by Murdoch to buy some shares in News Corporation.[1] And Murdoch was sufficiently impressed by ABC's programmes to buy some of them for his Australian television stations.

When Murdoch went to live in New York in the early 1970s he became close friends with the multi-millionaire John Kluge, who owned Metromedia, a group of successful television stations in seven major cities across the United States, as well as radio stations and entertainment companies.[2] In 1983 Murdoch was one of the investors who helped finance Kluge when he turned his business back into a private company. Murdoch was a prominent guest at Kluge's wedding in 1981 and Kluge continually encouraged Murdoch to go into American television.[3]

Kluge's argument to Murdoch was persuasive. He told him that News Corporation was ideally placed to start a fourth television network. It already had an established news operation in the United States, which could be combined with Metromedia's television stations and a film studio. Such a combination would guarantee the flow of news and entertainment programmes and the means of distribution – the basis of a fourth network. This chimed with Murdoch's own thinking. He had already been considering this. Back in 1982 he had said to a News International executive that he thought he could 'get 20th Century-Fox'.[4]

Unlike commercial television in Britain, broadcast television in the United States is highly fragmented. Across the States there are hundreds of television stations, many of them owned locally. As these are relatively small companies

101

they cannot afford to produce expensive drama and games shows or run an international news service, so these and other programmes are bought in from independent producers, film studios and news organisations. In a free market, companies could be expected to buy up a large number of small stations to get the benefits of economy of scale and national coverage. A company owning, say, 100 stations across America would have guaranteed outlets for its programmes, would be able to use its buying muscle to keep programme costs low, and would be able to sell advertising nationally.

In the past some American companies had been quick to see the potential for setting up a network of television companies across the States. However, the founding fathers of American television were concerned about the dangers of concentration in such a powerful medium. They were determined to stop the natural drift towards concentration and control by a few companies. No network company is allowed to own more than twelve stations, with a maximum coverage of 25 per cent of the United States. So the three network companies increase their reach by signing up affiliated stations who take network-provided programmes for specified hours of the day during which time the network companies can sell advertising.

Murdoch saw a way of exploiting the rules by becoming, in effect, a mini-network. The FCC rules prohibited any 'network' and its affiliated companies from syndicating or acquiring a financial interest in programmes which it produces or buys for its network. However, these rules only applied when the 'network' broadcast more than 15 hours a week to 25 stations in more than 12 states. Provided he stayed under the 15-hours-a-week threshold he could have the best of all worlds. Fox could make and syndicate its own programmes and they could target them at the rich prime-time hours, rather than transmit all day like the three majors. Once again, he had found a way to exploit the rules of a heavily regulated industry, all in the name of a free market.

By the time Murdoch was planning his assault, the three networks, ABC, NBC and CBS, had ruled supreme in the United States for decades. There had been several attempts to enter this market but all the previous hopefuls had retired hurt and significantly poorer. But by the early 1980s the networks were vulnerable to attack by a resourceful and well-capitalised competitor like Rupert Murdoch. The network companies and their affiliates were losing market share of both audience and advertisers. Though they competed vigorously with each other, they did so within the confines of a comfortable cartel. Inevitably, the overheads of the established network companies, which had been protected from effective competition for so long, were high.

This was just the sort of complacent establishment with an unprotected underbelly that Murdoch found irresistible. It was tailor-made for the Murdoch theory of market penetration. He would do what he had done all his life. He would start a new network company, operate it on a very tight budget and offer the public something they were not getting from the existing suppliers. It was a formula he had used to devastating effect, taking the *Sun* from a minor paper to the best-selling daily in the English-speaking world.

His belief was that he could broadcast attractive programmes, which did not necessarily need to be expensive. Such a network would inevitably attract a great deal of attention. The viewers, who were becoming increasingly dissatisfied with the diet they were getting from the existing networks, would switch on. Because his cost base was so much lower he would be able to offer cheaper slots, and the advertising would inevitably follow. Others had tried and failed but he was not put off – after all, he was gambling other people's money. The opportunity to put the theory into practice came along in 1985, when half of 20th Century-Fox Film Studios came on the market.

Back in June 1981 the wealthy oil tycoon Marvin Davis had indulged his passion for movies by buying 20th Century-Fox. By 1984 it was in trouble. Senior management was in revolt, losses were mounting and Fox's bankers were putting on pressure to bring in new management.[5] Davis was in a corner. He turned for help to one of the legendary Hollywood film executives, Barry Diller. Davis's timing was fortunate. Diller was falling out with his bosses at Gulf and Western, owners of Paramount Studios. Although Diller was on the way out, Davis didn't know this.

Because of the huge sums of money available, Hollywood attracts some of the smartest brains and toughest negotiators in the United States. Barry Diller is one of them. He negotiated brilliantly, making Davis concede everything to secure his services. In desperation Davis signed a contract probably unparalleled in the power it surrendered. The five-year contract was signed on 1 October 1984. Diller was paid $3 million a year, as well as receiving a generous range of executive perks. The money was good, but the contract contained two other important provisions which were exceptional, even by Hollywood standards.

First, although Davis and Diller were to be 'in frequent and regular contact', they were only required to meet twice a year. Second, Diller effectively could leave almost whenever he liked and could leave automatically if Davis sold more than 20 per cent of the studio.[6] In practice this gave Diller a virtual veto over the future ownership of Fox and put him in a very powerful position if he ever fell out with Davis. And this being Hollywood, inevitably they did.

The reason was money. Diller's contract committed Davis to putting in enough money to finance new Fox films. Davis had other ideas of how to spend his money. The only solution for Davis was to bring in a new partner. Rupert Murdoch had already made enquiries to see if Fox was for sale, so Davis rang him. Murdoch agreed to buy a half share for $250 million – $162 million paid to Davis directly and $88 million of 'new money' to go into the studios. Diller, of course, could ruin the deal by leaving, but he talked to Murdoch, whom he knew only slightly. He liked him and signed a new contract, which gave him even greater power. He became the highest-paid executive in News Corporation, after Murdoch himself. It also made him unique in the Murdoch empire: he was his own master. Murdoch's role was limited to consultant and adviser.

Within weeks of the deal with Davis, Murdoch was offered Kluge's Metromedia stations. As a result of taking Metromedia private, Kluge was heavily in debt and needed to sell. Diller knew Kluge, had sold programmes to him and had previously thought of making a bid for the Metromedia stations.

At the end of March 1985 Diller held a small cocktail party in his Los Angeles office. Kluge was there because he was attending the annual investors' conference organised by the financier Michael Milken for his many clients at Drexel Burnham Lambert. Murdoch was there because he was on his way from Australia to New York. Diller asked Kluge if the rumour that he was selling his TV stations was true. Kluge said he was willing to sell some of them. Within ten days Murdoch had agreed on behalf of Fox to pay Kluge his asking price of $2 billion for the stations in New York, Chicago, Boston, Washington, Houston, Dallas and Los Angeles. The conditional contract was signed at the beginning of May 1985.[7] It was conditional on approval from the FCC.

There were two remarkable features to these deals: the

speed with which they were done and the price paid. The Metromedia deal valued the company at about fifteen times profits. This was high. At that time television stations were changing hands at around ten times profits. Until then Murdoch had a reputation in the United Kingdom for never over-paying. There were two reasons why he paid so much. First, Metromedia provided a unique opportunity for his grand plan of creating a fourth network. There were other bidders hovering in the wings and, if they succeeded, then Murdoch would have missed his chance completely. And he had no way of knowing whether the chance to establish his network would come round again. Metromedia's stations exactly fitted his requirements. They were in the top ten areas of America, representing a quarter of America's television audience.[8] A core of strong stations like these would provide the basis for a network company.

But there was another reason to hurry. Murdoch's plan ran foul of the American broadcasting regulations. There was a limited amount of time for him to get official approval before Kluge went and found another buyer.

There were two regulatory problems for Murdoch. He was an Australian citizen, and only Americans are allowed to own television stations. Second, News Corporation owned several newspapers in the same areas as the Metromedia stations, and American broadcasting regulations specifically forbade this. Barry Diller raised these difficulties with Murdoch at his office in the *New York Post*, just before the deal with Kluge was done. Murdoch brushed them aside. The expansion of News Corporation had been built on his extraordinary ability to leap over any regulatory hurdle. With characteristic chutzpah, he told Diller that the nationality issue 'was not a problem' and he would figure out how to deal with the cross-ownership rule.[9]

On the face of it, this was going to take some figuring. It

was difficult to see why Murdoch believed he could succeed where everyone else had failed. No one had ever before managed to persuade the Federal Communications Commission that they should be allowed to own both a newspaper and a television station in a major city, let alone a non-American.

Murdoch, however had good reason to believe that he had more than a sporting chance. Ronald Reagan had been re-elected in 1984. His Administration's policy of deregulation was in full swing and fully applauded by Murdoch's papers. His papers' support for Reagan had already won the appreciation of the President. After the 1981 inauguration he sent Murdoch a presidential plaque, thanking him for his help.[10] At a dinner in the same year, Congressman Jack Kemp said appreciatively, 'Rupert used the editorial page and every other page necessary to elect Ronald Reagan President.'[11] This support continued throughout Reagan's Presidency. Journalists on Murdoch's papers both in the United States and in Britain had been forced to give President Reagan, and his transatlantic ally Mrs Thatcher, almost uncritical support. Murdoch went to great lengths to make sure that his enthusiasm was not only appreciated at the White House, but was equally felt elsewhere in the Administration. At a lunch for government leaders he had impressed a Washington lawyer as a man of 'enormous vision'. The lawyer was Mark Fowler.[12]

In March 1985, Fowler was the Reagan-appointed chairman of the FCC. He shared Reagan's commitment to deregulation, which neatly coincided with Murdoch's aspirations. Past American administrations had seen rules against cross-ownership as a way of increasing diversity and choice. Fowler saw them as obstacles to freeing up markets 'to serve consumer needs'. For him all the FCC regulations were 'fair game'.[13] His policy was to go through the rule book and eliminate every rule unless there was an overwhelming reason why it should stay. Over four years he got rid of 70 per cent of the rules and regulations that governed American broadcasting.

Though Murdoch had a powerful supporter in the White House and an FCC which was ideologically in agreement with him, his proposed deal was still not a pushover. Over the spring and summer of 1985 he had to fight his corner vigorously to get a waiver of the cross-ownership rule. He signed up some of the best media lawyers in Washington to fight the case. It was a fight which again revealed his uncanny knack of getting the regulators to bend. But the fight itself meant that his longer-term ambitions were frustrated.

News Corporation made its first application on 22 June 1985. At this stage Murdoch had applied for American citizenship but was still an Australian. On the face of it, he was barred at the first hurdle. Only Americans were allowed to own TV stations. The FCC was limited by its own precedent. In 1982 Efren Palacios had made an application to run a new commercial station in Texas. Like Murdoch his application for citizenship was pending. The FFC told him: 'Although your application for citizenship is pending, you are not yet a citizen and, thus, you are statutorily barred from holding a broadcast licence. For this reason your application can not be granted ... consequently your application is dismissed.'[14] Things had clearly changed by 1985. Murdoch received no such letter and the FCC started work considering his application. Efren Palacios failed because his name was not Rupert Murdoch and he was not a close ally of the Reagan White House. But this was only the first example of the preferential treatment Murdoch was to receive from the FCC.

Murdoch's application for citizenship also received preferential treatment. As might be expected, he hired the best immigration lawyers in the United States and his application went through in almost record time. On the day on which he made his formal appearance in the Federal Court in New York to receive his citizenship he entered not from the public hallway but from the judge's chambers. Murdoch's declared pleasure at becoming an American citizen[15] contrasted oddly with some earlier protestations. In 1980, when the Australian Broadcasting Tribunal was investigating Murdoch's suitability to own Australian television stations, he said:

> I regard myself as an Australian, serving an Australian company with large interests around the world. It is necessary for the pursuit of my duties at this time to spend more time out of Australia than in it. So far as I am concerned that has no bearing on my love for this country or my feelings towards it or my Australianism.

And when asked whether he was going to become an American citizen he said: 'I think I have stated many times that it is not my desire.'[16] By 1985 times had obviously changed. Murdoch, the great pragmatist when there was· a deal he wanted, had clearly changed as well.

Whereas giving up Australian citizenship and becoming an American was easy, he still had a much more substantial problem with the cross-ownership rule. This had been established by the FCC in 1975 to guarantee the diversity of both ownership and viewpoints which the FCC regarded as central to a democratic society.[17] In the years since, the FCC had allowed a few cross-ownership cases through, but they had never granted such a waiver to a new entrant to broadcast television. Murdoch wanted the FCC to grant him a waiver which would allow him to own both a daily newspaper and a television station in two major cities, Chicago and New York. And he wanted it to last for two years. This was an unprecedented request. The FCC had never agreed to such a proposal before. No newspaper company entering the broadcast television business had been granted a temporary waiver, and previous waivers to television station owners had been for only eighteen months.[18]

In the past the FCC had granted waivers only in exceptional circumstances – when they were likely to increase diversity or when the television station, newspaper or radio station could not survive by itself. None of these arguments applied in the News Corporation case. Murdoch had already ruined this argument himself by stating on record that the *Chicago Sun-Times* was nearly twice as profitable as when he had bought it in 1983.[19]

News Corporation ran two arguments in defence of its claim to have two years to sell the newspapers in Chicago and New York. First, a rapid sale would reduce diversity, and second, it would reduce the amount News Corporation could expect to receive.[20] This case was supported by the claim that there were not many potential buyers for the two newspapers. It is hard to see how they could make this claim with a straight face.

Within days of Fox's planned takeover of Metromedia being announced, a Murdoch aide, Howard Rubenstein, said 'The phones have been busy. [Murdoch] is considering offers.'[21] The *New York Times* quoted an anonymous Murdoch spokesman as saying there were 'several "serious" offers'.[22] The names of British press barons Robert Maxwell and Lord Rothermere were mentioned in reports about the possible buyers for the *New York Post*. In the case of the *Chicago Sun-Times*, a Murdoch representative had actually met one of the possible buyers, a consortium led by lawyer William Singer, who had been a previous bidder for the title.[23] And Sun Publishing of Canada had also said that they 'might be interested'.[24]

Given the amount of interest and the speed with which

News Corporation themselves had managed to buy seven television stations, it was clearly going to be difficult to argue that there was no market for other media properties like major newspapers. They were challenged on this by the public interest lobbying group Media Access Project[25] and so took professional advice. The advice News Corporation received was just what it needed to hear. Despite appearances, it was, in fact, difficult and time-consuming to sell newspapers and to 'maximize the financial result' (i.e. make as much money for News Corporation as possible). Two years would be needed.[26]

The advice came from the New York investment adviser, Stanley Shuman, who was also a member of the News Corporation board. Indeed Shuman himself advised News Corporation not to put the papers on the market until after the FCC had made up its mind.[27] In other words, News Corporation produced as an expert witness their own director whose own advice was making it hard to find buyers. Despite the absurdity of this, the FCC accepted News Corporation's case: 'We recognise that market forces associated with sales of daily newspapers may be different from those affecting broadcast properties making them more difficult to sell and therefore believe that a waiver for a period of 24 months would be appropriate here . . .'[28]

The FCC's willingness to accept News Corporation's word on this was another remarkable case of special treatment. On previous occasions when this had been claimed, the FCC had demanded details of a company's attempts to sell as well as accounts showing the profits and losses of the papers in question. News Corporation was not asked to provide this. Furthermore, the FCC did not think it necessary to impose strict reporting conditions on Murdoch's behaviour during the waiver period, even though they accepted that he was a person who had 'changed his earlier

111

stated intentions'.[29] The changes to which the FCC referred were his broken promises over the purchase of *The Times* in London (see Chapter 3) and the purchase of the Melbourne television station in Australia (Chapter 2). In the case of *The Times*, he had made written and binding commitments to the British Government guaranteeing the editorial independence of the paper and then broken them. In the case of the Australian television station he had broken the rules about multiple shareholdings in television stations. Despite this record, which was not challenged by News Corporation, the FCC swept his waiver application through. Last year, Mark Fowler told us that: 'What he asked for seemed reasonable and I still think was reasonable'.

There is little doubt that in this case the private interest of Murdoch was allowed to triumph over the public interest, as it had previously been defined by the FCC. Fowler summarised the reason for his decision by saying that he wanted to avoid Murdoch having a 'fire sale', that is, one that involved selling the papers at a knockdown price.[30]

This decision was a substantial concession to Murdoch because it was a very hard case to argue. The FCC's job was to ensure that there was diversity in local areas and to safeguard this diversity by preventing cross-ownership. A key point against Murdoch was that he had entered into a voluntary agreement and knew what the regulations were when he made the deal. The Washington-based Media Access Project argued that to allow a waiver which meant that he would get a higher price for his papers was, effectively, like handing News Corporation a public subsidy.[31] Over the summer of 1985 News Corporation and its opponents argued out this case in various submissions to the FCC with references to the eighteenth-century economist Adam Smith, the other side's economic naivety and ever-obscurer past cases of the FCC.

The Media Access Project, run by a nimble-brained lawyer, Andrew Schwartzman, kept News Corporation on the hop. Schwartzman turned the company's free market ideology back against the FCC. He argued that a distress sale, the thing Murdoch feared, was actually good for diversity as it lowered the price and brought more potential buyers into the market.[32] This was a telling point, but News Corporation argued it would do the opposite: by pushing down the price of a newspaper nearer to its asset value it would make it more likely for the owner to close the paper down, so reducing diversity and choice.[33] 'The waiver requested should be granted to minimise the potential that the important contributions to diversity represented by *The Chicago Sun-Times* and *The New York Post* will be impaired or lost altogether,' read one of News Corporation's submissions, going on to say:

> If sufficient pressure to sell hurriedly is exerted, the value of the physical assets of the papers – the land, buildings, plant and the like – will very likely be the upper limit on purchase offers. In such an environment either the seller . . . or the buyer . . . might very well cease operation of the papers and liquidate its physical assets.[34]

This argument quickly backfired on News Corporation and put Murdoch on the defensive. To the untrained legal eye this read like a threat to close the papers. It contrasted oddly with Murdoch's earlier statements that the *Chicago Sun-Times* was at least twice as profitable as when he bought it. When challenged, News Corporation quickly denied this interpretation at the end of August, saying its submission to the FCC was just 'lawyers' language'.[35]

By now it was clear that the FCC examination of the bid for Metromedia was a charade. But there was one final hiccup for Murdoch. It emerged that he did not actually have the money lined up to buy the Metromedia stations after all. When Murdoch applied for the stations to be transferred to Fox he was asked a standard question about his financial ability to complete the takeover. He said that he had the financial muscle but that the deal needed the approval of the holders of $1.375–$1.4 billion of bonds in Metromedia.[36] Unfortunately for Murdoch this approval was not forthcoming.

These bonds had been issued to help Kluge take Metromedia private in 1984. The issue had been handled by Drexel Burnham Lambert, the specialists in such high-yielding (junk) bonds. It was their junk bond expert Michael Milken who had tipped off Diller that Metromedia was for sale. It was they who assured Murdoch that there would be no trouble with the bond holders. Only a few days after Murdoch and Kluge signed, Milken told him that he could not get the agreement.[37] Murdoch's search for a solution was nearing an end when Schwartzman drew the FCC's attention to the financing problem. Just in time, News Corporation came up with an alternative plan to pay for Fox by a new issue of preference shares in Fox (See Chapter 11). But the fact remained that Murdoch had been allowed to give one of the sketchiest accounts of his finances ever given in a major deal being considered by the FCC. By now the whole Murdoch network plan was out of the bag. He had bought out the remaining 50 per cent share in 20th Century-Fox and on 6 October 1985 announced his intention to start a 'fourth network'. In September he had become an American citizen and at the end of November the FCC gave the two year-waiver which he sought. Getting the waiver had taken longer than both he and Fowler had expected.[38] This was to prove decisive because although Murdoch had won the battle he had lost the war.

The war Murdoch wanted to win was to get a permanent waiver so that he would never have to sell either the Chicago or the New York papers. He wanted to do something which had never been done before – he still wanted to own a daily newspaper and a television station in two major cities. In May 1985 Murdoch had been asked by an Australian magazine if he would be selling these papers. He replied: 'We will, unless the law is changed and there have been some mumblings about that . . . when you start looking forward to the number of years [comprising a temporary waiver] and you watch how the legislation is changing in that whole broadcasting area – we'd hope for the best.'[39] Murdoch's hope was that by the time the temporary waiver came to an end, the FCC would have been able to make his temporary waiver permanent.

In January 1987 Fox bought a seventh television station WFXT (formerly WXNE-TV) from the Christian Broadcasting Network. This took Fox into 24 per cent of American homes. It also gave Senator Edward Kennedy the chance to clip Murdoch's wings. Unfortunately for Murdoch, he had not accounted for the legislative ingenuity of Senator Edward Kennedy. Just as Congress was about to break for Christmas, Senator Edward Kennedy tacked a clause on to the end of a Bill going to the White House for signature. It prohibited the FCC from giving anyone a temporary waiver from the cross-ownership rules. Kennedy's piece of mischief was clearly aimed at Murdoch whose *Boston Herald* newspaper was a constant irritant to Kennedy on his own patch. Kennedy had disliked Murdoch from the early 1980s when he ran against President Carter only to see himself pilloried in Murdoch's *New York Post*. Revenge was sweet. Kennedy was attacked for behaving in an underhand way and a federal judge upheld Murdoch's complaint that the amendment was unfairly aimed at him. However, it was a temporary victory because the eventual legislation enshrined the principle that whilst the FCC could grant temporary waivers, it could not grant permanent ones. The 'mumblings' of which Murdoch spoke had been silenced and he had to sell both the Boston television station and the *New York Post*.

Although Murdoch had a film studio which could make some of the films for Fox Television, and he had the core of television stations to broadcast them, he still needed more than this. He needed more stations, more programmes and, most importantly, more advertisers. Through the autumn and winter of 1985 Barry Diller held a series of luncheons for the most successful television producers in the United States, so they could meet Murdoch and hear about the plans for the fourth national television service. In January 1986 Murdoch announced his plans officially.

The original concept was kept deliberately simple. Throughout the 1980s the FCC had increased the number of independent TV stations from 112 in 1980 to 270 in 1986. It also changed the rules to allow a station group to own up to twelve stations, provided it did not cover more than 25 per cent of the homes. Programming could then become affordable by these stations and this would lessen the grip of the majors. This was the chink that Murdoch and Diller sought.

One of the first recruits was David Johnson. After a lifetime in the networks he wrote to Barry Diller, having read a piece in the *Wall Street Journal* about his plans. He told Diller not to make the same mistakes as the networks. Johnson's argument was that running a network station is 'a conceptually elegant and simple business. You lease programmes, up-link them to affiliates and you sell the advertising'.[40] This exercise did not require five thousand people. Murdoch and Diller agreed.

As always with every Murdoch operation, Fox Television started with very low overheads. The total payroll was not much more than twenty people and even by the time it went on the air by the end of the year, it still employed only 100 people.

It was a real shock for many of the early recruits when they discovered just how hard they had to work, compared to the life they had experienced in the networks.

The sales pitch was to broadcast just one or two nights a week in prime time, between 8 p.m. and 11 p.m. and aim at a young blue-collar audience.

One of the first tasks was to get independent stations around the country to sign up as Fox affiliates. It was not an easy task, as many were already committed to buying programmes from elsewhere. But all the independents knew that programming costs were rising and Fox's main selling pitch was that they could provide cheaper programmes and thus improve the independents' profit margins. When it came to describing the programmes, that was a bit trickier because Fox had nothing to show its prospective customers and a very unclear idea of what programmes it was going to make. The independents asked what the programmes were going to be. Fox's salesmen, with true Murdoch chutzpah, told them: 'We don't know what they're going to be, but they're going to be good'. David Johnson is a charismatic talker and one of the smartest selling brains in the network. In his view Murdoch's name was crucial: 'The mystique associated with his name was the glue that held that part of the effort together. People wanted to meet him.'[41] He believes it was the Murdoch name that opened doors. 'Without his name', he argues, 'we would have got thrown out of a lot of offices.'

Without any programmes to show, the sales pitch concentrated on the economics of the industry. The 270 independent television stations were Fox's target. They were told that if the present trends continued and programming costs continued to rise, the future looked bleak for them. Many of these stations had been tremendous investments to the people who owned them and this argument had a strong appeal. The independents were offered two-year contracts, in which they could take Fox's programmes at prime time and late night as well as any other special programmes the company might make.

The sales team's job was made slightly easier in May 1986 when Fox announced one of its main programmes, *The Late Show*, presented by the abrasive comedienne Joan Rivers. Rivers was a national name as the host of the successful *Tonight* show on NBC. Signing her proved that Fox were real players in the network television game. Fox went on the air on 9 October 1986 with 95 independent stations signed up. Theoretically these covered 85 per cent of television homes, more than Fox had originally expected to reach. But in fact many of them had very weak signals and CBS, one of the network competitors, reckoned that they only reached 55 per cent.[42]

Fox's programmes were a disaster. They looked just like any other network programme – but worse. David Johnson now admits that 'there was not a full appreciation of the fact that to get people to change their viewing habits, which in some cases were thirty-five to forty years old, you have to give them a reason to switch.'[43]

Fox's programmes did not provide that reason, because by and large they were made by all the same sorts of people who were making programmes for the other networks. As a result Fox were not delivering on any of their promises. They were not delivering better programmes. They were not delivering the promised audiences, and as a result of this they were not delivering the promised level of advertising.

The affiliated stations around the country started to get restless. David Johnson and his team went on another round of visits to try and persuade them not to pull out. One station did. Fox managed to cover it up by claiming that it was Fox which had decided to cancel the affiliation. Again it was the Murdoch mystique that encouraged the stations to stick with

Fox. 'We spent a great deal of time saying – don't worry, things are going to get better. Rupert Murdoch is pouring hundreds of millions of dollars into this effort, in the end there is going to be a terrific pay-off.'[44]

The cost of Fox was indeed high. News Corporation's accounts for the year which ended in June 1987 show that Fox had already cost around $40 million – quite apart from the $2.5 billion cost of buying Metromedia and 20th Century-Fox. By the summer of 1987 the station was losing about $2 million a week, almost twice what had been projected.[45] There was no sign of a turnround and, worse, no sign of a strategy to deal with the problem.

The formula for the unsuccessful *Late Show* was changed in May 1987 when Joan Rivers was replaced as the host. This single event attracted huge amounts of unfavourable publicity for Fox. As always, Murdoch found a way of turning disaster into triumph. The Annual Report for the year to June 1987 told the shareholders that 'the exposure the show received has helped to firmly establish in the minds of the television audiences the identity of the stations affiliated with Fox.' As Fox was in the middle of an exceptionally unpleasant row with Joan Rivers, the report went on to tell the shareholders what a success it now was with celebrity hosts. Within three months they knew that the 'revised format incorporating more comedy, novelty and singing acts' was 'an attractive option for local and national advertisers'. The show was cancelled. It was then replaced in October 1987 by the *Wilton North Report*. When this also flopped the *Late Show* was brought back.[46]

No one could see any sign of an end to the enormous cash drain. There were endless public expressions of confidence. But in the view of one senior executive, who saw the weekly financial figures, the company was within weeks of collapsing.[47] Murdoch held on. In the year to June 1988

Fox's total losses were over $90 million. News Corporation managed to disguise this by an accounting sleight of hand (see Chapter 11). The company was only able to afford the cash drain because by now Murdoch's gamble in moving his British papers to Wapping was beginning to pay off. In 1988 the British end of his newspaper operation made profits of over £120 million – four times as much as before the move.[48] These profits did not go to pay for the losses, they just meant that News Corporation had the money to pay the interest on its massive debt. Murdoch guessed that provided he continued to meet his payments to his bankers, he could let his gamble run a bit longer. He needed a lucky break.

In early 1988 he got it. Fox at last discovered a successful programme formula which gave them the niche they were searching for. It is surprising Murdoch did not find this niche right at the start. Fox began to do on television what Murdoch's papers had done for years. The programme which started the recovery was *America's Most Wanted*. The programme reconstructed an unsolved crime, often in the same lurid tone that had been the hallmark of his tabloids round the world. The programme was not just sensationalism. It had a social purpose. Viewers were asked to ring a police phone number if they had any information which might help. The show was a success. The same formula has been sensationally successful in Britain with BBC's *Crimewatch* programme. The programme was tested in Sacramento. In April 1988 it was on the Fox network. *America's Most Wanted* was an instant success. After thirteen shows, thirteen criminals had been apprehended. Barry Diller loved it. It looked like nothing else on network television and it was incredibly cheap, only $125,000 a show.[49] Not everyone in Fox agreed with Diller. They thought that *America's Most Wanted* was 'not network' material. That was, of course, exactly Diller's point. Besides, it was Fox's best-rating show. It has remained one of the bankers in the Fox schedules. By 1990 News Corporation could boast that it had led to the capture of more than 100 criminals.

America's Most Wanted was given a name. It was called 'tabloid' or 'reality' television. This was Fox's unique appeal to viewers. Other programmes with similar production values quickly followed. *A Current Affair*, a sensationalist news programme, was run in New York in June 1986 and then put on to the network in June 1987. Gradually Fox's stations began to get some market share. The ratings started to climb. In February 1988 Fox had only 6 per cent of the network audience. In May it was 7 per cent; by November up to 8 per cent. By now Fox had something else going for it. Following Murdoch's purchase of *TV Guide* in August, Fox was treated as a network company in the magazine. This was important. With 16 million copies sold each week *TV Guide* dominated the television listings market. Although *TV Guide* paid Fox no editorial favours, this listing helped its profile.

Fox had discovered a way of breaking the 'least objectionable programming principle' which had characterised American network television for years. The established networks, with the lion's share of the audience, pursued a programme policy which aimed to offend no one. Fox, aiming at a smaller niche market of young blue-collar workers, seemed not to care. The formula was similar to Murdoch's tabloids. He wanted to shock and amaze, scandalise and vulgarise. This was what the audience wanted. The most important thing for a new network was to be different, so that it got noticed. If the viewers noticed, then so would the advertisers. Soap operas like *Married . . . with Children* and later the wildly popular cartoon series *The Simpsons* confronted some of the traditional family values which made successful programmes like *The Cosby Show* such saccharine viewing.

121

The irony of this development was clear. Some of Fox's programmes were genuinely anti-establishment and were dubbed 'guerrilla television' or 'counter programming'. They espoused values which were different from those of the conventional right-wing proprietor Rupert Murdoch. To some extent this was because the running of Fox was out of his hands. Barry Diller's contract specifically limited Murdoch's role to that of adviser and consultant.[50] Unlike newspapers where he could go down on the floor and change anything he did not like, he could not do that with television. He knew little about the nuts and bolts of the industry and so was completely at Diller's mercy.

By 1990 Fox was making profits and was a recognised success. However, by now the other networks had caught on to the attractions of the Fox style of programming. They too started to produce counter programming and guerilla television. This now represents a major threat to Fox. The other network companies are much larger and they have the resources to take the formula further. With News Corporation now desperately short of spare cash, it remains an open question whether Fox can compete with this. Murdoch may be in the familiar position of a new competitor who has managed to carve out a small share of a large market but can't get any further because the big producers can do everything he can and have more money to do it.

6

HWT and Queensland Press

'I think it would be a pity if I grew any bigger in Australia. There are now basically three groups in Australia and that's too few already. If I were to grow bigger and take over one of the other groups . . . that would be against the public interest . . . The fewer there are, the worse it is,' Rupert Murdoch told an interviewer from *More* magazine in 1977.[1] Privately he told another journalist: 'Monopoly is a terrible thing – till you've got it.'[2]

Nearly ten years later, in 1986, the noble public sentiments of his magazine interview were forgotten. He put his private thoughts into action and made a takeover bid for Australia's largest media group, the Herald and Weekly Times (HWT), the company his father had built up and chaired, but never owned. His small shareholding was sold to pay death duties. The takeover of HWT would make Sir Keith's son the world's largest newspaper publisher. It would also give him a monopoly position in Australian newspapers, owning 14 of Australia's 19 capital city and national dailies. This gave him 76 per cent of total circulation of Australian papers. It sent a long shiver through Australia's newspaper community. In future, there would be three classes of journalists in Australia: those who worked for him, those who had worked for him and those who would work for him, one day.

For two months Australia was transfixed by the takeover battle, which brought in all the big names in the country's media. It was a battle in which Murdoch demonstrated all his prodigious skills for manipulating the regulatory authorities. But it was also a bid which showed his fallibility. He made several crucial tactical errors which have haunted him ever since. The price he eventually paid started the slide into the financial crisis which has gripped him throughout 1990.

Before this takeover, Murdoch's control of the Australian media was surprisingly weak, both in newspapers and television. According to a former Fairfax editor, V.J. Carroll:

His papers, with the exception of the *Australian* on Saturday, were struggling. The *Sydney Daily Mirror* was fighting a battle of attrition with Fairfax's *Sun* for a shrinking retail advertising market; the *Daily Telegraph* had lost ground to the *Sydney Morning Herald*. In Brisbane his recently established *Sun* had done Queensland Press a favour by forcing it to enliven its heavy-weight *Courier-Mail*. The *News* in Adelaide had always been overshadowed by the *Advertiser*. Only his Sunday papers in Perth and to a lesser extent in Brisbane and his two very successful magazines *New Idea* and *TV Week* were leaders in their market. His Channel Ten television stations in Sydney and Melbourne were erratic.[3]

With fierce competition against all his major titles, Murdoch's Australian base was vulnerable. He had to strengthen his grip on the newspaper market. He had to do what he had done in Britain. He needed to embrace that 'terrible thing', monopoly, and dominate the market. But his choices were limited.

'He knew that if he was ever going to have publishing strength he had to put News Limited with HWT. He couldn't take over any other company because they were all run by families. HWT was the only one with a democratic share register,' explains the former HWT chief executive John D'Arcy.[4]

HWT was a perfect fit for Murdoch. It owned fourteen metropolitan newspapers including the leading papers in Adelaide, Brisbane and Melbourne. Besides, it also had two television channels, seven radio stations, over a hundred country and suburban papers and nearly twenty magazine titles.

Kerry Packer had already sold his two newspaper titles, the *Daily Telegraph* and the *Sunday Telegraph*, to Murdoch, though he had kept hold of the family media company, Consolidated Press. That only left the Fairfax empire, and that was not for sale because the family controlled the majority of shares. Fairfax was much smaller than HWT, but it did have some prestigious publications and also owned television and radio stations.

Murdoch decided to bid for HWT while celebrating Thanksgiving at his home in Aspen, Colorado. There must be something in the clear mountain air which helps Murdoch focus on his targets. It was while celebrating Thanksgiving in Aspen six years earlier that he had decided to bid for Times Newspapers in Britain.

While skiing down the slopes near his home he had two things on his mind. He knew that the Australian entrepreneur Kerry Packer had already been in serious talks to merge his Consolidated Press with HWT. If Packer was successful this would severely limit Murdoch's expansion plans.

Murdoch had also been nursing a vital piece of inside information he had picked up two months before in September. The Government Treasurer, Paul Keating, had taken time out of the International Monetary Fund meeting to tell Murdoch privately that the Australian Government was going to change the cross-ownership rules for media. The new rules would prevent newspaper owners in a metropolitan city also owning a television channel. The formal announcement about the changes had been made only a couple of days before Thanksgiving. Now everyone else knew as well. Murdoch did not know how much time he had left to restructure the Australian province of his worldwide empire. In future, media organisations would have to choose between being 'prince of print or queen of screen'. As far as Murdoch was concerned, newspapers were still the main financial focus, taking 40 per cent of all advertising dollars spent in Australia.[5] Murdoch chose print.

Under the proposed new rules, this left him with a fairly simple choice. He could either sell his Sydney papers, the *Telegraph* and the *Mirror*, or his Channel Ten-10 television station in Sydney. There was no cross-ownership conflict in Melbourne. He owned a television station there, but no newspapers. He already had problems over his ownership of the television stations. He was being challenged in the courts over his ownership of both the Channel Ten television stations in Melbourne and Sydney. Under the Australian Broadcasting and Television Act, a foreigner could only own 15 per cent of a television licence. Since 1985 Murdoch had been an American citizen – a move he made so he could buy Fox Television under the American ownership rules (see Chapter 5).

Murdoch's change of citizenship was to become a central

issue throughout the HWT takeover. He had traded in his Australian passport for an American one to satisfy one set of legal requirements, only to discover that he had exposed himself to the same set of legal problems back in Australia.

Once he had made his decision to bid for HWT, Murdoch took off for Melbourne, arriving on 2 December. He had arranged to meet his top corporate advisers in the Regent Hotel. The arrangements were so secret they had registered under false names. Their cover was so good that initially no one could find each other. When they finally met up, Murdoch went through the figures with them. He had written them down on the back of a menu on his flight over from the United States.

The offer was A$12 per share, valuing HWT at A$1.8 billion. HWT shares were trading at A$8.30. The offer was pitched at thirty times earnings and more than three times HWT's quoted net tangible assets. But media analysts reckoned the assets would be worth much more if HWT was broken up. Some estimates went as high as A$1.7 billion. Murdoch was not the only one to spot this. The HWT directors knew it too and so did other potential bidders. Murdoch's bid unlocked all the doors to HWT for the first time. But it also opened them to everyone else as well. And unfortunately for Murdoch one of the items he did not include in the sums he had done on the back of his airlines menu card was Robert Holmes à Court, whose cunning would thwart Murdoch at every turn.

Holmes à Court had already made an attempted takeover bid for half of HWT in December 1981. Murdoch's last dealings with Holmes à Court had been over his half purchase of Ansett Transport Industries in 1979. Then, they had had a gentlemen's agreement but one which had left Holmes à Court A$11 million richer. This time there was no agreement. But once again Holmes à Court would walk away with the cash. His interference in the 1986 battle for HWT was to cost Murdoch A$1000 million more than he had originally planned to pay. And although no one realised it at the time, the HWT purchase helped to begin the slide into the financial crisis which was to engulf Murdoch in 1990.

But in the beginning, on 3 December 1986 when the bid was announced, Murdoch looked like a winner. He gave the HWT board just seven hours to make up their minds whether or not to accept his offer of A$12 per share, or two News Corporation shares or two convertible notes for every three HWT shares. In the formal offer letter to John Dahlsen, the HWT chairman, he wrote: 'No such offers whatsoever will be made, however, unless the board of HWT indicates to News Corporation Limited, prior to 5 p.m. today, that it will recommend acceptance of the takeover offer subject to there being no higher offer from any third party.' As far as Murdoch was concerned, he had made them an offer they could not refuse.

The HWT board recommended Murdoch's bid to the shareholders 'in the absence of a more attractive offer'. There was no higher offer. But the day after the bid, Holmes à Court, who already had a stake in HWT, bought 3 million HWT shares. The following day he had discussions with the HWT board but did not make a counter-bid.

But more importantly Holmes à Court had a 10 per cent stake in Queensland Press, HWT's largest shareholder. Holmes à Court knew that to make a successful bid for HWT you had also to make an outright bid for Queensland as well. HWT, Queensland and its third largest shareholder, Advertiser Newspapers, had a complicated set of cross-shareholdings (see Appendix III). This structure was designed to protect the company from unwelcome takeovers, as well as a device to leverage the share price in an unwelcome takeover. The way it worked was this: if someone bid for HWT, this increased the value of its main shareholder Queensland Press. But as HWT also held shares in Queensland Press, this in turn made HWT more valuable. In a hostile bid this structure acted like a ratchet pushing up the value of each company. Ironically, this structure of cross-holdings had been put in place because of the stock market antics of one man – Rupert Murdoch.

Back on 20 November 1979, Murdoch had made a A$126-million bid for half of HWT. This valued HWT at A$250 while Murdoch's News group was only valued at A$150 million. The entire takeover attempt lasted a mere two days. In a hasty defence, friends of the company swung into action. Enlisting the help of Fairfax, the HWT management started to buy HWT shares at a higher price than Murdoch had offered. They hoped that this tactic would stop Murdoch getting the 51 per cent majority he had said he was after. By the end of the second day, the share-buying had cost the Herald-Fairfax alliance more than $53 million, most of it borrowed.[6]

On 22 November a record A$71-million-worth of HWT shares were traded. But the major action took place in the morning when almost 7 million HWT shares valued at A$35 million were bought and sold in just thirty minutes. What neither the HWT alliance nor the market knew was that Murdoch had decided to withdraw his bid. His decision was influenced by the intervention of the Trades Practices Commission which threatened to seek a court injunction against News unless it stopped buying HWT shares for a month so it could look into the bid.

Murdoch's team ran a smart selling operation. They outflanked the HWT camp by selling through a stockbroker who had not been involved in the affair, while at the same time maintaining one of News's own brokers in the market. At the height of the frantic bidding, the News group secretly unloaded their shares onto the unsuspecting HWT camp, which thought it was still locked in combat.

By the end of the day the stunned 'victors' were staring at a book loss of about A$20 million. Murdoch, on the other hand, had unloaded his shares at a profit of more than 3 million dollars. He proudly revealed his coup and announced that he was no longer interested in the Herald organisation.[7] It was the biggest turnover in a single stock in the history of Australian share markets and was hailed as the share market coup of the decade. News of the bid was reported in *The Australian* on a scale usually reserved for war or disaster. It also gleefully reported Murdoch's A$3-million coup.

The HWT directors were humiliated. They were determined that this would never happen to them again. Any bid in the future would have serious problems because the friends of HWT now lifted their original stake from 15 per cent to 35 per cent. After Holmes à Court's aborted bid in 1981, Advertiser Newspapers had taken a large stake. By 1986 two of HWT's associated companies, Queensland Press and Advertiser Newspapers, had increased their stakes to 24 per cent and 11.8 per cent respectively. In turn, HWT owned 46 per cent of Queensland Press and 38 per cent of Advertiser Newspapers.

Murdoch had scored an own goal. He may have made 3 million dollars in 1979 but because of his aborted bid he had to pay a much higher price in 1986. In his bid for HWT Murdoch expected to pick up all the cross-shareholdings and therefore control of all the affiliates. But Robert Holmes à Court had worked out you could achieve the same result by targeting Queensland Press instead of HWT. Murdoch's first mistake was his failure to see this danger. Only three days after Murdoch had stunned corporate Australia with his offer it became increasingly clear that the prize was not going to drop gently into his lap.

Once the battle for HWT got under way, it stopped being simply a financial matter. The future of Australian newspapers was at stake: 'The battles for HWT were conducted on several fronts: the stock exchanges, in the courts, before government tribunals, on the front pages and in the boardrooms, in private meetings and over the telephone systems of Australia and North America.'[8]

But in the two weeks following Murdoch's bid nothing much happened. Holmes à Court made noises about a bid but did nothing. Murdoch and his papers enthused about his cash or share swap offer. But without a counter-bid there was no comparison to measure it against.

On 11 December it looked as if Murdoch had made the major breakthrough he needed. The New Zealand financier Ron Brierley (later Sir Ronald) sold him his 12 per cent stake in HWT for A$12 per share. This eliminated one important rival as well as giving Murdoch a strategic stake in HWT. Rather surprisingly, he had not built a large stake in HWT before his bid.

Then on Christmas Eve he received an early Christmas present from the Trades Practices Commission (TPC), the body controlling monopolies and mergers in Australia. The TPC said it would not block the bid if Murdoch sold certain papers. Later on in the bid it specified the papers it would accept Murdoch selling. They were either News's papers or HWT's papers in States where they would together dominate the market. These papers would be in Adelaide, Brisbane and Perth. This was quite a good deal for Murdoch as the papers he owned in two of these cities were under pressure already from the papers he was trying to buy. If his bid was successful, he could keep the best papers and sell the weaker papers in each city. There was a public outcry at the Commission's decision, but the Commission believed that it had little room for manoeuvre.

131

The Trades Practices Commission's public duty is to stop monopolies. But under the Trades Practices Act there was no public interest clause and the Commission could not rule out the bid, as a whole, in the national interest: it had to decide on a State-by-State basis. This was a result of a change made in 1977 by Malcolm Fraser's coalition Government which had considerably weakened the Act. Today, Fraser deeply regrets these changes.[9] Under the new Fraser-introduced rules, a monopoly was defined as existing when a company could behave in its own market quite independently of pressure from a competitor or suppliers. In other words, a large market share by itself did not establish a monopoly, so if a company didn't have the capacity to act independently it was not dominant. With such a weak definition of monopoly and no public interest clause, the TPC believed that if Murdoch sold certain newspapers he would be within the law. The objections to the decision were vociferous, but the then chairman, Bob McComas, who took the decisions, says: 'There isn't any doubt in my mind that a large part of the comment was due to the person behind News rather than the acquisition itself. It is important to recognise that there was a particular feeling about the takeover which in no way related to the law.'[10]

Throughout his career, the regulators had stepped in to help Murdoch at crucial moments, and they had just done it again. It would not be the first time, either, in the bid for HWT. Given the green light from the Trades Practices Commission, Murdoch started to look around for buyers.

But before he could celebrate his victory, Holmes à Court moved against him. He offered, through his Bell group subsidiary, J.N. Taylor Holdings, A$13 per share, compared with Murdoch's A$12. This valued HWT at $2 billion. The price of HWT for Murdoch instantly increased by over A$150 million. Murdoch had no one to blame but himself.

He should have dealt with Holmes à Court in the beginning. Holmes à Court did not want HWT as a whole. He just wanted HWT's West Australian Newspapers and its television channel, HSV7. Murdoch said that he thought Holmes à Court's offer was 'silly' and was 'an attempt to punish me for not selling him some of the company's assets at a discount by the back door by private negotiation.' Murdoch was adamant that: 'In no circumstances will we deal separately with Mr Holmes à Court.'[11]

Holmes à Court's response was to turn the screw. He increased his cash offer to A$13.50 on New Year's Day. The price of HWT for Murdoch went up by at least another A$77 million. J.N. Taylor also offered a share swap which valued each HWT share at A$14 – much higher than News's offer.

The next day the HWT board met at 10 a.m. to consider whether to switch its recommendation from Murdoch to Holmes à Court. Murdoch's reaction was to ambush the meeting. His first words were 'surprise, surprise'.[12] He then spent an hour arguing his case – to no avail. For once, the famous Murdoch charm failed. He had seriously under-estimated HWT's board's determination to get a good price for its company. The HWT board recommended the Holmes à Court offer 'in the absence of a more attractive offer'. Dahlsen, the chairman, told reporters that the directors had switched to Holmes à Court's offer 'because it's the highest cash offer on the table'.[13]

On 4 January the battle for HWT took another dramatic turn. Fairfax announced a $910-million takeover bid for Queensland Press. Fairfax could not afford to let Murdoch win HWT. With just five capital city papers Fairfax would be Murdoch's only, much dwarfed, competitor if he won. Even if it couldn't stop Murdoch, Fairfax might be able to come out with some spoils from the battle. The bid was designed to complement Holmes à Court's bid for HWT and lock out Murdoch. Fairfax's offer of $20 per Queensland Press share compared with a price of $11 per share before Murdoch's bid for HWT. There were two crucial conditions to the Fairfax offer. Firstly, Queensland Press had to accept Holmes à Court's bid for its 24 per cent holding in HWT. This was, in effect, a condition that Holmes à Court win HWT. Secondly, Holmes à Court had to vary his offer for HWT so that Fairfax could buy HWT's 46 per cent stake in Queensland Press. Murdoch had been outflanked.[14]

But Murdoch then received some inside help from an unexpected source. The Government Treasurer, Paul Keating, who had earlier secretly tipped off Murdoch about the changes in the cross-ownership rules, decided to get involved. On the Sunday when Fairfax made its bid for Queensland Press, Keating and a friend were visiting Holmes à Court. Keating was in the room when Holmes à Court took phone calls from Fairfax's general manager Greg Gardiner concerning the Queensland bid. Keating has since said that Holmes à Court let him in on the inside of this deal, leaving him with a good understanding of both Holmes à Court's and Fairfax's intentions.[15]

Keating used his knowledge to good effect. He warned Murdoch that Holmes à Court was serious and told Murdoch if he wanted Holmes à Court to pull out he would have to do a deal with him over West Australian Newspapers, the company he wanted. In this way both men would get what they wanted out of the deal. And of course both would have good reason to be grateful to him. It was a smart move.

Keating says his intervention was critical in persuading Murdoch ultimately to come to a deal with Holmes à Court. Both men listened to Keating because of his position. His negotiating strength was that Murdoch would need his approval, under the Foreign Investment Review Board rules, for the bid to go ahead. However, Keating knew that he could not ultimately stop Murdoch because the Prime Minister, Bob Hawke, was determined that Murdoch should get approval. But just to show who was boss, Keating says he delayed the approval for a month. Ken Cowley was, according to Keating, constantly on the phone complaining about the delay.[16]

As Keating himself admits, his intervention left Fairfax exposed and ultimately lost it control of Queensland Press. Keating believes that he could have similarly intervened to force Murdoch to deal with Fairfax over Queensland. But he did not; he wanted to see HWT broken up and Fairfax hurt.[17] For this reason he had not tipped off HWT and Fairfax about the cross-ownership rules in advance, but he had told Rupert Murdoch and Kerry Packer.[18] Keating had been on friendly terms with Murdoch for several years.

Even in early 1991 Keating was still helping Murdoch. When members of the Labour Party's Communications Committee called on Keating to set up a media ownership inquiry because of fears of Murdoch's media domination, Keating refused. He argued that it would unnecessarily antagonise Murdoch's newspapers before the next election.[19]

Keating was not alone in his dislike of HWT and its papers. The majority of the ruling Labour Party shared his view. Despite Murdoch's behaviour in 1975 when his papers had run a hysterical campaign against the Labour Prime Minister, Gough Whitlam, the Labour Party now saw Murdoch as a mate and HWT as the real enemy. The Prime Minister, Bob Hawke, whom Murdoch had seen immediately after making the HWT bid, was extremely bitter about the virulent campaign the *Herald* had run against the Government. Keating was furious over personal attacks in the Fairfax papers.[20]

One ex-HWT director believes that Fairfax and HWT

were naive not to court politicians in the way that Murdoch had done. They had stayed away from Canberra to prove that they were independent of the Government, unlike Murdoch's and Packer's media empires. They paid the price. When in 1986 John D'Arcy, then chief executive of HWT, asked Hawke to dinner with the HWT executives, he was told that the Prime Minister would be busy for a whole year. In 1990 Murdoch got different treatment. When at a week's notice he sent out an invitation to many politicians in both parties asking them to come to a party in Canberra, few refused.

During the bid for HWT, the Labour Government was not the only party that wanted to keep the support of Murdoch's papers. Only one Liberal MP spoke up against the takeover – the Opposition Communications spokesman Ian MacPhee, who was told to shut up by the Opposition leader John Howard, and was later pushed out of the party. As former Prime Minister Malcolm Fraser says: 'The Opposition and the Labour Party did not do anything to stop him. It was an expedient move for both parties.'[21]

Although Murdoch realised he might have to do a deal with Holmes à Court, he carried on with his bid for HWT regardless of the new bid by Fairfax for Queensland. On the night of 7 January News Limited lodged a new Part A document with Victorian Corporate Affairs. The Part A is the formal offer document required under law. This document was to replace the original Part A document lodged on Christmas Eve. The changes involved the difficulties Murdoch had under the Broadcasting and Television (B & TV) Act. The Act prevented a newspaper group owning more than two television stations. Murdoch's acquisition of HWT's two TV stations would put News above this limit. News now said that it intended to sell the television stations within a six-month grace period.[22] (This grace period had been brought in as part of the 'Murdoch amendments' – see Chapter 2.)

136

But Murdoch had an additional problem. He had recently become an American citizen to allow him to buy television stations in the United States. Under the Australian B & TV Act a foreigner was not allowed to control more than 15 per cent of a TV channel. So even if News sold the HWT stations in six months as the B & TV Act allowed, it would still be illegal for Murdoch to own them for that period. And it was debatable whether the six-month grace period was available to a foreigner. Murdoch acknowledged in the new Part A document that he and his company News Limited were foreign for the Act's purposes.

The next day Holmes à Court's solicitors were threatening legal action unless Murdoch and News confirmed their status under the foreign person clause of the Act. They sought an injunction to prevent Murdoch sending out the Christmas Eve Part A document until Murdoch's status under the B & TV Act was clarified – But Holmes à Court and his solicitors did not know about the new Part A or that the Victorian Corporate Affairs Commission had quietly helped Murdoch. In an unusual and unexplained action the Department allowed Murdoch's lawyers to file and despatch the formal offer document just twenty-four hours after registration instead of the statutory fourteen days minimum. Before Holmes à Court knew anything about it, later that evening and into the night, trucks from TNT, Murdoch's Ansett partners, were rumbling out with the revised offer document for the thousands of HWT shareholders scattered around the country.[23]

This dispensation from the Corporate Affairs Commission was absolutely vital. With the shareholders in possession of the new offer document, Murdoch stormed the Queensland board meeting less than forty-eight hours after registering the document with an offer for HWT shares that could be accepted immediately.

Fifteen minutes before the Queensland board met,

137

Murdoch rang its chairman, Keith McDonald, and asked if he could speak in person to the directors. This came as a surprise as Murdoch's papers had said he was in Los Angeles. But, in fact, he had been in New Zealand, where he chartered a private jet to Brisbane. Murdoch's advisers were there to meet him. Murdoch had entered the Queensland offices through the back door and got lost. When he finally found the Queensland directors they were amazed by his new offer. Murdoch said he would raise his HWT offer to A$15 per share, outdoing Holmes à Court's offer of A$13.50. This new offer valued the company at A$2,350 million. He also topped the Fairfax bid for Queensland Press, saying his family company, Cruden Investments Pty Ltd, would pay A$23 a share, valuing Queensland Press at A$1,050 million. But the Cruden offer was conditional on the board accepting his new offer for Queensland Press's 24 per cent of HWT within three hours, by 5 p.m. Murdoch left the room after twenty minutes instead of staying to convince the directors to accept his bid. It was, he later acknowledged, a serious mistake. Because in the following three hours everything changed.[24]

That afternoon Holmes à Court's solicitors realised what Murdoch had done. They had an injunction which prevented Murdoch sending out his offer document for HWT, but it only prevented the original Part A document from being despatched. It did not cover the Part A which the TNT trucks had been busily distributing around the country. The solicitors sought an injunction preventing Murdoch acquiring more than 15 per cent of HWT on the grounds that Murdoch's foreign citizenship could otherwise put HWT's television and radio stations at risk.

While his lawyers were fighting the case in front of a judge, Holmes à Court and Fairfax were ringing the Queensland board to improve their offers. By late afternoon Holmes à Court got the injunction. Queensland Press's solicitor was

contacted and told that if Queensland Press accepted the
News bid Holmes à Court would take court action including
requests for forced divestiture. But although the Queensland
board decided that it could not accept Murdoch's offer for its
HWT shares, the HWT board decided to switch its
recommendation from Holmes à Court to Murdoch 'in the
absence of a more attractive offer'.[25]

Murdoch's chances of a quick deal were dead. 'The only
mistake I made was in giving them three hours instead of
one,' he said. According to one of his own papers, Murdoch
complained that the directors allowed themselves to be
intimidated. Counsel for Holmes à Court remarked acidly:
'Apparently the complaint is that they allowed themselves to
be intimidated by someone other than him.'[26]

Murdoch had hoped to get control of HWT and
Queensland Press before the court battle. Possession was
nine-tenths of the law. He believed that he stood a much
better chance of winning if the battle in the courts took place
after he had taken control of HWT. He assumed that no
court would try to unscramble the deal even if it found that
News Limited was in breach of the Broadcasting Act.

But just in case, Murdoch's lawyers had come up with an
alternative to get around the B & TV Act. Murdoch may have
seen himself as a global citizen, but clearly he could not be an
American to the American authorities and an Australian to
the Australian authorities. On 9 January his lawyers came up
with a solution. They restructured News Limited. News's
solicitor Dawson Waldron sold a shelf company, Votraint No.
275 Pty Ltd, to News Corporation, which then transferred to
Votraint its Australian and HWT bidding company, News
Limited. All voting preference shares in Votraint were held
by another of the law firm's nominee companies, Travinto
Nominees. Travinto would be controlled by three men who
would have voting rights over the company, which meant they

139

would control Votraint and therefore News Limited, until News's problems under the B & TV Act[28] had been negotiated. This meant that the 'foreign person' Murdoch would no longer be deemed under the Broadcasting Act to 'control' the Herald's television and radio licences if News acquired more than 15 per cent.[27]

This was the second time Murdoch and his lawyers had adopted a twin ownership structure to get round the law. They had done it before to allow News Corporation to continue to hold the Channel Ten television stations' licences in Melbourne and Sydney. This was still being challenged before the Australian Broadcasting Tribunal and in the Federal courts. The new restructure was open to legal challenge in the same way. And who would believe that Murdoch would give up control of his company?

On 10 January the injunction on Murdoch's share-buying was lifted and Murdoch promptly moved beyond 15 per cent. He acquired another 2.5 per cent from Associated Newspapers of Britain, whose chairman, Lord Rothermere, was an HWT director. Another HWT director, Sir Laurence Muir, swapped his HWT shares for News Corporation shares. Other shareholders started to follow the lead of the directors. The scales were tipping in Murdoch's favour.[28]

Whilst the financial and legal battles were being fought in public, the political battle was being settled in private. Murdoch could have been stopped under the Foreign Takeovers Act which gave the Treasurer, Keating, the power to stop the acquisition by a foreigner as 'contrary to the national interest'. The Foreign Investment Review Board (FIRB) was the Government agency that advised the Treasurer on whether or not to stop a bid under the Act. The Act says a foreign investor must notify the FIRB if he/she proposes to buy more than 15 per cent of a company. News is believed to have argued two things: one, that it was not a foreign company; two, even if it was, it did not matter because it had behaved as if it was a foreign company and complied with the rules. This rather tortuous argument was accepted and the Government announced on 13 January that it would not impede Murdoch under the Foreign Takeovers Act.

This decision was crucial in helping Murdoch take over HWT. Once again the Government Treasurer, Keating, was to prove invaluable to Murdoch. He abdicated responsibility at the time by arguing that the FIRB had recommended the bid. Four years later he had a different story. In December 1990 Keating contradicted his previous statements, claiming that the FIRB recommendation was 'non-committal'. One ex-adviser to a minister said: 'The FIRB is just a couple of civil servants shuffling through papers. They didn't actually make a recommendation. They thought it was too hot to handle.'[29] Several years after Murdoch got HWT, a former Liberal MP and a critic of the takeover, Ian MacPhee, obtained the FIRB recommendation. It had been heavily censored. It was impossible to see what the board had recommended.

The decision certainly wasn't a surprise to Murdoch. 'I was having a drink with Murdoch before the bid,' recalls John D'Arcy, then the chief executive of HWT and later to join the board of the Murdoch parent company, News Corporation, 'and he said it was inevitable that the takeover would happen. He said that the globe was awash with money and that he didn't think there would be any problem with the Government authorities. Once the Government put their stamp on it the various authorities just went along with it.'[30]

While the court battles continued, Murdoch and Holmes à Court had decided that the battle was getting too expensive. By lifting his initial bid by A$3 to A$15 a share Murdoch had increased his bid by over A$500 million. But it still was not enough to guarantee victory against Holmes à Court, who still had a credit line for A$2 billion and could therefore push Murdoch further. Murdoch was forced to swallow his earlier words of not doing a separate deal with Holmes à Court. On 11 January the two camps talked. By the 15th they had to come to a deal. The terms were these: Murdoch would sell to Holmes à Court HWT's Perth morning and afternoon papers, the *West Australian* and the *Daily News*, for $200 million, and its television station, HSV7, for $260 million. In return Holmes à Court would sell Murdoch his HWT and Queensland Press shares, stop bidding and drop his legal actions. Holmes à Court made a A$108-million profit.

Murdoch was still nervous about what Fairfax would do; he immediately phoned the Queensland Press chairman, Keith McDonald, to tell him of the peace settlement and reinstate his offer of A$23 per share for Queensland and A$15 for its 24 per cent stake of HWT. At 11 p.m. the Queensland board decided to accept Murdoch's offer. He now had over 40 per cent of HWT.

In the meantime he had been busy still trying to appease the Trades Practices Commission. He found his answer in David Gonski. David Gonski is an astute corporate lawyer and successful too, judging by his 38th-floor office with its antique furniture. He had a key position in Frank Lowy's Westfield Capital Corporation which held a controlling stake in Northern Star Holdings (NSH). NSH was a medium-sized media group with a string of regional papers, magazines and radio stations.

Gonski, like so many others, was scurrying around the HWT carcass early in 1987, hoping to pick off whatever scraps Murdoch would not be able to consume. He had his sights set on the Channel Ten television stations in Melbourne and Sydney. '[Murdoch's] office was like a supermarket,' said Gonski. 'It was quite embarrassing. They were all there trying to buy bits and pieces.'[31]

We wanted the Channel Tens in Melbourne and Sydney, even though they were the worst houses in the best street, though even this could be an advantage as they could only get better. There were at least three other buyers for these stations and to get them we would have to offer something else and the one thing we could do was relieve Murdoch of some of his other properties.[32]

They offered to buy the Brisbane *Sun* and his father's old paper the *News*. Gonski negotiated firm guarantees on access to printing facilities and distribution. Northern Star was not interested in buying and running its own presses. It was much cheaper all round if Murdoch did it. But more important were the put options and indemnities Gonski negotiated. This meant that if losses were incurred by the paper during a set period, then there was scope to defer the fees owed to News for production.

Gonski asked for this deal because there was not sufficient time to carry out the normal due diligence and he wanted some sort of protection if things went wrong. But he says that 'it wasn't a great risk to Murdoch'. The conditions were very tightly drawn. There had to be audited accounts. There were provisions to adjust the figures if there was any expansion of the business. There was a let-out if there was gross negligence on the part of the management. Furthermore Murdoch knew a lot about these businesses – the Adelaide paper he had run since he started, the Brisbane paper he had started from scratch. Both papers were profitable.

And because Murdoch planned to keep the HWT papers in Brisbane and Adelaide, he could crush the paper he sold if necessary, so what he lost on the roundabouts he could regain on the swings. Finally, Murdoch was to take a 15 per cent shareholding in Northern Star and put News Limited's chief executive, Ken Cowley, on the board of Northern Star. (Cowley did join the board but had to come off when the cross-ownership rules came into effect.)

The deal, which was finalised on 9 February, enabled him to get HWT, keep the TPC off his back and at least choose a friendly, rather than ferocious competitor. How friendly it was became a nightmare for the TPC when Northern Star decided to sell the papers when the cross-ownership rules became law. It also had later serious financial ramifications for Murdoch.

But before Murdoch could celebrate this and the acceptance of his offer to Queensland there were other hurdles put in his path. Although Holmes à Court had now stopped his litigation, his previous actions were still niggling away at Murdoch. He had caused the Australian Broadcasting Tribunal (ABT) to gather for a conference on 16 January. Holmes à Court had planned to use the ABT to pressure Murdoch by encouraging the tribunal to hamper Murdoch the American. Section 92M of the Broadcasting Act gave the Tribunal wide powers that could have been a significant obstacle to Murdoch. If the tribunal was convinced that the scheme the lawyers had dreamed up to separate the foreign Murdoch from the bidding company News Limited was a pretence, then it could be argued that he was in breach of the Act. If so, it was arguable that HWT's licences for HSV7 and ADS7 Adelaide were in jeopardy because Murdoch would have breached the Act by exceeding the 15 per cent holding allowed to foreigners. If they ruled against Murdoch there was a possibility that his takeover would not succeed.[33]

The ABT was waiting for the Federal Court's ruling on the legitimacy of the legally similar News restructure which had claimed that Murdoch was not in control of the company that owned the Channel Ten television stations in Melbourne and Sydney. The Federal Court's decision on 20 January was

144

bad news for Murdoch. It gave a wide interpretation to the expression 'control of a company'. It said 'control' meant 'power to direct or restrain what the company may do on any substantial issue'. This meant who had the ability to appoint directors, though not necessarily directing what they did, because presumably those directors would act in the best interests of those who had appointed them. Control of a company could therefore mean the ability to direct takeovers and sell assets even if the person did not legally control the company. With this definition, Murdoch clearly controlled News Limited, the company which was attempting to acquire HWT's television licences. Murdoch could not argue anything else. Only the week before, Murdoch's papers had applauded their proprietor as the hero for his solo role in the deal with Holmes à Court.[34]

Although this was bad news for Murdoch, the Federal Court had only been asked for an advisory opinion which would not commit the Australian Broadcasting Tribunal to any particular course. The good news for Murdoch was that Advertiser Newspapers had decided in principle to accept News Corporation's offer for its 11.8 per cent stake in HWT.

But the next day Fairfax bid $16 per share for the whole of HWT and won a new injunction in the Victorian Supreme Court restraining News from registering its HWT shares. During the hearings Justice Beach said that the talk of restructuring News Limited was just a 'sham'. He argued that it seemed apparent that Murdoch was in control of News. Murdoch appeared to be 'the one' who was talking about selling TV licences and had been 'making statements as if he owns HWT and he is a foreign person'.[35]

The ABT reconvened on the 22nd and announced an urgent inquiry into whether Murdoch actually controlled News Limited or not. Crucially, the Tribunal gave Murdoch the chance to settle the matter beyond dispute. The Tribunal did not order News to stop buying HWT shares. It did not believe this was necessary. The ABT ordered HWT not to sell any assets, register any shares, appoint any directors, give any information to News group companies or hold any meetings without three days' notice. This meant that, for at least the ten days before the 'urgent inquiry' was to start, News Limited could continue to receive acceptances from the HWT shareholders even though they could not be registered. By the time the inquiry started Murdoch would have received acceptances for over 50 per cent of HWT.[36]

On the same day Fairfax's offer was rejected. The HWT board thought that, although Fairfax's offer was a dollar a share higher than Murdoch's, some shareholders might prefer News Corporation shares. They also argued that it seemed inevitable that Murdoch would receive acceptances of over 50 per cent of the capital of HWT, therefore it was unlikely that Fairfax would get the 51 per cent it needed.

In the meantime Murdoch and his advisers had come up with a plan that would, they hoped, solve their problems with the ABT and Fairfax. On 28 January, the eve of the Supreme Court hearing into Fairfax's claims that the News offer was illegal and misleading because of Murdoch's citizenship, News announced that it had lined up buyers for HWT's radio and TV stations. This would mean that even if there was a breach of law it would only be momentary.[37]

When the ABT met for its 'urgent inquiry' on 2 February, it listened to this new argument from News. But this ploy was superseded by the anouncement that HWT's John D'Arcy and John Dahlsen were planning to sell the television stations themselves. Murdoch, the American, would no longer be in control, or dealing out licences like a pack of cards.

The next day the Tribunal made its decision – it decided to do nothing. It wanted HWT to be free to find a solution to 'the current situation'.[38]

The day after Murdoch was relaxing at Cavan and enter-
taining the American Newspaper Publishers' Association with
some HWT directors and his political buddies who had done
so much to help him in the takeover, Keating and Hawke.[39]

By the beginning of February, just as it seemed that Murdoch was finally going to secure his prize, Fairfax's lawyers discovered that Queensland Press and Advertiser Newspapers
had breached the Stock Exchange rules by agreeing to sell their
strategic stakes in HWT to Murdoch. The breach involved a
rule that prohibited a company from selling a major asset to one
of its substantial shareholders without the prior approval of
other shareholders at a general meeting. Murdoch was a major
shareholder in both companies and neither had held a general
meeting when agreeing to sell the major asset of their stakes in
HWT. Again the regulatory authorities came to the aid of
Murdoch. The boards of the Adelaide and Brisbane Stock
Exchanges retrospectively waived the breaches of their rules.

By this time, Fairfax, like Holmes à Court, had realised that
it was better to do a deal with Murdoch and at least come out of
the battle with something. On 6 February Murdoch agreed to
sell the Brisbane television station HSV7 to Fairfax for A$320
million. Murdoch got Fairfax off his back.

The problem for Murdoch was that he had already promised
the same television channel to Holmes à Court in their deal.
Holmes à Court made him pay. He released Murdoch from the
January agreement to sell him the station for A$260 million, but
extracted an expensive concession: he would get West Australian Newspapers for $140 million instead of A$200 million.
'This was a ridiculous price as they were worth three or more
times that . . . but Holmes à Court had him in a vice,' said John
D'Arcy, chief executive of HWT.[40]

Finally, on 7 February, after a bruising and expensive
sixty-seven days, Murdoch had won, but at what cost?

'Murdoch thought the takeover was effective from day one

when he made the fantastic offer of A$12 a share,' says John D'Arcy. But D'Arcy was amazed that Murdoch and his fellow directors didn't realise that the HWT board would do everything possible to get the price up. After all, it was their legal duty as directors to do the best for their shareholders. 'We kept Holmes à Court in the picture as a lever although we never believed he would go ahead with the bid. He always plays the share register. But by keeping that alive we were able to push Murdoch up.'[41]

It was Murdoch's fault that Holmes à Court had had him in a vice all along. His major and most costly mistake was at the beginning of the takeover battle. 'It was a tactical error not going for Queensland Press at the same time as HWT. It cost him A$3 a share by not doing it, in other words A$450 million. Plus the A$600 million he had to pay for the shares of Queensland Press not owned by HWT. If he had gone for it at the same time it would have been all over the first day,' says D'Arcy.

The entry of Holmes à Court and the Fairfax bid for Queensland put Murdoch in a predicament. His bid for HWT had stretched him financially. Just before Christmas 1986 he had agreed the terms of the loan from the Commonwealth Bank of Australia. They agreed to lend News Corporation A$1,120 million but there were conditions. The total value of all News Corporation's debts were not to exceed 110 per cent of the company's net assets and the secured borrowings were not to exceed 25 per cent of the value of the net assets. In addition, the loan was only for two years and A$250 million had to be repaid within six months.[42] There was also a share alternative – two 'notes' convertible into News Corporation shares for every three HWT shares.

It is important to remember that an overriding principle for Murdoch was keeping control of his empire. He must have calculated that picking through the complex cross-holdings it was unlikely that enough of the convertible loan notes would be issued to substantially reduce his grip on News Corporation. Holmes à Court and Fairfax upset this delicate situation. Holmes à Court bid A$13.50 a share for the HWT shares. His chances of success seemed high as the largest shareholder, who held 24 per cent of HWT, was under pressure to accept. This shareholder was, of course, Queensland Press. There was only one bid for Queensland – from Fairfax, which was willing to pay A$20 a share if the Queensland board accepted the Holmes à Court offer for HWT.

So for the Queensland board the choice seemed simple: A$20 a share for the shareholders if they went with the Holmes à Court/Fairfax deal or nothing for their shareholders but a big stake in News Corporation if they accepted Murdoch's offer.

The only hope for Murdoch was the Queensland chairman, who favoured the News Corporation offer. But he had been told by the National Companies and Securities Commission that the Queensland board must keep the interests of shareholders paramount. In addition, Holmes à Court – who owned 14 per cent of the Queensland shares – was threatening legal action if his offer was not accepted.

In these circumstances, Murdoch had to bid for Queensland Press and had to bid more than A$20. His problem was that News Corporation didn't have the money and, given the conditions imposed on the loan to bid for HWT, it didn't seem very likely that the bank would lend it to him, especially as he was going to need even more cash for an increased HWT bid to knock out Holmes à Court. The alternative was to make a bid with News Corporation shares or convertible notes. This option was very unattractive.

No one knows precisely what calculations Murdoch did on the back of an envelope or menu, but the following is the 'worst case scenario' he could have painted. To outbid Fairfax he might have to offer shares which would make each Queensland share worth around A$23, compared with the

A$20 cash bid from Fairfax. Together with the share alternative he was offering for HWT and allowing for the elimination of the cross-holdings, on 'worst case' assumptions this could have involved issuing almost 100 million new News Corporation shares to new outside shareholders, including Holmes à Court. This could have had the effect of reducing the Murdoch holding in the company from 46 per cent to around 25 per cent. As Murdoch was not the only shareholder in Cruden, his effective interest in News Corporation would be very low. To stop this happening, Murdoch had to find some more cash. Where could he turn?

There was only one place – the family investment company, Cruden. However, Cruden did not have any cash – it only had a shareholding in News Corporation. The Commonwealth Bank was, however, willing to lend money to Cruden, on the security of its shareholding in News Corporation. In addition the bank was to take a charge over the Queensland shares which Cruden bought and, to be quite sure, got a guarantee from another Murdoch family company.[43]

Murdoch started getting money out of HWT as soon as possible. He sent a bill to HWT for A$14 million for his advisory services which went straight to a News Corporation offshore company. It was a big surprise to those paying, as he had only been around the company a couple of days in the six months after he took the company over. Conveniently the bill was sent before 30 June, when the company's year ended – the payment took the profits out of the company and away from the taxman (see Chapter 11).[44]

Murdoch was now the most powerful newspaper magnate Australia had ever seen. But the Trades Practices Commission felt rather pleased with itself. Having entered the complicated HWT takeover it felt it had emerged victorious, believing that with Murdoch's divestiture of certain papers it had sown the seeds for effective competition in years to come.

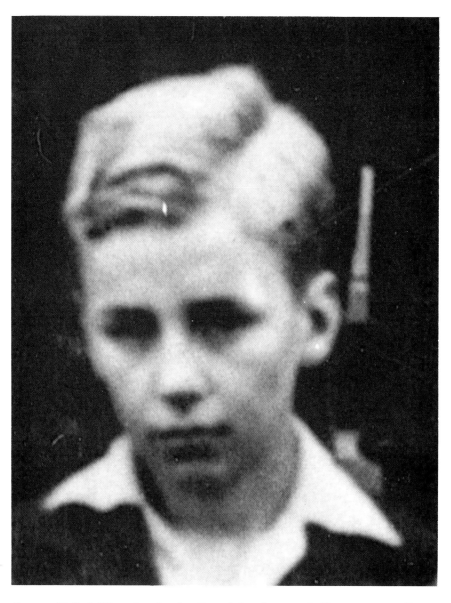

A youthful Murdoch during his days at the expensive Geelong Grammar School. *(Geelong Grammar School)*

Murdoch kisses his mother, Dame Elizabeth. 'Britain will perhaps learn to know that he's a pretty good chap.'
(Popperfoto/Reuter)

**Murdoch takes over the Sydney *Daily Mirror* in May
1960. The *Mirror* was a crucial landmark in his rise
in Australia.** *(Keystone Press Agency)*

Murdoch with his loyal wife, Anna. They met when she was a junior reporter on one of his Australian newspapers. *(Rex Features)*

Murdoch at the launch of the 'breezy, not sleazy' *Sun* in November 1969; a year later, the first Page Three girl appeared. *(Press Association)*

Mutual admirers. Editorial support was matched by government reward when Murdoch's takeover of Times Newspapers was rushed through the House of Commons without reference to the Monopolies Commission.

(Universal Pictorial Press and Agency)

Prime Minister Hawke forgets his earlier statement to ex-Prime Minister Gough Whitlam: 'You're going to regret the day you got into bed with Rupert.'

(Herald and Weekly Times)

The *Sun*, renowned for its lurid headlines, surpassed itself with 'GOTCHA'. Its heartlessness shocked many but Murdoch approved, saying, 'I rather like it.'

TODAY
Rain, windy, 50-55

TONIGHT
Partial clearing, 40

TOMORROW
Partly cloudy, windy, 50-55
Details, Page 2

TV listings: P. 103

NEW YORK POST

METRO
TODAY'S RACING

FRIDAY, APRIL 15, 1983   **30 CENTS**   ★   © 1983 News Group Publications Inc.   Vol. 182, No. 129

30 cents beyond 50-mile zone except L.I.   **AMERICA'S FASTEST-GROWING NEWSPAPER**

ABC AVERAGE
SALES EXCEED   **960,000**

HEADLESS BODY IN TOPLESS BAR

Gunman forces woman to decapitate tavern owner
PAGE TWO

SENATE OKAYS PREZ'S PICK FOR ARMS CONTROL
PAGE FIVE

Koch plans to hire 1,000 more cops
PAGE THREE

TAXING DAY FOR 1 MILLION IN N.Y.
PAGE SEVEN

Post Photo by Marc Vodofsky

Taken kickin' and screamin'

An angry Juan Emilio Robles tries to kick a photographer yesterday as detectives took him in to be booked for the murder last year of Chase Manhattan exec Kathleen Williams. Robles, a hulking 20-year-old ex-con, is accused of stabbing the 30-year-old victim during a bungled robbery attempt on a stairway in the Waldorf-Astoria Hotel in midtown. Story on Page 14.

Murdoch exported his tabloid formula to America, but while it increased the *New York Post*'s circulation, it lost advertisers. *Newsday* quoted a space buyer for the top store Bloomingdales saying to Murdoch, 'But Rupert, Rupert, your readers are my shoplifters.'

The Queen congratulates Rupert Murdoch at the bicentenary celebrations of *The Times* despite having taken legal action against the *Sun*, the first time she had ever done so against a newspaper. *(Associated Press/Topham)*

Barbed wire is removed from the entrance to the News International plant at Wapping following the ending of the year-long dispute. 'Managements were weak and the unions so strong that someone had to do something.' justified Anna Murdoch. *(Press Association)*

A humble Murdoch posing with the Simpsons, one of the programmes that helped save Fox Television.
(Universal Pictorial Press and Agency)

Murdoch managed to get a satellite dish for his London home to watch his Sky Television. Unfortunately for him, Westminster City Council ordered it to be removed.

(Press Association)

Murdoch's previous policy of expansion became one of closure, selling and merger in the 1990s. Here he is announcing the amalgamation of four of his Australian papers into two. *(Herald and Weekly Times)*

A worried-looking Murdoch before a meeting with his bankers in November 1990. *(Robert Pearce/John Fairfax Group)*

CUSTARD SPIES

Snoopers report dinner ladies who dollop it over puddings

EXCLUSIVE

By ANDREW PARKER

BARMY burghers have hired snoops to check whether dinner ladies serve custard on TOP of school children's puddings instead of on the side.

The spies also make sure they dish up **APPLE PIES** with sultanas and that they slice their **CARROTS** to a regulation size.

The caterers are even **FINED** small amounts of money for breaching the strict food presentation "enhancement" code drawn up by Labour-controlled Sandwell Council, West Midlands. Already 17 schools in the borough have been busted after caterers were caught pouring custard **OVER** fruit flans and crumbles.

But the pudding policy got a tart response yesterday from dis-custard governors at one school, Springfield Infants.

A governor, Derek Crump, said: "This is making a laughing stock of Sandwell education department."

And Tory councillor Roger Woodhouse said: "Making a fuss over custard being on top of a pie is barmy.

"Most children like it better on top."

Attractive

The schools' caterers, Direct Services, are made up of council employees who launched an in-house company.

A spokesman explained: "Three monitors tour schools to check on meal presentation.

"Points are deducted for poor presentation and money deducted from our budget."

Yesterday Sandwell education spokesman David Badger defended the pudding code.

He said: "Our food experts believe custard served on the side of a plate is more attractive.

SUN

SCOOBY the mongrel dog sent a raider packing after owner Tina Smith, 19, had sprayed deodorant in his eyes at Sinfin, Derby.

SPOT

PRESENT ARM

An artificial arm torn from Brendan Swann, 24, by muggers has been returned by a Sun reader who found it in a street at Ilford, Essex.

BEFORE *Pal asked when baby was due*　AFTER *Slimline Lynn is 3½stone lighter*

Slim Lynn boobs with her husband

TRIM Lynn Barnes won a slimming title yesterday and confessed: "I've really boobed with my husband!"

Lynn, 31, who shed 3½stone in five months, has lost **SEVEN INCHES** off her bust — to the disappointment of hubby Wayne.

She added: "I know he misses them. But now I've got curves he's never seen before!"

Mum-of-two Lynn weighed 12¼stone and had a 41inch bust — until a neighbour looked at her tum and asked: "When's the baby due?"

Shocked Lynn, of Barnsley, Yorks, joined a slimming club. She said: "I knew I was too fat. But it was only when the neighbour thought I was pregnant that it really sank in."

Now Lynn, who beat 5,000 others to become Northern Slimmer of the Year, weighs 8st 12lbs — and her bust is 34ins. She said: "It's wonderful."

Wayne, 31, added: "She's like a new wife. But I miss her boobs."

CLIFF COMFORTS PAL

Continued from Page One

since he was 16, added at his home in Kinver, West Midlands: "Cliff was a great inspiration to me.

Wife Jill, 29, who works in an antique shop, has moved out of their home and is staying with friends.

A pal said: "She is bearing up very well — the break-up is amicable."

Born-again Christian Chris first played Saviour's Day — which looks set to be the Christmas No.1 — to Cliff in the star's Rolls-Royce.

He said: "He loved it and said it would be a Christmas hit."

Hit

CHRIS'S bad luck continued yesterday when he was involved in a road smash.

He was unhurt in the prang near Derby.

A kind-hearted motorist drove him to BBC radio station WM in Birmingham where he due to play.

OLD-TIME COP

A driver who sped off as a meter warden tried to book him got a suspended sentence at the Old Bailey yesterday for "furious and wanton driving" — a charge from 1861.

Tracey Elvik was the Page Three girl for 19 December 1990, the day a Citicorp memo was sent to the dozens of banks involved in the rescue talks. Part of the banks' security was the Page Three trademark. The banks were as exposed as the women who boosted the circulation of Murdoch's British papers.

But then the TPC's dream of a competitive press suddenly started falling apart. In August 1987 Northern Star announced that because of the cross-ownership rules it was bowing out of the newspaper market and selling the metropolitan papers it had bought from Rupert Murdoch to a small management consortium. The TPC had no say in the matter. The papers, the Brisbane *Sun* and the Adelaide *News*, were gift-wrapped and handed to Frank Moore and Roger Holden respectively.

Under the TPC's rules, Murdoch could neither own nor control these papers. The arrangements between the new proprietors and Murdoch raise serious doubts about Murdoch's commitment to maintaining his obligations to the TPC.

Both Holden and Moore had previously run the papers for Murdoch. With a few changes they took over all the agreements for printing, distribution and leasing that Northern Star had negotiated with Murdoch. Northern Star arranged the finance for their buyouts through Citibank, one of Murdoch's consortium of lenders to News Corporation. Moore and Holden stated how grateful they were to the bank. Neither mentioned their gratitude to Murdoch, who was effectively underwriting the venture.

News Corporation guaranteed the loans which Citibank made to the two new proprietors. This meant that if they could not repay the money, News Corporation would. At this time the arrangement was not made public, though it should have been. The guarantee was clearly a contingent liability for News Corporation – money it might have to pay in certain circumstances. Such liabilities should be disclosed in a company's Annual Accounts. No trace of these contingent liabilities can be found in News Corporation's Accounts. In its latest financial results the A\$35 million loan to the proprietors was written off. In September 1991 we asked the company to explain the write-off and its omission as a contingent liability but it refused to answer (see Appendix IV).

But the guarantee was not the only support Murdoch gave the Adelaide and Brisbane papers. At present, Holden and Moore only own the mastheads of their papers and employ the journalists and the advertising staff. Murdoch owns the computer systems into which the journalists type their stories, the presses on which the papers are printed and the trucks and distribution systems which get the papers onto the streets. He also employs the compositors who make up the pages of the papers. Apart from that they are independent titles.

Early in July 1988 the Adelaide *News* staff moved out of their Murdoch-owned building in North Terrace into a Murdoch-owned building adjacent to and joining Murdoch's *Advertiser* paper. In Brisbane Moore's papers at least operate out of their 'own' building although it and almost everything in it, including the presses, is owned by News Corporation.[45]

Though Murdoch and Moore are theoretically in competition, they have ordered their publishing businesses for each other's convenience. In Brisbane, Murdoch closed his after-noon paper, the *Telegraph*, but kept his morning paper, the *Courier Mail*, open. Moore then changed his morning paper, the *Sun*, into an afternoon paper, where it would not compete with Murdoch's paper. Brisbane now has one morning and one evening paper, each owned by a separate proprietor. Moore claims there was no collusion. It was just good business sense and that he had been planning the move long before the *Telegraph*'s announced closure.[46]

But the most audacious deal to come out of the HWT takeover is Queensland Press. After the bid battle was over News Corporation owned HWT outright, which in turn owned 46 per cent of Queensland Press. The remaining shares in Queensland were owned by Cruden – which had made the bid to knock out the Fairfax offer for the company. From Murdoch's point of view this was fine – he controlled both News Corporation and Cruden.

But there was a problem: as a result of its bid for Queensland, Cruden had a bank loan of A$340 million. As its only assets were shares in News Corporation – which paid very low dividends – and the shares in Queensland, paying the interest on this loan was going to be a problem. However, in 1987 a solution appeared. There was a buyer for over 42 million of Cruden's shares in News Corporation, representing 16 per cent of the total number of shares in issue. The buyer was willing to pay a price of A$16 – a total cost of A$670 million. The problem for the Murdoch family was that they would lose control of 16 per cent of their company. Well, not quite: the buyer was Queensland Press, the company controlled by Cruden itself and News Corporation.

For Cruden this was a good deal – they lost no control of News Corporation but, after repaying the loan raised to bid for Queensland, they were A$330 million better off. For the outside shareholders in News Corporation it was a different matter. Before the deal was done, News Corporation owned 46 per cent of Queensland – a moderately successful news-paper company, making profits of around A$70 million, with no debt. Afterwards it was barely profitable because of the interest on the debt, and the asset it had bought was in a highly volatile stock exchange investment – News Corporation. This was clearly a deterioration in the value of News Corporation's investment. The Murdoch family may not have minded because they received a cash injection, but for the other shareholders – who received nothing – it was a rip-off. As one analyst remarked 'News Corp has geared an associate purely for the purpose of providing a capital injection to the major shareholder of News Corp – Cruden Investments.'[47]

By any measure this was an extraordinary deal and we asked Murdoch to explain it. He replied:

Against the background of Queensland Press's history

153

of investment in media company shares, the Queensland board took up the opportunity. They apparently took the view that, together with HWT's existing holding of convertible notes in News Corporation, the shares would give Queensland a substantial position in probably the most successful and dynamic media company in the world.

He added: 'No member of Cruden Investments' board or members of the Murdoch family participated in the Queensland decisions, or was present when it was made.' (See Appendix II.)

This explanation must be rejected as unsatisfactory on several grounds. The attempt to paint Queensland as an independent company is unconvincing. It was run as 'a fully integrated part of News Limited'.[48] The loan which Queensland raised to make the share purchase came from a subsidiary of News Corporation (A$170 million) and from a consortium of banks (A$500 million). The bank loan, which was secured on the News Corporation shares, was also backed by a letter of comfort from News Corporation.[49] There is no way in which News Corporation could not have known about the investment its associate company was making.

In addition, from July 1987 Murdoch was a director of Queensland Press, along with his right-hand man in Australia, Ken Cowley. Even if Murdoch was not present at the meeting at which the decision was made, it is not hard to imagine what happened. One ex-Queensland director told us: 'There were News Limited directors on the Queensland board, they would have had a captive audience for any suggestion or recommendation they made.'[50]

The investment has, of course, proved disastrous. The value of News Corporation shares has fallen and the income of Queensland Press only just covers the interest on the loan.[51]

154

7

Sky: The European Dream

'What it's going to look like is either a bloody battlefield with a lot of red ink strewn around, or a brilliant success,' Rupert Murdoch told the *Washington Post* in a 1983 interview. He had just bought a majority stake in Inter-American Satellite Television Network, renamed it Skyband and leased transponders on the American SBS 3 satellite. The FCC waved through his application, allowing him to launch a totally unregulated direct broadcasting by satellite (DBS) service.

There was the usual Murdoch bravura in the annual report of News Corporation. He told his shareholders: 'Within a few months we expect to be operating the first satellite-to-home broadcast network in the United States.' Murdoch's plan was to beam at least five television channels across the United States. The target audience was the 26 million American homes who could not get television programmes on cable. Each subscriber would be equipped with a big dish, between 1 and 1.8 metres in diameter and an indoor box of tricks to

155

decode the signal. Murdoch wanted to be first in the market. He believed, quite rightly, that the competitive advantages from being first were enormous.

The initial plan was to transmit bought-in programmes to around two million Americans. Eventually, News Corporation would close the circle and make the programmes itself. This was to be one of the first steps in a major expansion of News Corporation, which would change it into a 'broadly based international communications company'.[1]

In 1983 he told his shareholders:

We are advantageously placed for a strategic move into satellite broadcasting at an early stage in the development of that medium. We recognise the uncertainties associated with any such pioneering effort. However, decades of experience of communicating the printed word in uniquely competitive and varied markets, together with considerable experience in conventional television broadcasting in Australia, have prepared us for expansion into the new forms of communication being opened up by advances in technology. We believe the potential rewards fully justify the risks.

As with other Murdoch ventures, enthusiasm and ambition ran ahead of the product.

New technologies are very exciting. In the long term, every major international corporation has to embrace them if it is to survive. But in the short term new technologies can be so expensive that they can threaten the survival of the company. Costs can quickly run out of control, the market becomes less than enthusiastic and the company suddenly finds that it has bet everything it has built in the past on trying to secure the future. Instead of dominating their market, the directors discover they are fighting for their survival. The pundits and the market who originally applauded their bravery and foresight now turn against them and they are dismissed as foolish gamblers chasing the rainbow. This happened to Murdoch's first satellite venture.

He tripped at the first step. Within six months, in November 1983, he closed down the operation.[2] The following summer, 1984, he told his shareholders that despite 'intensive effort and considerable investment . . . we felt that the risks involved in proceeding last year exceeded the potential rewards'.[3] Neither the technology nor the programmes could be delivered at a price which made them attractive. Even for Murdoch, the great global gambler, the odds were too long.

The cost to News Corporation was A$20 million, a cheap lesson for Murdoch to get himself on the learning curve. This was not the only bet Murdoch lost in 1984. In his own words, News Corporation had made 'a serious misjudgement' on the international money markets and failed to cover itself against large currency fluctuations. Basically, News Corporation had bought large forward currency positions. They had committed themselves to buying huge amounts of dollars at fixed prices today. The exchange rate moved against News Corporation and the losses were large.

Murdoch was not the first to be seduced by the potential of huge rewards from the international money markets and he will not be the last. But he quickly learned that these markets are cruel and unyielding. Unlike his other businesses, he could not solve his problems with a phone call to a sympathetic regulator. Murdoch told News Corporation's shareholders that the company had now changed to a more prudent policy of keeping a balance between the currencies in which they earned their money and the currencies in which they borrowed. The policy of buying large forward currency positions was stopped. In future News Corporation would always hedge its currency positions, so it did not get caught again.[4] These were brave words, but this early painful lesson on the currency markets did not stop Murdoch. He just got better at it (see Chapter 11).

Murdoch is a consummate gambler. The extraordinary thing is that he appears to take each decision in isolation, assessing each bet on its merits. So although two of his big decisions in 1983–84 had gone wrong and cost the shareholders (including himself) a great deal of money, he had already taken another, far greater gamble. This gamble would cost far more than the losses on Skyband or on the international currency markets. Murdoch was hooked on satellites. Though he closed down his American satellite operation in November 1983, he had already opened up a second front. On 28 June 1983, News International plc, the British-registered company which owned his British newspapers, put £5 million into a British company called Satellite Television plc (SATV) in return for which it got 68 per cent of the votes.

This initial investment was tiny but was a crucial part of a move into electronic media. Throughout the early 1980s Murdoch had been defining his business and looking to the future. The message was clear. In the past, media empires had been built on paper, which formed the medium for mass market products like newspapers and magazines. In future, media empires would be built on silicon. While he had been expanding his newspaper and magazine empire, a new world-wide multi-billion-dollar industry had grown up around him. The mass production of the silicon microchip and the extraordinary computer advances this provoked had revolutionised the communications industry. The currency of this revolution was electronic. The coinage, in future, would be the microchip. After a lifetime career in the inky world of newspapers, Rupert Murdoch knew that this was his future.

He knew that opportunities like this only came, perhaps, once in a lifetime. This new electronic world was like the Wild West before the railroad. The first entrepreneurs who had built the railroad had established family dynasties which dominated for generations to come. Murdoch wanted his share.

Unless he embraced this new technology, he knew that News Corporation could not survive. His research told him that by 1983 as many as 60 per cent of Americans worked in information-related jobs, compared to only 17 per cent in the 1950s. This meant that News Corporation had to become electronic as well. And that meant two things: television and satellite. He needed to expand heavily into television. But temperamentally it was satellite that really appealed to him. Like Murdoch himself, a broadcast satellite did not recognise national boundaries or accept the diktats of politicians. This was the new territory, the new frontier. The expansion into satellite was the cornerstone of an ambitious global plan to expand into every area of communications, whether it be papers, magazines, books, television, films, satellite or cable. In future Murdoch wanted to control both the product and the means of distribution. It was a desire of breathtaking audacity. He wrote: 'It will engage the best of our present creative and managerial skills with a forceful new technology, placing the Company in an excellent position to benefit from a revolution that is changing the way we live, the way we work and the way we are entertained.'[5]

The move into space was one of the first steps in the master plan. In 1983 Murdoch announced that he had decided to devote 'a large part' of News Corporation's earnings to satellite.[6] In fact his initial investment was quite modest, less than £10 million a year. The 'large part' would come later.

In Britain he had an unlikely kindred spirit: Norton Louis

159

Philip Knatchbull Romsey. Lord Romsey was one of Britain's aristocratic rich. He was also a satellite fan and one of the first people in Britain to own a dish. At that time, SATV was a fledgling company run by a group of believers including Lord Romsey and some of his friends, and supported by a couple of merchant banks. In 1983 they had a choice between Rupert Murdoch and a deal with Racal/Ferranti. The board was split, but Romsey voted for Murdoch, who won. Romsey is convinced he made the right decision. 'Without Rupert Murdoch there would have been no satellite television,' he says.

In the early days SATV broadcast the Sky Channel on the Orbital Test Satellite, OTS. There were no rules. The directors lobbied throughout Europe and little by little secured permission to broadcast. There were few dish sales and the programming was distributed through local cable stations.

Along with his fellow directors and shareholders, Murdoch had a vision that one day satellite television would become something much more important in everyone's lives. His first few million were just the down-payment on what turned into a multi-million-pound gamble. Within six years the losses on his European satellite venture had run out of control and nearly crippled the empire. News Corporation and its shareholders are still paying the price and do not yet know for certain whether the gamble will ever have been worth it.

Despite the unfailing support of his newspapers in Britain, particularly the best-selling *Sun*, which has loyally supported Sky throughout, it is doubtful whether Murdoch can achieve the breakthrough he desperately needs much before the mid-1990s. Whether the patience of his bankers lasts until then is another matter. New ventures like Sky are expected to lose money in the early days, especially those riding on the bleeding edge of a new technology. As Murdoch predicted with his first satellite venture, there has been 'plenty of red ink' strewn around. He hoped the venture would break even early on. But the early hopes of brilliant success have always eluded him. His problem has been that he has never been able to stop the bleeding, which turned into a major haemorrhage in 1988. From day one, his European satellite venture established a trading pattern which has remained unchanged ever since. Increasingly heavy losses have been followed by increasingly large transfusions of money.

The story has been vintage Murdoch. Both he and his bankers believed that he was a far-sighted pioneer who had a vision which allowed him to go where others feared to tread, keep his nerve and emerge triumphant. He could see things few others could see. When Murdoch looked at European television in the early 1980s he did see something few others had seen. While others had seen a stable market dominated by state-run television networks and controlled by tight legislation, he saw cosy monopolies, which offered a very limited range of programming. European television, self-satisfied and cocooned in regulation, was everything he hated. In Murdoch's eyes this was a sleepy market waiting to be attacked. State-run television was worthy and run by well-meaning liberals who saw television as a medium which was dangerous and had to be controlled. Even in Britain, commercial television (in which he had once had an interest back in the 1970s) talked of public service broadcasting while enjoying a comfortable cartel which guaranteed them easy profits.

The joke was that in Germany everything was forbidden except that which was allowed. In France everything was allowed except what was forbidden. In Italy everything was allowed including what was forbidden. The same spirit which drove Murdoch to smash the restrictive practices of Fleet Street propelled him into the skies over Europe. The electronic signals from his satellite transponders would break through the bureaucratic fog the same way his trucks would later smash their way through the picket lines at Wapping.

For the first four years, Sky Television (then still called SATV) was a modest affair. It lost around £7 million a year but, crucially, it was beginning to build an audience, however tiny.

Initially, it broadcast entertainment programmes on one channel to the whole of Europe. By 1984 it reached 1.6 million European homes. Murdoch proclaimed the ratings were 'excellent'.[7] He knew that ultimately success depended on getting strong support from the advertisers. Optimistically he declared to News Corporation's shareholders: 'While we have not yet reached break-even, Sky Channel has already achieved a level of support from both viewers and advertisers that merits our continued investment.'[8] It is difficult to see where Murdoch's optimism came from. In 1984 SATV's actual advertising revenue was just over half a million pounds. Operating costs were £5.5 million.

By 1985 Sky Channel broadcast to four million homes in twelve European countries: Holland, Belgium, Switzerland, Finland, Norway, Denmark, West Germany, Britain, France, Austria, Sweden and Luxembourg. Programming was extended to 10 hours on weekdays and 11½ a day at weekends, with a target of 18 hours a day by the end of the year.

The emphasis was on entertainment, children and music for the youth market. It all seemed wonderful. News Corporation paraded its typical European viewer. Ad van Rin, 35, was the editor of a weekly Dutch fashion magazine. His wife, Corrie, worked in a laboratory. 'We like watching American comedy shows never seen here. It's a bit like travelling to another country for a holiday,' said Ad van Rin.

Murdoch, his shareholders and his bankers could feel

reassured that this was the future. The van Rin family had three daughters and Sky could hook them with pop music. Murdoch boasted that: 'Sky Channel remains the only station to broadcast English language programming to cable stations across Europe and is now attracting many multi-national advertisers. Measured audience research and rating surveys show its programming has tremendous appeal.'[9]

The viewers turned on, but the advertisers stayed away. The Sky accounts, which were publicly available but unpublished, continued to tell the same old, rather bleak story. In 1985 advertising sales were still only £2.8 million but trading losses were £8.8 million. By 1986 Murdoch was claiming that Sky Channel, 'the Group's pioneering pan-European television service based in London', was broadcasting to seven million homes across fifteen European countries. This was two million more than its nearest rival, but the actual number of regular viewers was tiny. In 1986 the advertising revenue had grown to £8 million but the operating losses were £5.7 million. By 1986 the accumulated deficit was £20 million.[10] Murdoch, as always, was undeterred. He claimed that Sky had succeeded in obtaining the audience, being 'most heavily viewed' in Holland, West Germany and Switzerland. He expected to reach nine million homes by the end of the year. He was expanding the service in countries like Belgium. Advertising revenues were 'coming through slower than expected'[11] but the future looked good. After three years of losses he tried to reassure his shareholders, telling them in the News Corporation 1986 Annual Report that Sky 'should be operating profitably by the end of the current fiscal year'. It was not. And even five years later, by 1991, it still had not begun to operate profitably.

Back in 1986 the problem for Murdoch was all too obvious. The advertising was not coming in but the daily costs of running Sky were beginning to escalate. By now, Sky was a substantial operation with a cost base to match. Though there were only 96 employees, there were studios in London and sales offices in Amsterdam, Frankfurt, Stockholm, Berne and London.

Sky was broadcasting 122 hours a week. The programmes were mostly American and bought through syndication – some from Fox Films, his Hollywood subsidiary. Sky made 40 per cent of the programmes in-house. These were mostly pop video, sports and children's programmes. One of their most popular programmes was *Sky Trax*. As with every Murdoch product there was no shortage of hyperbole. *Sky Trax* 'is for European kids what MTV[12] is to America's'. The flagship pop video programme was called *Here Comes The Weekend*, presented by Gary Davies who worked for BBC's Radio One during the week. It was the usual format for this kind of show. A collection of videos, some inane chat and studio guests. *Sky Trax* did not command the audience to attract major stars. Instead it settled for middle-rank performers like Samantha Fox, the *Sun* Page Three pin-up, whose large breasts and happy smile had made her a favourite amongst the paper's readers. Murdoch loved it all. For him, 'Sky Channel is the only truly private commercial television station in Europe and Gary Davies' *Sky Trax* is just the sort of thing Europeans cannot get on their state-run networks'.

By 1986 Sky could proudly boast that it was the third most popular channel in Holland. According to Jane Perry, the head of media research for the advertising agency Young and Rubicam, who has made several lengthy studies of the European advertising market, 'it was only in countries like Holland, where there was a basic level of English comprehension and a rigid state television network, that channels like Sky had a chance to succeed.' Sky started to make ten hours a week in Holland, with shows like *Eurochart Top 50* from Europe's largest discotheque, the

Escape Complex in Amsterdam. But this was formula television, which could have been made anywhere in Europe. By
the end of 1986 Sky was broadcasting to 9.5 million homes,
giving it a claimed audience of over 20 million viewers.

But, despite all the claims, the advertisers remained unimpressed. News Corporation's 1987 Annual Report talked of
Sky now reaching 9.7 million homes and maintaining its
'leadership in pan-European television'.[13] On the face of it,
this was an exciting claim. As with many of the stories in his
newspapers, the truth was more banal. Sky was a leader in a
field of one. No other satellite broadcaster had tried to set up a
pan-European service on the Sky model. Every other
European broadcaster knew what should have been obvious.
There was no pan-European audience for an English language
television service – even if you gave it away. Murdoch's vision
of a pan-European advertising market was not shared by the
people who mattered most – the advertisers. As with his
rapidly aborted adventure into American satellite, neither the
audience nor the advertising were there. Looking back on
those days now, Lord Romsey, who was a director throughout
this period, says: 'The great weakness of the business plan was
pan-European advertising. The reality is that there is little
pan-European advertising on television.'

As always, News Corporation remained upbeat, claiming
significant and increasing viewership levels, particularly
among children, though Murdoch did admit that advertisers'
acceptance had been slow. By 1987 his problem was clear. For
every pound Sky took in advertising revenue, it lost two. To
break even, Sky needed to hold its costs steady and at least
double the advertising take. Though advertising had risen in
Britain, it was falling in Europe. According to Murdoch's
claim of the year before, Sky Channel should now have moved
into profit. Instead in 1987 it made pre-tax losses of
£10,198,801 on a turnover of £10,246,211.[14]

By now, Sky's accumulated losses were just over £28 million – quite a modest sum for a new venture of this size. The losses had been covered by rights issues, underwritten by News International, which had given Murdoch 83 per cent of the company, and by an overdraft of a further £10 million. But Murdoch remained confident. The News Corporation Annual Report for 1987 said: 'Sky has not yet become profitable, but it is strongly pursuing strategies to build viewer and advertiser support. Over the next five years, Sky Channel's potential audience is expected to grow to more than 19 million viewers.' It never happened.

Murdoch hung on because he believed a pan-European market, a market where advertisers would buy advertising for every European country from one supplier, was inevitable. Provided Sky kept its position as the leading pan-European broadcaster, then he would dominate this new market and clean up. Much of his optimism was based on the rapid growth of advertising revenue across Europe throughout the 1980s. The optimistic argument went like this. As new media, like satellite television, appear, so advertisers want to take advantage of it. However, advertisers will still continue to use traditional forms of advertising like newspapers, magazines and terrestrial broadcasters. So Murdoch believed the overall volume of advertising would inevitably increase as advertisers began to use the new medium as well as their usual sources.

This was a very seductive argument for Murdoch. If true, it meant that his new ventures like Sky could expect, in the future, to be swamped with advertising. It also meant that his existing core products, like his newspapers and magazines, could also expect rising advertising revenues. There was a basic flaw in the argument. There was no pan-European advertising market. The market was more complex than it first appeared.

There had been an explosion of advertising revenue across

Europe throughout the 1980s. But this advertising had been national not international, local not pan-European. Crudely put, Italian companies advertised in Italy and German companies advertised in Germany. Even when German companies advertised in Britain they made different adverts, which would appeal to British consumers. The Mercedes car is marketed in Britain as the final word in class and luxury for the executive at the top of his or her chosen profession. But in its home country of Germany it is sold as a solid and reliable family car. Critically for Murdoch, European advertising was domestic, even for international, pan-European products. Even world-dominating multinationals like Coca-Cola do not run the same campaign throughout Europe. Worldwide campaigns, like 'I'd like to teach the world to sing', use the same bank of shots but have a different cut depending on the target country. The same applies for all other mainstream pan-European products.

Jane Perry's view is that 'like many Americans, Murdoch looked at Europe with American eyes'. Both he and his advisers took the classic American view of Europe – that it is just like America, except that some of them speak a different language. But Europe has never been a single advertising market and never will be. In Perry's judgement, 'there were no immediately accessible pan-European advertising budgets for European television. He anticipated that the existence of a pan-European audience for television implied a demand for pan-European advertising. At the time it was a common belief and he would have liked it to be so,' she says.

Throughout the early 1980s there had been a pan-European advertising market but it was so small it barely showed on surveys. It covered car hire, airlines and the kind of luxury goods bought in duty free shops. These were not the same consumers who would watch Gary Davies interviewing Samantha Fox on *Here Comes The Weekend*.

And because advertising agencies have different strengths in different countries, it is rare for a major campaign to be handled by the same agency across Europe. The pattern usually is for multinationals to use two or three agencies across Europe. It was not in their interests either to encourage one-stop shopping by their clients. 'What we didn't realise – naively – was that it was not in the interests of the advertising agencies to give power to their clients in this way. With one exception, they only ever paid lip service to the idea,' argues Lord Romsey.

Crucially for Sky's European dream, multinationals organise their advertising budgets on a national basis. Advertising follows sales. And the advertising budget for each country is set according to the level of sales. And that means that national managers are extremely reluctant to give up part of their national budget to fund an international advertising campaign which may not benefit their sales figures and will not therefore affect their annual bonuses.

At that time the technology was not sophisticated enough to transmit multilingual versions of the same advert on the satellite. Whilst Sky was happy that everyone in Europe got the same programme, the advertisers were not. But while Sky could not provide the viewers with the programmes they wanted, other new commercial stations were springing up across Europe to give the viewers the programmes in a language they wanted to hear.

In Jane Perry's words, Murdoch and his advisers 'underestimated the legislative ingenuity of every European country'. While Britain, Australia and the United States had a fairly 'free skies' broadcasting policy as regards satellite, the continental Europeans did not. As soon as satellite television became a threat in the early 1980s, every European government responded by opening up its markets. The arrival of satellite led to an explosion of commercial television throughout Europe, both terrestrial and satellite. These new commercial stations put great pressure on the existing state-run networks which responded by scheduling more light entertainment. Murdoch had achieved his avowed aim of freeing up the market, but suddenly found that it had become a rather crowded place. Advertising follows sales, and advertisers chase audiences. The new commercial television stations across Europe began to deliver both audiences and sales. Sky, with its English-language programming, missed out on the advertising bonanza it had helped to provoke.

And there was little Murdoch could do about it. His political clout in Europe was zero. He has always been reluctant to operate any of his businesses in a language he does not understand. He therefore did not own any papers or television stations on mainland Europe. Consequently, there were no politicians or regulators he could manipulate. It was inevitable that he could not defeat powerful media empires like Bertlesmans or Berlusconi on their own territory.

He retreated back to Britain, to a country where he already had a dominant position in daily and weekly newspapers, a close friend at 10 Downing Street, Margaret Thatcher, and where the natives spoke a language he understood. But whilst he had been broadcasting his European dream from a satellite with a footprint that covered Europe, the British Government was looking for a broadcaster to bid for the first of five new high-powered satellite channels, which were to start towards the end of the decade.

There were several bidders, including a consortium led by Sky, but in the December 1986 the British Government announced the winner to be, British Satellite Broadcasting (BSB). This consortium included Pearson (the publishers of the *Financial Times*), Granada (the entertainment group), Virgin (the record company) and Amstrad (the consumer electronics company). BSB quickly announced a four-channel package and a launch date, September 1989. Murdoch's Sky Channel now had serious competition in Britain. BSB was far richer than Sky and represented a serious threat.

But then Murdoch was offered a chance to beat BSB and he took it. Salesmen for another satellite, the Astra, called on Sky, trying to sell space on their new satellite, which was much more powerful than the one he was using for Sky Channel. The Astra would give him four channels instead of one and, even better, it was due to be launched in spring 1989, six months before the BSB satellite. The Astra footprint covered Britain and western Europe. The salesmen were pushing at an open door. In Lord Romsey's words, 'it was cheap and cheerful and would do the business'. Murdoch decided to go for broke and took four transponders (i.e. channels) on the satellite. Murdoch guessed quite correctly that there was only going to be one winner in the sky wars. If he could get into the market six months before BSB, that winner would be him.

Someone else agreed. Richard Branson, of Virgin, at that time had £30 million invested in BSB. As soon as he knew that Murdoch was going onto Astra he looked round for someone to take his BSB shares. He must have played the card game, Old Maid, as a child. In this popular British game the crucial trick is to pass on the Old Maid card as soon as possible. If you are left with it at the end, you lose the game. Branson added a million pounds on, to cover his costs, and found a willing taker: the Australian multi-millionaire entrepeneur and yachtsman Alan Bond. Branson celebrated with champagne. As he remarked recently, 'I think it was the last deal of any size that he [Alan Bond] did.'[15]

The directors of BSB were horrified by Murdoch's arrival. They had bid for a satellite monopoly in Britain. In return they had agreed to use an untested and expensive new technology, D-Mac, and an unlaunched satellite, Marco

170

Polo. Under the terms of the licence, media groups were limited to a 20 per cent share in BSB. But now Murdoch was planning to remove their monopoly, use the technology of his choice and own the business 100 per cent. BSB shouted foul. As far as they could see, Sky and BSB were the same: both were British based, both were targeted at Britain, both used a British up-link to their satellites and, crucially, both were dependent on the British advertising market. They went to see Mrs Thatcher to ask her to intervene and keep to the terms under which they had originally agreed to become involved. They received a short lecture on the virtues of competition and were sent away. Once again the rules of engagement had been tipped in Rupert Murdoch's favour by an ever-grateful Prime Minister.

By now, Sky had also begun to take in sponsorship fees, payments by companies to underwrite the costs of a programme in return for credit at the end. This, as well as an increase of £1.4 million in advertising revenue from the UK, helped to boost Sky's income in 1988 to £12,629,166. But the pre-tax losses were £8,452,544. The 1988 News Corporation Annual Report was, as always, upbeat. Sky channel was now seen in more than 12 million homes 'throughout Europe'. It went on, 'audiences in the UK and Europe will be able to receive an appealing array of programming options.' The number of cabled homes which could receive Sky was expected to reach 15.7 million in June 1989. Sky was 'still not profitable', but the Report boasted that its reach and market penetration had exceeded expectations. The number of homes receiving Sky had doubled in the previous two years.

The graphs attached pointed up the exciting vista of the growth of European advertising, particularly in West Germany where advertising expenditure had grown by 15 per cent between 1981 and 1986, and France, where it had grown by 37 per cent in the same period. The kindest thing that can be said about this was that it was terribly misleading. Sky was not going to reach these exciting and lucrative European markets. The pan-European dream was over. Though the number of channels had quadrupled, Sky's audience had suddenly shrunk. Sky's real plans were revealed in the small print of a 20-F filing News Corporation made with the Securities and Exchange Commission in Washington.

A 20-F is an annual report in which companies are obliged to provide details of their operations. This showed that although the sports channel could still be seen across Europe, the Sky movie channel would only be available in Britain and the Republic of Ireland. The news channel would only be available in Britain. Because Sky could not clear the transmission rights on some of the programmes, the upgraded Sky Channel would only be available in Britain, the Republic of Ireland, Holland, Belgium and Scandinavia. The upgraded Sky Channel would therefore miss out on the lucrative advertising markets of Germany, France and Austria, though it is highly doubtful whether there was any significant advertising take from these countries even when Sky was targetting them.

The 20-F filing finished with the chilling sentence: 'In contrast to the present Sky Channel whose principal audience has been in continental Europe, News International expects that the principal audience for Sky Television's four channels will be in the United Kingdom.'

The News Corporation Annual Report, filed under Australian rather than American rules, was also dated June 1988. It told a completely different story. The shareholders were sold an exciting vision of 'Sky Television's determination to stay at the forefront of the changing European television scene, and offer more opportunities for advertisers to reach a pan-European audience.' Quite how Sky could do this when its primary audience was now contained in 400,000 homes in Britain and Ireland was not explained.

8

Pie in the Sky

Murdoch's retreat to operating satellite television just in Britain was one of the biggest risks of his career. He committed News International to an annual expenditure of around £100 million a year on Sky Television when he knew the company had only two basic sources of income: subscriptions to the movie channel and advertising. The movie channel faced a major problem. Britain already had a very advanced market in video rental so Sky was effectively trying to break into an existing market. They had to persuade people to stop going to the local video shop, where they paid a couple of pounds for a video of their own choosing, and instead to spend considerably more to receive someone else's film selection via a satellite dish.

Any projections about subscription income were only guesses. Murdoch knew a bit more about the state of the advertising market in Britain. In the twelve months up to the announcement, he knew that Sky's total revenue from

174

advertising in Britain was just over £3.8 million. The whole plan depended on the mass production and marketing of the dishes by his favoured supplier, Amstrad. None had yet come off the production line.

To begin with, the money flows in Sky were all one way – outwards. Sky signed a ten-year lease costing £74 million with British Telecom for four transponders on the Astra satellite to be launched the following spring.[1] It was a risk he could only take because he controlled such a big chunk of the News Corporation equity. As he has said since:

> The fact is that if our family had let our stake down to 20 per cent, there would have been a bunch of investment managers who would have risen up and fired me when I started Fox Broadcasting in 1986 and again when I got in to Sky in 1988. If you don't have a major, major shareholding, you can't take the same risk.[2]

Taken in isolation it was, in Lord Romsey's words, 'a staggering gamble'. It was an even bigger gamble when set against the other risks Murdoch was taking in News Corporation. His fledgling network company, Fox, was still draining cash; he was committing News Corporation to buying new printing equipment in Britain; and the month after the Sky launch announcement he sat down for lunch with Walter Annenberg to start negotiations to buy Triangle for just short of $3 billion. These were heady times.

Sky's marketing plan was to broadcast free of charge to dish-owners, with only the movie channel being paid for on subscription. There was to be no scrambling so that everyone would be able to receive the pictures free once they had bought a dish and paid the subscription fee.

David Johnson had been one of the six key figures who

dined with Rupert Murdoch back in March 1986 at the Mandarin Chinese Restaurant in Beverly Hills when Fox Broadcasting was born. Murdoch brought him to England to take a look at Sky. What Johnson saw horrified him.

I always felt that Rupert had a tremendous intuitive marketing sense. I think if Rupert has a fault, it is to someway be taken in by his own mystique. If there's one person you don't want to be enchanted by the mystique of Rupert Murdoch, it's Rupert Murdoch. The mechanics of the business didn't interest him.

It was the mechanics which Johnson thought were all wrong. He was worried that Sky was giving its product away too cheaply. He believed that Murdoch had made a critical mistake in copying the American broadcast television model. This model – like British commercial television – worked on the principle that you secured as much distribution as possible and then sold advertising on the back of it. In Johnson's view this model was inappropriate for Sky. Rather than secure its revenue from advertising, which is very sensitive to recession and competition from other sources, Sky should have followed the American cable model and secured the bulk of its revenue from leasing the dish and the decoder. It should have only relied on advertising for a small part of its income.

'There it was, this economic model lying there for someone to pick up and run with. And the fact is, it was not picked up and run with. In fact Rupert and his people started all over again and made the same mistakes which cable made in the United States,' Johnson says. Murdoch's team at Sky ignored two fundamental lessons from American cable. 'The first one was to retail the dishes, that was an absolute no-no,' argues Johnson. 'Cable didn't do that. What cable did was they leased a box to you and you pay for that every single month.' That guarantees the steady stream of revenue. The second mistake which Johnson identified was not making the system 'addressable', i.e. building into it the ability to switch off a non-payer. Instead Sky adopted a policy of sending workers out to remove the dishes from non-payers. Apart from the poor image this created, it was an expensive drain on Sky's resources. A great fan of television in all its forms, and a key player in the success of Fox, Johnson remains disappointed that Sky did not get a better start. 'The thing that I think is too bad about that was, you shouldn't have been in the position of learning from scratch. That model was there for all to see,' he said.

But Murdoch was taking a much longer-term view. He had already rejected the more cautious policy of leasing just one transponder and continuing broadcasting as before. The Sky board went along with his more ambitious plans. Murdoch did not believe that he would ever get market share if viewers had to pay from day one. And he did not worry that Sky would not make a profit for several years. The policy was to get the dishes out as cheaply as possible and build market share. He believed that the advertising would inevitably follow. Besides, he knew that every household that bought an Astra dish would not buy a BSB squarial. Once the Astra satellite was settled in geo-stationary orbit, he knew that BSB was dead.

The press launch in June 1988 was a lavish affair. Rupert Murdoch and Alan Sugar, whose company, Amstrad, was to make the dishes, appeared after an expensive multi-screen video presentation with simulated rocket smoke to the background music of Carl Orff's opera *Carmina Burana*. Murdoch held a model of the Astra satellite and Sugar held a small umbrella. 'We are seeing the dawning of an age of freedom,' Murdoch declared.

There was a bravura performance from Murdoch. Sky would be relaunched with four channels, instead of one. Sky Channel remained a general entertainment and arts channel. To these he added a feature film channel, a news and current affairs channel and a European sports channel. When he took the journalists through a glowing account of Sky's future he must have known that he had committed News Corporation to an annual spend of at least £100 million when Sky's advertising revenue from Britain for the previous twelve months had been just over £3.8 million. It was going to be a long haul.

Three months later he held another press conference to announce among other things that viewers were going to have to pay for the movie channel. The Murdoch papers treated this as a triumph. *The Times* ran it under the headline 'Satellite channels to cut advert costs'.[3] The *Sun's* piece did not mention it at all but told its readers that the Sky four-channel package was the 'dawn of a new age of freedom for the viewer and the advertiser'.[4]

Sky's first twelve months were extraordinary times. The operating costs of the venture were £100 million a year.[5] Effectively, Murdoch had quadrupled Sky's output, increased its costs tenfold, but cut the 'audience' from the whole of Europe down to Britain.

Having failed to secure any serious pan-European advertising income he now had to focus on Britain. The numbers of 'viewers' he put in the News Corporation Annual Report would no longer run into millions. But although, the numbers of viewers was dramatically smaller, crucially, the advertising market was much larger. Once Sky concentrated on Britain it theoretically offered advertisers a much larger

178

audience for an English multi-channel television service. However, it was a huge risk to take. It would require Murdoch's legendary nerves of steel as well as the almost as legendary indulgence of his bankers.

By the summer of 1988, before the satellite was launched, Sky was broadcasting to a claimed audience of twelve million homes across Europe. The running costs were around £20 million, just under £2 a home. The advertising income reduced the loss to under £1 a home. But after the launch and the restructuring, Sky was focused on 400,000 homes in Britain for an annual cost of more than £100 million: more than £250 a home. Sky was now losing £225 on each home, as opposed to just under £2 the previous summer.

But eight months later when the Astra satellite was settled in orbit above the earth, few people in Britain could see anything at all. Despite the earlier promises of flooding the shops with cheap dishes at £199, there were few available. It was a marketing disaster. The Murdoch papers struggled to find a positive angle. Under a headline reading 'Sky launch boosts demand for dishes', *The Times* told its readers that the Council for the Protection of Rural England was worried about 'forests of intrusive satellite dishes springing up across the rooftops of England'.[6] The *News of the World* was more basic: 36 column inches were devoted to a picture of five semi-naked women under the headline 'Dishes Galore'. It was captioned 'Skybirds are taking off'.[7] The *Sun* continued the theme during the week, with a Page Three 'Dish of the Day' feature – naked women holding satellite dishes.

Two months after the launch, there was a further blow to Sky's marketing chances when a crucial deal with Disney fell apart. Back in November 1988, Murdoch and the Sky executive chairman, Andrew Neil, had announced that Sky had concluded an impressive deal with Disney. Sky would

179

start a Disney Channel the following August, as well as up-grading its film channel. It planned to turn the two channels into a £12-a-month subscription package. It was a marketing masterstroke. Sky would broadcast Disney's unparalleled range of children's programming and Disney also would contribute films from its Hollywood subsidiary, Touchstone. There was even something in it for Sky's bankers. Disney would put up half the funds for Sky Movies. Murdoch and Neil had beaten off their rivals, who were also trying to conclude a deal with Disney. They both looked mightily pleased with themselves as they posed for the photographers in front of Disney characters.

But the relationship with Disney was strained from the start. There were reports that Sky faced problems raising the cash and Disney wanted to renegotiate the deal. By May the partners could not resolve their differences and the deal fell apart. Sky filed suit against Disney for $500 million in damages and a further $1 billion in punitive damages. It was a terrible blow to Murdoch. The Disney deal would have given him an unassailable market position in Britain. The Disney name would have encouraged thousands of parents to subscribe to keep their children happy. Murdoch tried to soften the blow by announcing that Sky planned a pay channel of 'classic films'. For once, the old Murdoch magic failed. Everyone knew that 'classic films' were old films that had already been seen on television at least twice.

The following summer, even though Sky's viewers were almost entirely confined to Britain and Ireland, Murdoch was still pumping out the European message. The News Corporation Annual Report for 1989 reminded the share-holders that Sky was 'launched to take advantage of the emerging liberalisation of broadcasting regulations in Europe'. The report had some good news for the shareholders, telling them that advertisers had 'welcomed the new opportunities'. Some of them might have done, but far more stayed away. What Murdoch did not reveal to his shareholders was that Sky's total advertising income for the year was just over £10 million. The previous year, before advertisers had 'welcomed the new opportunities', it had been just over £12 million.[8] The end of the European dream was confirmed in the figures. European advertising had dropped by a third from £6.3 million in 1988 to £4.3 million. Advertising revenue in Britain was just £5.2 million. Who was fooling whom? Was Murdoch just fooling the shareholders or was he fooling himself as well?

Sky's total losses took off into orbit along with the satellite. Between 1985 and 1988 losses had averaged around £8 million a year. In 1989 they were just over ten times as much – £81,264,000.

The analysts were horrified. Murdoch's accountants, Pannell Kerr Forster in Sydney, did their best to perform some cosmetic surgery on the Accounts. By 1989 the investment in Sky had reached $154,767,000. These losses came largely from day-to-day running costs and the lease on the satellite. But under Australian accounting conventions News Corporation was allowed to define these losses as a new business start-up cost. Accordingly they were capitalised until the operations were started on a commercial basis.[9] This meant they could be taken out of the profit and loss account and therefore not affect the crucial pre-tax figure which would grab the headlines when the results were announced.

The unpublished Sky Accounts in Britain used the same sleight of hand but provided far more details of just how grim the position had become. According to these accounts the pre-tax loss in 1989 was just £5.5 million. It was much worse than this. Costs of £62.6 million had been deferred. The bank loan and overdraft was £98 million.

As with its attack on the European market, Sky was struggling against the existing broadcasters. It was competing directly for viewers with the BBC and both ITV and Channel 4 for advertising and viewers. Sky was making little impact. When he launched the new four-channel Sky in June 1988, Murdoch laid out his blueprint for the 1990s. He told the journalists that his apartment in New York was hooked up to cable offering him thirty channels. Some of it was 'pretty awful', but much of it was 'enormously satisfying'. When in Britain, on the other hand, he said: 'I come in every night and find very little to satisfy.'

His problem there was that even after eighteen months of transmission, there was little on Sky to satisfy his potential viewers. Sky was struggling to survive. Sky Movies were given away free for a preview period. There was endless support from the *Sun* and other Murdoch papers. The sales pitch stressed the new and innovative programmes, but the reality was banal. *Jameson Tonight* was a week-night talk show presented by Derek Jameson, a former editor of the *Daily Express* who had become a radio and television celebrity. The current affairs programme was called *Target*. It had two presenters, Norman Tebbit, a former chairman of the Conservative Party and a strong supporter of Mrs Thatcher, and a middle-of-the-road Labour MP, Austin Mitchell.

Neil Kinnock, the Labour Party leader, and a long-term hate figure for Murdoch newspapers, immediately fired Mitchell from his position as a front-bench spokesman. This minor story was splashed all over the front pages of the *Sun*, *Today*, by then a Murdoch paper, and even *The Times*. Without a trace of irony, the *Sun* even reported that Sky had sent Kinnock a bottle of champagne thanking him for all the free publicity. The *Daily Mail* and the *Independent*, neither of which are owned by News Corporation, failed to see the exciting significance of the story and did not carry it.

Austin Mitchell soon blotted his copybook with the Sky management by a joke attributed to him. *Question*: what is the difference between Sky Television and the Loch Ness Monster? *Answer*: More people have seen the Loch Ness Monster.

The war between BSB and Sky was far more exciting than anything either of them ever broadcast. From the start they began to snipe at each other, complaining of each other's 'misleading' advertising. They sneered at each other's equipment and each other's movies. At the heart of the row was Murdoch's dominant position in British newspapers and his papers' slavish support for Sky. BSB's spokesman complained: 'Apart from the fact that there seems to be an editorial tie-up between News International and Sky Television, can it be right that Sky takes large amounts of advertising space in those papers?' Sky's spokesman countered: 'BSB can dish [sic] it out but can't take it. They started a negative advertising campaign in which they rubbished our technology, they are about to launch the biggest knocking campaign in history, and yet they are posing as having been the victims of some media campaign against them.'

On the day Murdoch and Alan Sugar launched the new Sky service, Anthony Simmonds-Gooding, BSB's chief executive, put out a statement saying: 'I think Murdoch's plan is just a load of junk. If I've got it right, he's going to come out with a receiver kit that is already obsolete the day it hits the markets.' It was difficult for anyone to take this knockabout stuff seriously. For a public trying to get to grips with a new technology it was all very confusing. Potential customers stayed away, as the row between the parties only served to promote a negative image of satellite broadcasting, particularly when they began to call in to doubt each other's parentage.

BSB commissioned a Manchester Professor, George Weddell, to produce a 'report' on the nature of the relationship between the ownership of Murdoch's papers and their editorial line. His report reached two conclusions. One, that there was a 'significant' body of material in Murdoch papers promoting Sky Television and of material 'unfavourable' to BSB. Two, Sky Television's advertising was placed almost exclusively with News Corporation newspapers. He was unable to discover whether this advertising was sold at favourable or market terms.

Murdoch complained about Weddell's report and asked why he did not investigate the relationship between BSB and papers which had a financial interest in. He did and found there was little evidence of any bias, particularly in the *Financial Times* which was owned by the Pearson Group, which in turn was a large shareholder in BSB. As added spice to the story, News Corporation owned 20 per cent of Pearson. In fact, the *Financial Times* remained scrupulously impartial throughout.

The truth was that, despite the hype, both companies were looking at a black hole in their balance sheets. Even though the British have an apparently unquenchable appetite for television, they still managed to avoid the exciting range of Sky's programmes. By June 1989, dish sales were negligible. Only 400,000 homes received Sky, and two-thirds of these were the 250,000 homes in Britain which already received cable television.

Sky was committed to a marketing policy of market share at any price. It was so desperate to establish any sort of audience that the programmes were given away free to Britain's small number of cable operators, though they did pay a fee to include Sky Movies. Dishes were given away free to all News International employees and to News Corporation's friends in the City. But the advertising on which this strategy depended was a mess. After years of struggling to convince advertisers and their agencies that there was an exciting pan-European market, the pitch had now changed. The advertisers were now being asked to book slots aimed essentially at a British audience, which already had plenty of choice from ITV and Channel 4. Advertising rates were heavily discounted to the point where Sky did not really have a rate card, but still the advertisers stayed away. Though many advertising agencies were well disposed towards Sky in principle, they were notoriously conservative in embracing new forms of media. Sky's terribly low ratings did little to excite them. And the low sales of dishes did little to excite Murdoch's bankers. Sky's losses were making a daily contribution to the ever-increasing debt mountain which now dominated News Corporation's balance sheet. By the summer of 1990 News Corporation's borrowings were £5 billion.

Murdoch went on the attack. His legendary chutzpah did not desert him. In July 1990, two years after the launch of the Astra satellite, he held a presentation to outline Sky's position. He conceded that Sky had already soaked up £250 million and might need a further £100 million. But he told journalists, 'We feel that we have proved ourselves. We have gone a long way further than we thought we could at this stage.' Three years after his last prediction of imminent profitability he added, 'It is conceivable that we would be in profit by the end of the next calendar year, 1991'.

Even for Murdoch, this was an extraordinary piece of bravado. Sky's losses were running at more than £2 million a week. In fact, Sky's overdraft the previous year had already reached £98 million. And by August 1991, after Sky had merged with BSB, News International's annual figures told a familiar story. Operating losses were still running at £1.5 million a week. These losses did not include depreciation costs or interest charges, which effectively doubled the figure.

But back in July 1990, News Corporation had already been having difficulty borrowing any more money (see Chapter 12). By now Sky had soaked up nearly £300 million of News Corporation's money. Within a month of talking to the journalists Murdoch had sat down for dinner to talk about what previously had been unthinkable – the merger of Sky with BSB. His old friend, the New York investment banker John Veronis, who had secured the Triangle takeover, brought the two sides together. He suggested to Murdoch that he have a private dinner with Peter Davis, the chief executive of Reed International and a shareholder in BSB.

The two met in a private suite at London's Claridges Hotel in late July 1990. In the same month the directors of Pearson, another shareholder in BSB, discussed a paper recommending merger between BSB and Sky. The talks continued in Australia in October when a 50-50 split was agreed in principle. The two sides reconvened in Bath at the end of October and the deal was announced on the weekend of 3 November. It was assumed (correctly) that the new channel would use Sky's Astra Channel. It would be the end of the squarial and BSB's new technology. BSB's chief executive, the ebullient Anthony Simmonds-Gooding, who had previously worked for Whitbreads the brewers and the advertising agency Saatchi and Saatchi, was not told what was going on. He turned up for work on the Monday after the deal was announced to find Murdoch sitting in his chair with his feet up on the desk.[10]

Neither the Home Office nor the Independent Broadcasting Authority (IBA), which licensed BSB, was given any warning. Peter Lloyd, the Broadcasting Minister, only learned about it when he read his morning newspapers.[11] Rupert Murdoch thoughtfully visited the Prime Minister, Mrs Thatcher, four days before the deal was finally signed to tell her what was happening. She did not think fit to intervene or inform her colleagues. Andrew Knight, the executive chairman of News International, claimed that the mention of the merger came 'at the very end of a general chat about international affairs'. Mrs Thatcher was reported to have taken notes during their twenty-minute meeting. Presumably these notes did not cover Rupert Murdoch's views of the international political scene. 'It's sheer fantasy and ridiculous to say that Rupert somehow asked her if it was all right', claimed Andrew Knight. The Opposition Labour Party disagreed and argued that her silence and non-intervention was tantamount to approval. The IBA was furious, but there was little it could do. Once again Rupert Murdoch had danced round the regulators. Sky transmitted on the Astra satellite from Luxembourg, without an IBA licence, and there was little political will on the part of the Thatcher Government to unwind a deal which had saved one of its most loyal supporters from the clutches of his bankers.

It was a brilliant deal for Murdoch. The new company, BSkyB, was jointly owned 50–50 between News Corporation and the old BSB shareholders. The existing nine channels were reduced to five and the war of words with BSB stopped. Though News Corporation got no cash for past losses, the deal put a limit on its exposure. Andrew Knight, allegedly Murdoch's chosen heir apparent, said Sky 'was the biggest single earnings hole we had and we have plugged it'. Frank Barlow, the chief executive of the shareholders Pearson, said:

'I characterise this as two bad businesses, which together make one good business.' Under the terms of the deal, when the newly formed company started to generate cash, 80 per cent of the first £400 million would go to News Corporation, with 20 per cent going to BSB. The next £400 million was to be divided equally between News Corporation and BSB and the third tranche of £400 million was to be split 20/80 between News Corporation and BSB. After that, the cash would be split equally. One of the attractions of this deal to News Corporation was that it got the lion's share of the first available cash but because it held only 50 per cent of the shares in the company, it could treat it as an associate company leaving most of BSkyB's losses out of its profit and loss account. Crucially, it was the Sky management which went in to run the merged company. The clash of cultures could not have been greater. While Sky's London headquarters in Osterley were spartan, BSB's architect-designed headquarters building near the River Thames in Battersea was a by-word for waste and extravagance. Like peasants storming the Royal Palace after the revolution, Murdoch's men took over BSB's Marco Polo Building.

Simmonds-Gooding talked of 'six Australians rampaging about and BSB staff being put to the knife in a very inhuman way'.[12] The Australians for their part were horrified. A story quickly went round Sky that BSB had spent more on carpets than Sky had spent on their buildings. It was an exaggeration, but it made the point.

Sam Chisholm, BSkyB's new chief executive, arrived with a fearsome reputation for toughness and brutality. He quickly made his mark. He lined up the BSkyB managing directors, asking each of them: 'Who are you?' and 'What do you do?' He told them not to talk to the press. 'Some of you may get a bulge in your trousers when you speak to journalists . . . but how you act with regard to the press will influence what I do about your termination packets.'

Chisholm cut costs quickly at BSkyB but the company still needed £380 million refinancing in March 1991. The original plan was to raise this as a loan but the banks wanted the shareholders to make guaranteed provisions of £200 million before they would make the loan, and it would take several months to arrange. BSkyB had to go back to its shareholders for the money. This put Murdoch in a quandary. Under the terms of the rescue package agreed with the banks in January 1991, News Corporation was prevented from putting any more money in to BSkyB.

Murdoch did not want to dilute his stake in the company, so he agreed to subscribe for his shares in kind – by providing, among other things, films from his Fox studios. This protected his stake in BSkyB. But he could only do this by effectively turning profits at Fox into shares in BSkyB. Reed International did not subscribe for its shares, but all the other BSB shareholders – Granada, Pearson and Chargeurs – stumped up their portion of the cash.

The prospects for BSkyB are still unclear. Costs will undoubtedly fall – the question is by how much. Though Chisholm's rottweiler style of management has dramatically cut costs, the really big saving may come from the amount BSkyB currently pays for film rights. Before the merger Sky and BSB fought a bloody and expensive battle to buy Hollywood films. Once BSB's chief executive, Anthony Simmonds-Gooding, realised that Murdoch was going to start transmitting on Astra before BSB, he devised a strategy to deprive Sky of the films it would need for its movie channel. He believed that if he bought up the movie rights from all of the major Hollywood studios, it would not matter that BSB came on the air after Sky. Sky would not have been able to transmit enough good films to build their audience. In the period before its launch, BSB would constantly advertise the wonderful movies it had bought and so kill Sky's sales. If it worked, BSB would then arrive with a blockbuster programme of movies and steal the market. It was a brave strategy but very expensive.

The Hollywood studios could not believe their luck. In the past, the possibility of income from UK satellite rights had never seemed even remotely likely. And now they had two companies, with apparently enormous wallets, bidding against each other. Whatever Murdoch bid in one room, Simmonds-Gooding sitting next door bid 10 per cent more. But in the end BSB had more cash and won. It signed up the majority of Hollywood studios – but at prices far higher than anyone in Hollywood could have imagined a couple of years before.

In the end, Sky and BSB paid up to 60 per cent more for their film rights than Canal+, the French subscription television company. This was extraordinary, as Canal+ is the largest pay-television channel in Europe, with a much larger subscription base than Sky and BSB. And where Sky and BSB cranked up spectacular losses at the end of the 1980s, Canal+ only showed high-quality profits. Where Sky and BSB shared a mountain of debt, Canal+ has a very strong balance sheet and a healthy cash position.

But when Sky and BSB merged, the story changed. Now there is only one buyer for Hollywood films and BSkyB is currently trying to extricate itself from the expensive, long-term contracts signed by BSB. At the heart of the negotiation is a five-year, $800 million contract signed between BSB and United International Pictures (UIP). BSkyB now argues that UIP, which negotiated for Paramount, MGM and Universal, acted in an anti-competitive way. The argument is that, by negotiating for all three studios, UIP were able to impose more onerous terms on BSB than if BSB had negotiated with each studio separately.

BSkyB's managing director, Sam Chisholm, spent much of the summer of 1991 over in Hollywood trying to cut a deal with the studios, in particular UIP. From April onwards, BSkyB threatened UIP with legal action under the Treaty of Rome finally issuing a writ in September 1991. If the European Commission rules that UIP broke those sections of the Treaty of Rome which guarantee free competition, then BSkyB could declare the agreement null and void. Worse still, they could fine UIP up to 10 per cent of its turnover. UIP is fighting the action. Gary Marenzi, president of UIP pay TV said: 'There is absolutely no basis for the suit. We have an agreement which we are confident will be upheld.'

However, this leaves Rupert Murdoch in a potentially embarrassing position. On the one hand, he wants the price of Hollywood movie rights to come down because this will benefit BSkyB, where he is a 48 per cent shareholder. Anything which makes it more profitable makes it less likely that News Corporation, as a major shareholder, will be asked to put more money in. However, wearing his Hollywood hat, he wants the price of UK satellite rights to be high because this benefits his film studio, 20th Century-Fox. Any punitive action against Hollywood by the anti-cartel department of the European Commission could also spill over to damage his Hollywood film interests. Owning a world-wide media empire has its problems.

But the real irony is that Sky Television itself has already run foul of the competition authorities in Brussels and is facing a suit for damages in excess of £55 million. The story goes back to the early days of Sky. The only genuine

European-wide channel in the Sky schedule was Eurosport, which was a consortium of Sky, News International and a group of members of the European Broadcasting Union, including the BBC and major television companies from France, Germany, Switzerland, Italy, Belgium and Ireland. Eurosport had competition. Screensport was another satellite-based European sports network. Like Sky it broadcast on the Astra satellite. Like Sky, Screensport had already absorbed a considerable amount of investment and was not expected to reach break-even until 1992, at the earliest, when it hit its target of 30 million homes. By 1989 it had 11 million subscriber households and broadcast in English, German, French and Dutch. Screensport and its majority shareholder, W.H. Smith, the British-based newsagents and media group, shouted foul.

They argued that the effect of the agreements between Sky and the European Broadcasting Union was to limit and distort competition. They filed their complaint with the European Commission, alleging that the Eurosport consortium had breached Article 85 of the Treaty of Rome. The Screensport complaint was that effectively two potential competitors for sports programmes, Sky and the European Broadcasting Union, had co-operated instead of competing, while at the same time denying Screensport access to programmes and some sports events.

Unlike Washington, Sydney or London, Rupert Murdoch has no influence in Brussels. In February 1991 the European Commission ruled that Sky had broken the Community's free competition rules. They wished to ensure a level playing field between broadcasters of sporting events, and ruled in favour of W.H. Smith and Screensport. The great free marketeer had been caught by the strict anti-cartel laws of the EC. The European Sports Network chief executive, Francis Baron, said that the decision 'is a total endorsement of our position and of the principle of free competition in the television market place. It will enable Screensport to compete in the market place for the first time on a fair basis.'

In May 1991 the European Sports Network filed a writ against Sky Television, the European Broadcasting Union and some of its more prominent members, including the BBC. They are seeking very substantial damages: in excess of £50 million. Much of this writ is directed against Sky and News International as 50 per cent holders in Eurosport. Eurosport was not included in the Sky/BSB deal. It went off the air three months after the European Commission decision against it.[13]

Over the Atlantic, Murdoch's re-entry into American satellite television collapsed in June 1991. The original plan had been for an 108-channel network costing US$1 billion. News Corporation and its three partners said it had died because the companies had 'different needs'. News Corporation's principal 'need' now was survival.

9

The Purchase of *TV Guide*

It was inevitable that Rupert Murdoch should go to America. As a young man he quickly tired of Australia. It was not big enough to give him satisfaction or to cope with his restlessness and ambition. But he was limited in choice as he would only operate in countries where he spoke the language.

Murdoch was a frequent visitor to America in the 1950s and 1960s, and it was on one of these trips that he walked round the print works of *TV Guide* and told his startled companion that he would return to buy it one day. But the first chance to move permanently outside Australia came in Britain when he bought the *News of The World* and the *Sun* in the late 1960s.

However, it was a short stay. The endless scandalmongering of the *News of the World*, particularly the serialisation of Christine Keeler's memoirs, meant that Murdoch and his wife, Anna, were cold-shouldered by polite society. Christine Keeler was a prostitute whose simultaneous relationship with a Russian spy, Eugene Ivanov, a black

194

pimp, Lucky Gordon, and the British Government Minister for War, John Profumo, had helped bring down the Conservative Government of Harold Macmillan in 1963.

English society was horrified that Murdoch, an outsider, should choose to reopen old wounds ten years after the event. His defence on television that the story would 'sell newspapers'[1] only confirmed their view of him as the 'Dirty Digger'. Three years later he confessed to Alexander Cockburn in an interview in the *Village Voice* that 'maybe I just have an inferiority complex about being Australian'. Feelings of resentment were continually reinforced. 'Just as we were being invited round to places we'd catch Lord Lambton in bed or something and we'd be barred from everything.' On top of everything else, his wife Anna's nervousness about living in London was continually reinforced by the memory of the kidnap and murder in 1969 of Muriel McKay, wife of one of her husband's executives. According to the confessions of the kidnappers, Anna Murdoch had been the intended victim. On a professional basis, Murdoch was continually exasperated by the recalcitrant behaviour of the Fleet Street trade unions, and the reluctance of the other proprietors to do anything about it.

There were good reasons for not settling in London. There were even better reasons for going to America. Murdoch loved the notion of America as the new frontier where hard work and application were more important than inherited status. This was the biggest media market in the world and there was no limit to his ambition. In 1973 he moved to New York with his wife and young family. The specific reason was to launch the *National Star*, but he first bought some newspapers in San Antonio, Texas. Murdoch heard about these from his friend, the tennis star John Newcombe. He was immediately captivated by the advanced technology they used.

The *Star* was a typical Murdoch product, a mass-market

general interest weekly magazine, focused on television personalities and other figures in the public eye. Produced largely by English sub-editors, it looked similar to the early *Sun*. Breezy not sleazy, its articles were the usual Murdoch mix of diet, health, fashion, films, astrology, human interest and excerpts from best-selling books. It was a formula Murdoch knew and loved. The *Star* received 90 per cent of its income from supermarket sales, with the balance coming from advertising. After a rocky start, its circulation peaked at 3.7 million in 1987 when it booked 524 pages of advertising over the year. He sold it in 1989 for $400 million.

At the other end of the social spectrum he picked up *New York* magazine in 1977 after a bruising confrontation with the magazine's guiding spirit, Clay Felker. *New York* was an up-market news magazine which was essential reading for New York's chattering classes. By the latter half of the 1980s it sold 430,000 copies a week. It was a raft for advertising which was responsible for three-quarters of the revenue.

But it was the Reagan years which were the years of great expansion for Murdoch and the years when he consolidated his relentless courting of American politicians. Mark Fowler, President Reagan's new appointee as head at the FCC, remembers a lunch for key Government leaders, hosted by Murdoch. Fowler was just the sort of person Murdoch needed to get to know. A smart Washington lawyer, he had been brought in to shake up the FCC. His brief was to go through the FCC rule book and remove 70 per cent of the regulations, opening up the television market to new players like Murdoch. The lunch was 'a get acquainted session, more or less'.

Fowler was a bit mystified to start with but went along to see what it was all about. What he knew about Murdoch at that time was largely vague and anecdotal. But he soon got the point. 'It became pretty evident fairly quickly that this

196

man had big plans, had an enormous vision of what could be and had the courage and apparently the wallet to back up these convictions. He saw things other people didn't see and was willing to take risks and was willing to pay some extraordinarily high prices.' By the end of the Reagan administration, Fowler's first impressions had been more than confirmed.

Throughout the 1980s Murdoch continued to buy consumer titles. He bought *New Woman* in 1984, *European Travel and Life* and *Automobile* in 1987. He also took a half interest in *Elle* with the French publisher of *Elle* in France, Hachette. *Elle* was the best performer, becoming profitable after two years' operation. Circulation rose by more than 50 per cent and advertising tripled. In 1987 it picked up a string of awards from the New York fashion critics, the American Society of Magazine Editors and the Columbia School of Journalism, as well as winning the National Magazine Awards for Design and General Excellence.[2]

New Woman was also a success. It was a monthly women's self-help magazine, dispensing help and advice predominantly to working women. When Murdoch bought it in 1984, almost all its copy came from books and other periodicals. He quickly changed the editorial format to concentrate on original material. This worked. The circulation began to climb from just over a million to just over 1,350,000 by 1990, with just under 1,000 pages of advertising a year. In 1986 as much as 55 per cent of income came from circulation, 45 per cent from ads.

But Murdoch did not just confine himself to consumer magazines. In January 1985 News America bought a group of business publications serving the aviation and travel industry magazines from Ziff-Davis at a price of $350 million. In April 1985 News America bought 50 per cent of Fox Film from Marvin Davis and the other 50 per cent just before Christmas in the same year. Total price $575 million. In March 1986 it bought six Metromedia television stations from John Kluge. Total price $2 billion (see Chapter 5). In April 1987 News America bought the publishers Harper and Row: price £300 million. But the big deal, part of Murdoch's 'expansionary lunge' was in October 1988, when News America bought Triangle Publications, the publishers of *TV Guide, Racing Form, Seventeen* and *Good Food* magazine, from Walter Annenburg: total price $2.8 billion. It was this last deal which really shocked the market.

On estimated sales, this deal put Murdoch's magazine division on a par with Time Inc., Condé Nast and Hearst magazines. It made News Corporation the second largest media conglomerate in the world behind Bertlesman of West Germany. For his followers it showed Murdoch's 'enormous vision'. Matti Prima, an investment banker at Henry Ansbachers, told Reuters: 'It's a brilliant manoeuvre on Murdoch's part. Murdoch has always been known to pay for quality and make it work.' But for Murdoch's detractors it was 'a deal too far', which would strain an empire already overloaded with debt.

The most extraordinary thing about this deal was the timing. Though Murdoch's British newspapers were throwing off cash in impressive amounts, his fledgling American television network was having little problem consuming it. In June 1988 Murdoch committed News Corporation to major expenditure on his Sky satellite television channel in Europe, when he knew there was little prospect of any return for several years. Yet only a month later he sat down for lunch with Walter Annenburg to mount the largest publishing deal ever.

Ambassador Walter Annenburg was one of the richest men in America. In many ways, Annenburg's business background made him the American equivalent of Murdoch. They shared a common inheritance. Like Murdoch, Annenburg had inherited a publishing business from his father. He admired and liked Murdoch, though there is nothing to suggest they were close friends. They both held similarly right-wing views. They shared a common friend whom they both helped a great deal: President Reagan. They were both notoriously mean payers and both liked to maintain a hands-on involvement with their businesses. But there the similarity ends.

Murdoch had built a sprawling empire, spread across three continents and encompassing newspapers, magazines, television, printing plants and an airline. Annenburg had stayed at home and concentrated on a handful of magazines. While Murdoch turned his hand to everything, Annenburg stuck to what he knew. Murdoch built an empire based on a mountain of debt, while Annenburg's was based on a mountain of cash.

He had inherited the *Daily Racing Form* from his father, Moe Annenburg. Moe Annenburg rose to be the circulation manager for Randolph Hearst, the American publisher who became the model for Orson Welles's classic movie *Citizen Kane*. Moe Annenburg was ambitious. He bought the *Daily Racing Form* in the 1920s and set up a wire service linking bookmakers with the track. By the 1930s he was a millionaire with a rapidly growing media empire. The Government stopped all that when it threw him in jail in 1940 for tax evasion and violating Federal gambling laws. The young Walter took over the business, settled the outstanding tax bill and started to rebuild the empire. He had a bronze plaque on his wall, which read 'Cause my works on earth to reflect honor on my father's memory'. This was a sentiment that Murdoch could easily relate to. His father's will said: 'I desire that my said son Keith Rupert Murdoch should have the great opportunity of spending a useful altruistic and full life in newspaper and broadcasting activities and of ultimately occupying a position of high responsibility in that field.'

In his business life, Walter Annenburg had three brilliant ideas. The first was to leave *Daily Racing Form* alone. It was the cash cow which funded the empire, and he reasoned quite correctly that the punters wanted their information in the same place every issue. According to Paine Webber analyst Kenneth Noble, it produced $2 million cash a week by 1988. Annenburg's second stroke of genius was to start *Seventeen* magazine in 1944. It was edited by his sister and aimed at teenage girls. Though it was cruelly nicknamed 'The Acne and The Ecstasy', it exactly fitted the rising post-war affluence and spawned a clutch of imitators. His third stroke of genius was to spot the extraordinary grip television would have on everyone's lives. He guessed that where there was a mass audience for one product there was likely to be a mass market for another. In 1953 he started *TV Guide*. It was hugely successful from day one. The first issue cost just 15 cents and sold an unprecedented 2 million copies. *TV Guide* became one of the most successful magazines in the history of publishing. By the mid-1970s it was selling around 20 million copies a week, the first magazine to sell a billion copies a year. It was phenomenally profitable.

TV Guide ranked third behind *Time* and *Sports Illustrated* on advertising revenue. The strong editorial line-up was seen by many in the industry as the key to its success. 'Their editorial is better than anyone else's (in the category). People read *TV Guide*. They're really fascinated with the behind-the-scenes stories,' was the judgement of Al Hampel, director of creative services for Hearst magazines.[3]

TV Guide's formula for success was as elusive as Coca-Cola, but there was little doubt that it was the editorial which separated it from the competition. Many local newspapers had begun to publish separate weekly television guides as part of the Sunday edition. The listings were complete but they did not make serious inroads into *TV Guide*'s circulation because the magazine offered an authoritative picture of the industry as a whole. In Hampel's view, the local papers only made 'a flimsy effort, editorially speaking, with a little article here and there'. *TV Guide*'s added value was its unique mixture of controversy, informed industry gossip, reviews, cheers and jeers. The typical reader was young, fairly affluent, with household income of $35,000 and some college education. Only half the sales came through subscriptions. A big chunk of the sales still came through supermarkets, but this was not a down-market publication. It had a full colour national section, which contained both the national and regional advertising, usually from big companies selling cars, cigarettes and packaged goods. The 100 regional editions were produced by a highly sophisticated computer system.

This allowed the magazine to pick up local advertising, principally from local television stations, local health clubs and local car dealers. *TV Guide* had an interest in 60 printing plants across the United States, plus its own distribution facilities. There were other attractions of *TV Guide* for Murdoch. It had computerised summaries of more than 20,000 movies and 150,000 programmes. According to John Evans, president of Murdoch Magazines in New York, 'this will provide an enormous database for a major electronic publishing company that he is forming'.[4]

By the summer of 1988 *TV Guide* published more than 100 geographically defined editions each week. Its listings section was comprehensive, covering nearly 1,300 broadcast stations and every major cable programming service across the United States. The circulation had softened, but was still just short of 17 million copies a week, with over 9 million of these coming from subscriptions. The subscriptions were more profitable because Triangle did not need to share any revenue with the distributors. *TV Guide* was pretty close to the elusive 'river of gold', which is every publisher's dream. No accounts are available because it was a private company, but estimates at the time suggested it was earning between $100 and $125 million a year. The gossip suggested that it gave its owner $1-million-a-week spending money.

In 1987 Annenburg indicated that he would prefer to sell the magazines than hand them on to his heirs. He told *Forbes* magazine that he was worried that his rich heirs 'do not necessarily have the lash of ambition on their back and become what I describe as well-fed house dogs'.[5] However, Annenburg sent out conflicting signals. At the beginning of 1988 he told one staff member that he was not going to sell. But he was now aged eighty and keen to expand his philanthropic interests. Within months he was sitting down with Rupert Murdoch to do exactly that. He was in no hurry and knew he could wait to get a good price.

As always, Annenburg's sense of timing was excellent. It was the right time to sell. Media properties were commanding premium prices. CBS Magazines had just been bought and sold within six months for a profit of $300 million and bankers were meeting little resistance to recent billion dollar leveraged buy-outs for television stations.[6]

Though it was a good time to sell, the number of potential buyers was small. There were few publishing companies in the world that were rich enough to feel comfortable with such a huge deal, at the price Annenburg wanted. Annenburg himself drew up a short-list of acceptable buyers which he gave to his banker, John Veronis of Veronis Suhler and Associates.[7] One of these was Murdoch and, according to Veronis, Annenburg wanted him to approach Murdoch first. It was a smart choice. Murdoch had been interested in *TV Guide* for twenty years.[8] Though News Corporation was already highly geared and had a deadline to reduce its debt the following summer, Murdoch's bankers were still prepared to indulge him. Annenburg knew that although Murdoch had a reputation for being a smart deal-maker, his recent transactions suggested that he did not negotiate too heavily on price.

Veronis first talked to Annenburg on 5 July 1988. He then approached Rupert Murdoch the following day. The next day they met at Murdoch's New York office. Veronis asked him if he was interested.[9] Murdoch jumped at the chance. 'We never talked to anyone else,' said Veronis. He did not need to. Annenburg had asked for around $3 billion and Murdoch was prepared to meet the price: 'A rather large sum,' as he described it.

Two days later Rupert Murdoch picked up Veronis in his plane out in the Hamptons, an exclusive and expensive beach resort on Long Island, New York. They flew down to Annenburg's estate in Pennsylvania to discuss the deal over lunch. According to Veronis, they discussed the editorial quality and future prospects of the magazines for two hours. 'Not once', claims Veronis, 'did the subject of price come up.'[10]

After three weeks of negotiations they finalised the details at Sunnylands, Annenburg's 273-acre home at Palm Springs, Southern California, in the first week of August.[11] For bringing the two parties together and negotiating the sale, Veronis Suhler and Associates' fee was a reported 0.75 per cent at either end: $45 million dollars.[12]

While the deal was maturing, Murdoch did something which would be inconceivable to the chief executive officers of major corporations in America or Britain. After he had opened negotiations with Annenburg, and the deal looked as if it would go through, Murdoch started buying call options in News Corporation shares. Buying call options is effectively betting that the share price is going to rise by a significant amount in the near future. A call option gives you the right to buy shares at an agreed price within a certain time period, usually three to nine months. If a share price is currently 90 pence, then the three-month call option price on £1.00 options might only be two pence. If the price rises to more than £1.02 then the buyer makes a small profit. If the price rises substantially, say to £1.20, then the buyer can make a great deal of money – 20 pence for every 2 pence invested. But if the share price does not rise enough to at least cover the stake money, then the bet is lost, once the time runs out.

Earlier in the year, in March, Murdoch had been selling News Corporation shares, unloading 1,350,000 shares held by his investment company, Kayarem, at prices between $24.00 and $25.25 a share. The proceeds of the sale were $32,543,500. But now he started gambling that the News Corporation share price would rise by a significant amount in the near future.

In all, he bought call options over 2,394,000 News Corporation Limited shares in two distinct periods. The first buying spell ran from 21 July to 29 July, that is, around the time that the deal was moving towards the point that he felt confident enough to bring in his advisers. The second buying spell was between 3 and 5 August, just before the deal was announced. He clearly felt confident that this was a good bet, because he kept buying even though the price was moving against him. His first 100,000 call options cost him A$0.65 each, his last 900,000 cost him A$1.35 each: A$1,215,000. In all his stake money came to A$2,845,250. Even for a multi-millionaire who used to bet on the toss of a coin, this was a very large bet indeed. For him to have been successful the share price would have had to rise by nearly 10 per cent (see Appendix V).

In a statement to us Murdoch wrote: 'I regard shares in

the News Corporation as a good investment and, despite our efforts to provide as much information as possible to the market regarding the company, typically undervalued by the market. This was my view at the time the call options were acquired.' Such purchases would have been illegal in Britain. The British Companies Act specifically prohibits directors of public companies from dealing in options in their company's shares.

The dealings would also have fallen foul of the Stock Exchange regulations which prohibit directors dealing in shares in what is called 'the close period', the period between the year-end and the publication of the annual report. Dealings at these times are prohibited because it is assumed that at this time directors have inside information denied to the rest of the market. In the case of News Corporation, the year-end was 30 June, and the Report and Accounts were published at the end of August. These dealings fall right in the middle of this period.

For someone whose newspapers have frequently applied the harshest judgements to those public figures who step from the narrow path of virtue, these were extraordinary deals. At the time he made the purchases Rupert Murdoch was in possession of two pieces of extremely price-sensitive information, neither of which was known to the stock market. First, he was in the middle of secret negotiations to pull off the largest takeover in American magazine publishing history. He certainly believed he was getting a great deal. He said of Triangle's titles: 'These publications are the most valuable and prized properties in the world.'[13] Second, given the tight financial control and reporting for which he is famous, he must also have known that his end-of-year figures were going to be much better than anticipated.

However, in his statement to us he denied any impropriety:

Those responsible for making investment decisions within Kayarem [his dealing company] and I are all well aware of our obligations under Section 128 of the Securities Industry Code. I do not see any reason why the transactions to which you refer would not have complied with that section of the Code, since I do not believe that those responsible for the decisions made in respect to the transactions had any price-sensitive insider information at the time of the transactions.[14]

Section 128 of the Australian Securities Code prohibits dealing in shares by insiders. It says:

A person who is, or at any time in the preceding 6 months has been, connected with a body corporate shall not deal in any securities of that body corporate if by reason of his so being, or having been, connected with that body corporate he is in possession of information that is not generally available but, if it were, would be likely materially to affect the price of those securities.

At the time Kayarem dealt, Murdoch was clearly in possession of information that would be likely to 'materially affect the price' of News Corporation shares if it was made 'generally available'. Neither his negotiations over Triangle nor his better-than-expected figures were 'generally available'. In other words, his deals were almost certainly illegal. The Australian authorities have taken no action against Rupert Murdoch. This, in part, appears to stem from their disbelief that he would run the risk of being caught by using the family investment vehicle to make the bet.

Buying the options was not the only risk Murdoch was taking. The Triangle purchase itself was a huge gamble. It dramatically increased News Corporation's debt without an

206

equivalent increase in its cash flow or earnings. It also made News Corporation heavily dependent on the health of the American advertising market, which was already beginning to weaken. If this continued the danger was that Triangle publications would not make enough to cover the interest on the money Murdoch had to borrow to buy the company in the first place. For Murdoch neither the gamble on the shares nor the gamble on buying Triangle were successful.

The timing that was right for Annenburg was wrong for Murdoch. The problem for Murdoch, the share-dealer, was that the Triangle deal stunned the market. It was a sensational deal which confirmed News Corporation's status as a major international company, but it also gave News Corporation a debt mountain the size of a small Third World country. The market was not sure how to respond. The influential Lex column in the *Financial Times* wrote:

> Mr Rupert Murdoch has rolled the dice once again, betting the near equivalent of his company's total market capitalisation. ... He has always been a maverick on the international publishing circuit but his $3 billion acquisition of Triangle Publications is a move which will surely test the nerves of even his most ardent stock market follower.[15]

When the News Corporation figures came out they were much better than expected. The markets were pleased and surprised, but there was no great leap in the share price. The market had already discounted the good news. The main problem for Murdoch was that once the Triangle deal was announced, there was disbelief that he could have added even more debt to News Corporation's already debt-laden balance sheet. Market-makers in News Corporation shares were already looking towards the future and wondering whether the latest roll of dice would pay off or not. The options lapsed and he is unlikely to have made any money on his private share deals.

It was not just his personal share gamble which failed to pay off. It is also highly doubtful whether the Triangle purchase has ever made any money for News Corporation. At the time many analysts, like Kenneth Noble at Paine Webber, argued that Murdoch had got a good deal, having paid around thirteen times earnings. 'There are times when it is advantangeous to pay a premium price for something that is really important to you,' he said. Like many of Murdoch's deals, it left people shocked by its presumption and its speed.

Three days after Murdoch spent $1,215,000 buying his last 900,000 call options on News Corporation shares, John Weisman, the Washington Bureau chief, was having dinner at his home with some friends when the phone rang at nine o'clock. It was David Sendler, the editor of *TV Guide*, who said: 'Sit down. Are you sitting down? We have been sold to Rupert Murdoch for $3 billion and it will be announced tomorrow.' When Weisman's guests heard the news one of them said: 'Don't worry – you won't be working for him in a year's time.'

Weisman was surprised by the news because earlier that year Walter Annenburg had said that he was not going to sell, saying 'we are all family'. Others attacked the deal straight away. Andrew Schwartzman, the executive director of the Media Access Project, a Washington-based public interest law group, argued that the purchase of *TV Guide* raised serious anti-trust questions. '*TV Guide* is the dominant medium for programme promotion. The potential for abuse is considerable,' he argued. Because News Corporation already owned Fox, there was the possibility that Murdoch would use *TV Guide* to favour Fox against the network stations. 'Any media conglomeration of this scope ought to set off warning signals at the Federal Trade Commission and the Justice Department.'[16] But Schwartzman did not hold out much hope of action by the Justice Department. 'I would not expect this administration to oppose a merger of this kind under any circumstances,' especially given that both Murdoch and Annenburg were friends and allies of the Reagan administration.

The fear that he would abuse the power of *TV Guide* and promote his Fox network at the expense of the other television companies was a real concern. Rupert Murdoch used his newspapers in Britain, particularly his best-selling paper the *Sun*, as cheerleaders in the relentless promotion of his Sky satellite television service.[17] Murdoch quickly countered Schwartzman's complaint by agreeing that the *TV Guide* editorial would be kept separate from his other interests. Of course, he had made exactly this promise when he bought *The Times* in 1981 and had then broken the undertaking (see Chapter 3 on the Times Newspapers purchase).

In the case of *TV Guide* there have been few favours paid to Fox. However, it always treated Fox with the respect it deserved as a network, when the major companies were disputing its claim to this. The reason for *TV Guide*'s impartiality is probably financial. *TV Guide* needs the advertising from the other television network companies. If the magazine trashed their programmes at the expense of Fox this crucial revenue stream would dry up very quickly.

After the deal, Annenburg's prepared statement said: 'I am very happy that my publications are passing to Mr Murdoch's company. I now plan to devote the rest of my life to education and philanthropy.' Later, in December, after the deal was completed, John Weisman, then a staff writer on *TV Guide* who had known Annenburg for many years, was visiting him in Palm Springs. He asked him why he sold. He said: 'It was too much to refuse. There was the prospect of doing so much good.' Murdoch said: 'These publications are the most valuable and prized publishing properties in the world. They have been brilliantly developed by Ambassador Annenburg and we plan to make them the cornerstone of a great American publishing company.'[18]

Annenburg has been as good as his word. Since the sale of Triangle he has given away many hundreds of millions of dollars in philanthropic good works. Rupert Murdoch, in contrast, has failed in his plan to develop a great American publishing company. As soon as he took over Triangle, the circulation of *TV Guide* started to fall and advertising revenue softened.

During the summer of 1991 he sold his American magazines – except *TV Guide* – for US$650 million. News Corporation took a loss of A$229 million on the deal.

10

The Trashing of *TV Guide*

The purchase of Triangle Publications was a fantastic gamble for Murdoch to take. According to a Murdoch spokesman, Howard Rubenstein, Rupert Murdoch planned to sell part of his shareholding in Reuters to pay for Triangle, but this only covered a small part of the $2,825 million cost. Half the purchase price would come from other asset sales, the other half from bank borrowings.

In the end he did not sell any Reuters shares but he quickly disposed of both the American *Elle* for US$127 million and the British version for US$30 million. The following summer he also sold the New Zealand book division for US$1,300 million and eight business magazines for a further US$825 million. He also raised a reported US$320 million from the sale of the Fox Plaza Building in Los Angeles. But as fast as the money was coming he was making big plans to spend it. He committed News Corporation to spending $1 billion on new printing plant for his British newspapers, the same for his Australian papers, and there were huge losses on Sky as well as the plan to increase production at the 20th Century-Fox film studios from five to twenty movies a year.

But Murdoch's timing was faulty. The world's economies were about to tilt into recession. Sales of *TV Guide* had fallen from their all-time peak of 20 million copies a week during the 1980s. By the time that Murdoch got hold of it, the circulation had steadied at around 16½ million copies a week. In the past, the Triangle publications, particularly *TV Guide* and *Daily Racing Form*, had been recession-proof. In the two previous recessions *TV Guide* had actually increased sales. But Murdoch changed all that.

Although it was a listings magazine, *TV Guide* carried serious feature articles. The tone of the magazine was like Annenburg himself – cool and independent, reserved and confident in its judgement. It did not feel beholden to the industry about which it wrote. The long-term editor, David Sendler, had turned it from a 'fan magazine' into a house magazine which recognised that television was a major phenomenon and needed to be treated as such. It was not afraid to grasp thorny issues. *TV Guide* examined how well the American television networks covered areas such as the Lebanon, and investigated how CBS News had broken its own code of ethics in the way in which it made a programme about General Westmorland and Vietnam.

There was clearly a mass market for this mixture of listings and serious, well-written, middlebrow articles. Many staff writers felt a sense of purpose in their work. They believed that for many of their readers, *TV Guide* was the only written word going into their homes each week. Despite its success as the best-selling magazine in the English-speaking world, the Murdoch team quickly decided that the existing editorial team were not giving the readers what they wanted. They knew better.

On 31 October Murdoch arrived by helicopter to take

charge. It was Hallowe'en. While millions of young American children were playing 'trick or treat', the staff of *TV Guide* knew they were about to play the same game. Except for them, there was no treat. If they had spoken to other Murdoch employees, they would have known what to expect. The style was, by now, distressingly familiar. He immediately began to force *TV Guide* into the traditional Murdoch formula for tabloid magazines. Unlike his dailies, a listings magazine could not shock and amaze on every page. But it could be taken down market, in search of the readership which Murdoch believed he instinctively knew.

Murdoch met the senior editors and executives in what was known as the Layout Room. On the wall were the next four covers of the magazine. Murdoch had a copy of the current issue in his hand, which had as its cover story a piece about the NBC autumn season. Staff writer Rich Turner had been allowed access to the meetings at which NBC decided on their season. It was a classic *TV Guide* piece. And it was a unique opportunity for a fly-on-the-wall account of how a major network scheduled the programmes which *TV Guide*'s readers would spend the next few months watching. Murdoch threw the copy of the magazine on to the table and said: 'Why do we have this on the cover? It's not a seller. It's too complex, too preachy, too editorial.' Dave Sendler, the Editor of *TV Guide*, asked him what he thought of the magazine. Murdoch's reply was typical: 'It is far too cerebral.'

This was a typical Murdoch speech. He had delivered it over the years to different groups of journalists round the world, after he had taken over their papers. There is no doubt that *TV Guide* had grown a little slow and stodgy. Murdoch had some good early suggestions to liven it up. He changed the order of the magazine. The shiny pages which carried the features were moved from the back to the front and the lead time was shortened from 35 to 18 days, with a target of 12

213

days by 1990. He added more pictures to the magazine. After that it was vintage Murdoch.

Within the first three months Murdoch sacked the advertising director, the circulation director, the business manager and the marketing department. Long-term staff writers watched in disbelief as the Murdochians took a winning formula and tore it up. The Murdoch team did not seem to have a coherent strategy other than to get circulation up by sensationalism. They seemed intent on taking the magazine down market to chase a market which *TV Guide* had never embraced. The whole theory behind the Murdoch approach was that *TV Guide* was a mass circulation magazine. He knew that the masses were not interested in 'preachy' articles. Like the readers of Murdoch's first American magazine, the *Star*, they wanted fun. They did not want worthy articles about television. They wanted the classic Murdoch diet of health, fashion, film stars' lives and loves, human interest and horoscopes. He knew that the readers wanted to know what foods their favourite star ate while watching his/her favourite soap.

John Weisman, the former Washington bureau chief, among others, believed this was a critical mistake. *TV Guide* had a dominant position because it had a good blend of accessible features, none of which was longer than 1,200 words, and comprehensive listings. *TV Guide* was a little magazine, sold on supermarket shelves, which had refined its product over 25 years. It knew what it was doing and where it was going. The 9 million readers who renewed their subscriptions each year felt comfortable with the magazine. Weisman's basic complaint is that the Murdoch people knew nothing about *TV Guide*. They had no idea who the readers were. It was not a business they understood or liked. In the past, people like former American Gerald Ford, President Nixon's former Chief of Staff Al Haig, and the novelist

William Styron had written for the magazine. But Murdoch took the view that the up-market readers were unnecessary and therefore they did not need big-name guest writers.

TV Guide had been successful because it had been an advocate for the viewers. It took up issues. It questioned why certain issues were ignored by the networks and asked why some people got a raw deal from television. The Murdoch team changed all this. 'They just wanted fluff,' said one long-serving journalist. An early story put up by John Weisman, which was killed, was about the new system of credentials for television reporters. In the past television reporters had had photo identifications. Now when they went to Congress they were issued with pass cards, which are put in the computer, like bank cards. But this meant that the Government could record who went in and who went out. In the past, *TV Guide* would have run this sort of story. But the Rupert Murdoch *TV Guide* would not publish it.

The critical stance which *TV Guide* had always maintained to the industry was being slowly watered down. The writers were told: 'We don't trash the industry which puts bread on our table.' In the past, *TV Guide* had never sold ads on the back of editorial, and was fiercely independent of the networks. The new editorial stance embraced advertorial sections, which were really just platforms for advertising. This attitude horrified the traditional staffers who were used to the more independent editorial line of their previous proprietor, Walter Annenburg, who would complain about articles but still publish them.

By now, no one in the editorial department at *TV Guide* was in any doubt about the Murdoch criteria for a good story. They were not about what makes people tick, but what they wear. They were not about how they have become who they are, but what is their favourite diet recipe. The questions how and why were no longer asked – only 'who?', as in 'Who is married to whom?'

215

At the beginning of November 1988, boxes belonging to Valerie Salembier, 43, the new publisher, started arriving outside *TV Guide*'s offices. Salembier was probably the woman who most closely fitted the archetypal model of the perfect Murdoch executive. Salembier started her working life as a receptionist at Time Inc. She then educated herself at college in the evenings, while selling advertising during the day for *NewsWeek*. She became *NewsWeek*'s first woman sales representative, after a row between Katherine Graham, the chairwoman of *NewsWeek*'s parent company, and Gibson McCabe, who was then president of *NewsWeek*. 'I was the result of Kay Graham throwing a leaded crystal ashtray at McCabe,' she joked after she had been appointed the first woman publisher of *TV Guide*.

But her great ability was the knack of being able to sell advertising in the most hostile markets. After a spell on *Ms* magazine she was put in charge of advertising at *USA Today*, where she quadrupled the advertising revenue during her stay. 'Valerie is simply the best ad salesperson I ever met,' said her new boss John Evans, the president of Murdoch Magazines. 'We hired her because she has the pragmatism to be able to put the magazine to bed every week and the vision to evolve it in the future.'[1]

She told an interviewer at the time: 'I think it's time for some . . . change. It could be a format change. Perhaps the infusion of just a little more fun. After all this is an entertainment industry first and foremost.' The words were hers. They could just as easily have been her magazine's proprietor's.

She had certainly adopted the Murdoch management style. Shortly after she arrived she had dinner with four of the sales people. She told them: 'Don't shit me; don't lie to me or you are out on your asses before you know it.' Later, when one of her staff asked her, 'Who can I go to if we have a disagreement?' she told him with a smile, 'You can take it to Rupert.'

Right from the start *TV Guide* split into two camps: the existing staff and Murdoch's team. One of the first big battles was the Christmas issue. Its theme was the Arthur Hailey book *Roots*. The 'Murdochians', as they were quickly nicknamed, ripped the editorial copy apart. The copy was cut to two-thirds its previous length and the serious stuff moved to the back and the less serious to the front. Murdoch employed another familiar strategy. He left the editor, David Sendler, in place, but brought in a shadow, Roger Wood, to second-guess and monitor his every decision.

Murdoch had used this strategy before. Roger Wood had earlier been the beneficiary of it on the *New York Post*. After the Murdoch takeover, Paul Sann, the executive editor for twenty-seven years, found that he had one of Murdoch's men sitting with him all day and every day.[2] Within a month, Sann resigned. Within six months, Wood was editor. Roger Wood was a Murdoch trusty, having been editor of the *New York Post* when the city was gripped by the killings of David Berkowitz, who became known as 'Son Of Sam'. The *Post*'s daily coverage became increasingly lurid, ending with the extraordinary incident when they secured some of his letters to a girlfriend and ran them under the headline: 'HOW I BECAME A MASS KILLER BY DAVID BERKOWITZ'. A power failure which led to some looting in parts of the city prompted the headline: '24 HOURS OF TERROR'. Faced with the kind of yellow journalism the city had not seen since the 1930s, the *Columbia Journalism Review* later complained that 'the *New York Post* is no longer merely a journalistic problem. It is a social problem – a force for evil.'

Murdoch did not care. 'I don't give a damn what the media critics say,' he told *More* magazine. And if Murdoch did not care neither did Roger Wood. He knew just what Murdoch wanted.

Wood was quickly dubbed 'The Shadow Number One' by

the staff. He spent his whole working day in Sendler's office. He read every story idea that came in and offered his own suggestions for the magazine. One of Wood's first brainwaves was to hire an astrologer who was given the job of charting the new shows. The astrologer had a keen sense of humour, informing *TV Guide*'s readers that the planet Uranus was the planet for television.

Wood also planned to bind food coupons to the back of the magazine and advertise them on the front. This was opposed by the sales department, which believed it would be a marketing disaster and send out entirely the wrong signals to the readers. But the food obsession continued and, for those who could afford food, Wood introduced diets. His declaration to the staff had a familiar ring to it: 'We are out to have fun,' he told them. It was not much fun for Sendler and there was a great deal of sympathy for him from the staff. The in-house joke was that *TV Guide* was like *Star Wars*. Wood represented the Dark Side and Sendler the Force. The staff, many of whom had been at *TV Guide* for years, were shell-shocked by the brutality of the Murdoch regime.

The staff of *TV Guide* were learning that for Rupert Murdoch old habits died hard. Many left. For those who stayed it was a tough time. Sendler himself was in a 'golden cage'. He had a generous contract which meant it was difficult for them to sack him except for misconduct or insubordination. If he argued too vehemently they could sack him. He was a small aggressive man who removed his frustrations with exercise. The staff joke was that within a few months he was bench-pressing 400 pounds and serving a tennis ball at 200 m.p.h. He stuck it for a year and finally left in September 1989. In contrast to the screeching Murdoch editorial style which by now was all too familiar round the world, his prepared statement was understated: 'We have had differences, but I have the highest regard for the professionalism of the Murdoch Magazines people and wish them all the best in their efforts for the *TV Guide*.'

By the end of November, Wood was not at *TV Guide*'s headquarters at Radnor all the time but sent long-range rockets down from New York when he disagreed with what was going on. By now they could second-guess his views on any subject. With Wood back in New York, a new Shadow Number Two arrived – Phil Bunton, from the *Star*. Bunton was another editor straight out of News Corporation central casting. He staggered the staff by asking a classic Murdoch question: 'Why does *TV Guide* need an editorial research department?' For someone who has worked all his life in newspapers Murdoch has a low regard for journalists, particularly those who regard themselves as 'writers'. And there were plenty of those on *TV Guide*. He called it 'élitist journalism'. He told a Newspaper Publishers' Association meeting in San Francisco that 'A press that fails to interest the whole community is one that will ultimately become a house organ of the élite engaged in an increasingly private conversation.'

In the 1989 News Corporation Annual Report, Murdoch told his shareholders that News Corporation's handling of *TV Guide* was the usual success story. Traditional Murdoch cost-cutting, 'operating efficiencies from its association with the group' had made it 'more profitable during the year'. The company had 'taken steps to enhance the value of the magazine to readers and advertisers and to counter strong competition from newspaper supplements and cable television guides'. Though he had made more money by cutting costs, he was not making it by earning more from increased sales. After twelve months of the old Murdoch magic, circulation was down.

In June 1988, just before he bought *TV Guide*, the total circulation was 16,940,877. By the summer of 1989 the

Murdoch team had been in place for ten months. The figures for their year-end made dismal reading. Total sales were 16,330,051, a fall of 610,826 on the year. The subscriptions had held steady to the previous summer's figure. But ominously for the Murdoch team almost all the fall in total sales was accounted for by the dramatic fall in single copy sales, which were 13 per cent down on the previous summer. The product might look breezier. But it was failing where it mattered most – on the news-stands and in the supermarkets.

In his speech to the Newspaper Publishers' Association, Murdoch mused out loud: 'I cannot avoid the temptation of wondering whether there is any other industry in this country which presumes so completely to give the customer what he does not want.'[3] It should have been clear to him, within the first twelve months, that his presumptions of what *TV Guide*'s readers wanted were wrong. But he was not tempted to return to the previously successful formula. The Murdoch team's response was to claim that the 'popularisation' was going too slowly. Murdoch told them: 'There are too many damned essays in the magazine.'

But as the editorial got shorter, so did the advertising. Advertising had held up pretty well until the summer of 1989, but then it dropped off sharply over the next twelve months. Between the summers of 1989 and 1990, the advertising take was 386 pages down on the previous year.

In May 1990, *Advertising Age* ran a story that Murdoch was sounding out prospective buyers for *TV Guide*. The story said that *TV Guide* had been in an 'ad page and circulation slump' since he bought it in 1988. It said the asking price was $2.6 billion, but informal bids were in the range of $1.5 billion to $2 billion. Murdoch was furious and bet the editor $1 million to prove his story. The bet was declined as the magazine's editor, Rance Crain, argued that he did not want to reveal his sources.

Throughout 1989 the sales force was reorganised. In the summer of 1989, Murdoch said that the 'editorial enhancements and extensive promotional support are expected to reverse the decline in single copy sales and restore the magazine's sales base'.[4] Still the sales kept falling. By the summer of 1990 total sales had fallen by more than a million in just two years. The total sale was 15,837,064 compared to 16,940,877 two summers before. Nearly all of this fall was accounted for by single copy sales. The populist revolution had failed.

As with other parts of Murdoch's empire, *TV Guide* faced new competition. The mistake of the Murdoch strategy for *TV Guide* was that it created the very competition which then successfully attacked the magazine. *TV Guide* had always had competition from local newspapers which also ran listings columns. But in the past, *TV Guide* had held its position because of the quality of its editorial. There were features and articles in *TV Guide* which readers could not get elsewhere. That was *TV Guide*'s unique selling point. But as it was dismantled and the editorial was replaced with recipes, horoscopes and tittle-tattle about the stars, this was removed. For many of its traditional readers, there was no longer any need to buy *TV Guide*. Many other magazines provided this sort of material already – and many did it a lot better.

Murdoch is rightly congratulated with the success of the *Sun* in Britain. He saw a gap at the bottom of the market which the *Sun* went for and triumphantly made its own. The *Sun* formula worked brilliantly in Britain in the 1970s and the 1980s. The weakness of the Murdoch strategy is that he has applies it relentlessly to the other papers and magazines, whether it is appropriate or not. What is most extraordinary about the trashing of *TV Guide* was that Murdoch had not learnt from his previous mistakes. He had done exactly the same before in the United States and paid heavily for it.

Murdoch's problem has been that he has often found it hard to resist the attractions of the gutter. He bought the *New York Post* in 1976 and turned it into the kind of sleazy paper Americans had not seen for thirty years. He never found the market he believed was there. More importantly, he did not understand that by going down market and adopting the editorial policy he used elsewhere, he lost the city's advertisers. Despite his reputation as the consummate newspaperman he was never able to stem the paper's losses and sold it in 1988 at a huge loss.

In 1983 he made the same mistakes all over again when he bought the *Chicago Sun-Times*. This was a very successful quality newspaper, which had a clearly defined editorial policy and a team of award-winning journalists, including one of America's most famous columnists, Mike Royko:

We knew that there had been publications that he basically left alone, like the *Village Voice*, and we thought that he might do that here, since this was a very successful quality newspaper. But as soon as his people started coming in, it was clear that this wasn't their intention. They came in like a bunch of pirates. It's unusual for a Chicago newspaper guy to view somebody coming in as a bunch of thugs – I mean, we're generally thought of as pretty hard-nosed newspaper people.[5]

When he bought it, the *Sun-Times* was running neck-and-neck with its main competitor, the *Tribune*, and had strong advertising and a healthy cash flow. But it was the same old story. Whatever had been done in the past, the Murdoch team knew better. Murdoch trimmed costs by getting rid of anyone regarded as surplus to requirements. After that, there was the usual game of musical chairs as editors and advisers were bounced in and out.

But the basic problem was that Murdoch's view of Chicago was closer to a black-and-white 1930s film than the city as it was in the early 1980s. 'I don't think he knew much about Chicago and his people didn't know anything about Chicago. People are always surprised when they come to Chicago and find out that we don't have gangsters running on the streets shooting people down. It's not a cow town,' argued Mike Royko.[6]

The Murdoch team believed that they knew the city and knew the readers. They did not commission any readership surveys or do any research themselves but they knew, for certain, that the existing editorial team were going about it the wrong way. Mike Royko: 'They had this idea that our readers were a bunch of people sitting round with tattoos on their arms and beer bellies, gawking at the television.' The new policy was one already familiar to readers of Murdoch newspapers in Australia and Britain: screaming headlines which would shock and amaze on every page. One early Murdoch stunt was to fill the front page with a picture of Cary Grant on a black background. People all over the city bought the paper, thinking he had died. It was his birthday. People were offended and the circulation began to drop fast.

When Murdoch bought the *Chicago Sun-Times*, the readership surveys showed in almost every area the *Sun-Times* had either caught up with or had overtaken the *Tribune*. But the key journalsits, like Royko, who had made the *Sun-Times* successful, jumped ship after the 'pirates' boarded. The circulation of the *Sun-Times* collapsed, and it has struggled ever since. Royko began a daily barrage against Murdoch from his new column in the *Tribune*, including the epic line that 'no self-respecting fish would ever be seen dead wrapped in a Murdoch newspaper'. Royko has one very interesting insight into Murdoch: 'He has never taken a poor paper and turned it in to a quality paper.' He has done it the other way round, though. The problem is that, sometimes, as with *TV Guide* or the *Chicago Sun-Times*, the market actually prefers a 'good' paper or magazine.

After three years Murdoch sold the *Chicago Sun-Times* for US$145 million, having bought it for $100 million three years earlier. If he had put the money in the bank his return would have been about the same. Since then, the paper has never really recovered from the magic touch of Murdoch and his 'pirates'.

Murdoch's foray into American big city papers was a disaster. At one point he planned to create a chain of papers on the Australian model. New York, Chicago and Boston were just the start. It was another 'big idea' out of touch with the way the market worked. In Chicago and New York he believed that an insensitive down-market drive was the way to succeed. It failed comprehensively.

By the spring of 1991, Murdoch had also had enough of American consumer magazines. Under the January rescue agreement with his banks he had to reduce News Corporation's debt by US$800 million. The bankers did not care how he did it, but in practice it meant that he had to sell some assets. He sold all his consumer magazines except for *TV Guide* and the loss-making *Mirabella* for US$650 million. It was the end of any dream Murdoch might have enjoyed of building a global empire which would operate like a one-stop shop for the world's major advertisers. When he bought Triangle he also believed he could compete with Time Inc., Conde Nast and Hearst Magazines. That dream was over too.

The buyers were a company called K-111 which was backed by the New-York-based leveraged buy-out experts Kohlberg, Kravis Roberts, who had previously put together the US$25 billion buy-out for RJR Nabisco. Under the deal Murdoch sold *Soap Opera Digest, Soap Opera Weekly, New*

York, Seventeen, Premiere, Automobile, New Woman and *European Travel and Life.* The highly profitable *Racing Form* was also included. The consensus view is that the price he got for the magazines and *Racing Form* was about the best he could achieve in a depressed market-place. But it was a long way short of the kind of price he might have got just two years earlier. News Corporation took a loss of US$225 million on the sale.

The bald truth was that Murdoch had paid far too much for Triangle. Even at the time, there were doubts as to the value of the deal. Reginald Brack, the head of Time Inc's Magazine Division, had looked at Triangle very closely as one of its major competitors. 'From everything we know about the company – which certainly is an outstanding property – this is indeed fully priced.'[7] Everyone working in the industry knew that 'fully priced' was a polite way of saying 'over-priced'. At the time Murdoch denied that he had paid too much and said he did not think banks would baulk at the deal.[8] He might have been better off if they had. Murdoch himself has described 1988 as the year of the 'expansionary lunge'.[9]

Why did this happen? An anonymous member of the Murdoch family attributed the failure to the departure of Murdoch's long-standing adviser, Merv Rich, who left in 1987. Speaking to the *Sydney Morning Herald* in February 1991, this person argued: 'For more than 20 years Rupert had a wizard [Merv Rich] looking after the finances. It meant if he took his mind off one aspect of News' finances he knew Merv would not only look after it but look for further opportunities.'[10] Certainly the explosion of News Corporation's spending has come since the departure of Rich. Murdoch himself has admitted that he probably paid US$500 million too much for Triangle.[11] Sceptics would say 'double that figure and he might be close to the mark'.

Because Murdoch's empire is so large, the Triangle fiasco

cannot be taken in isolation from the rest of the empire. Although Murdoch said in 1990 that he had paid off most of the Triangle debt, this was irrelevant. He had made major spending commitments elsewhere throughout the empire, without counting on the economic downturn. 'If we'd thought all these things were going to happen at once, in these times, we might have postponed our capital development.' More to the point, if he had not done the Triangle deal, many of his current problems would be less acute.

Looking back on the deal it is hard to understand why Murdoch bought Triangle, apart from the fact that it was available and it fitted in to his plans for global self-aggrandisement. One of his former executives has told us that Murdoch had no coherent strategy for the magazine. It is possible that Murdoch saw the potential of the state-of-the-art computer software which Triangle owned. It can produce 106 different magazines a week, catering to the variation in listings through the States. If Rupert Murdoch wanted to produce a European-wide listings magazine then this would have given him a technological lead over his rivals.

But as the magazine's publisher, Jo Cece, admitted in October 1990, many of the 'synergies' which had made the purchase so attractive had not succeeded. Murdoch had long nursed a dream of turning News Corporation into a one-stop shop for advertisers. But the plan to combine *TV Guide*'s rate cards with the other consumer magazines in the group and offer multiple booking had failed. This was not so surprising, as the rates were too different. The plan to offer advertisers a joint package of *TV Guide* and Fox had also been dropped.[12]

The previous June, Murdoch had claimed in the News Corporation Annual Report that *TV Guide* had posted record profits, despite flat single-copy sales and a poor advertising climate. Partly because of the recession, *TV Guide* lost revenue from traditional heavy advertisers like car and tobacco manufacturers. Not surprisingly, given the new editorial line, advertising from the networks was strong. He later predicted that *TV Guide* would have earnings of US$155 million for the following year, an increase of 6 per cent. The problem is that the profits from Triangle do not go much further than to cover the annual payments on the debt News Corporation took on to buy the group.

And Murdoch is locked in. In the current recession it is doubtful that he could sell it for even the same price he paid in 1988. In the words of Heather Goodchild, the media analyst for Standard and Poor, the credit-rating agency in New York, '*TV Guide* could only be purchased by a very large buyer. The market is weaker and it's harder for any potential buyer, even one with reasonably decent credit, to get financing.'[13] And even if he could find a buyer, finding an attractive price is going to be harder still. The consensus opinion is that he would not get the price he paid for it. 'That's a reflection of both the weakness in the overall market, a decline in *TV Guide*'s own ad pages as well as some controversy about what he's done to the editorial format,' argues Ms Goodchild. And that's the rub.

When Annenburg sold to Murdoch he did so because he believed he was getting a strong management and a visionary for the next century. Rupert Murdoch assured Annenburg that he would keep its quality. *TV Guide* was Annenburg's dream, which he ran as an enlightened patriarchal despot. At the time of the deal he said he was 'very happy that my publications are passing to Mr Murdoch's company'.[14] More recently he was asked by an old employee what he thought. He said: 'It's his toy', adding enigmatically, 'The one thing we always had was quality.'[15]

11

The Debt Machine

When Rupert Murdoch's father, Sir Keith, died in 1952 his son inherited control of News Limited, a small company which owned two papers in Adelaide, the *News* and the *Sunday Post*. Through the family investment company, Cruden, the Murdoch family owned 46 per cent of News Limited. Cruden itself was owned by Keith Murdoch's widow and her four children – three daughters and one son, Rupert. By this mechanism Rupert, despite his father's doubts about his ability, was in control of News Limited. Forty years later the position is almost unchanged: Cruden still owns around 45 per cent of News Corporation and Rupert Murdoch is the unchallenged boss.

There is one important difference: today News Corporation controls worldwide assets valued at A$20 billion. This is probably a unique phenomenon in modern capitalism. There is no other company of comparable size which has grown so much but remained in the unchallenged grip of one person. The great names of business – Marks, Sainsbury,

228

Ford – may still serve on the boards of the companies which carry their name. They may still have substantial shareholdings in their companies, but these holdings are much smaller than when they took charge of their companies, as they have needed to issue more shares to raise extra capital to finance the business. Even more remarkable, News Corporation's growth has relied heavily on takeovers. Few, if any, companies of News Corporation's size have been able to mount an active takeover programme without issuing more of their own shares in return. News Corporation has never done this.

There are many reasons why Murdoch has been so resistant to giving up any control over News Corporation. Some biographers have attributed it to his desire in some way to make up for the fact that his father never had much of a shareholding in the Melbourne *Herald*, the paper which he had made successful. One former friend is quoted as saying 'Rupert was determined not to repeat his father's mistakes. No one would ever gain control over his business.'[1] But there is a more mundane reason. When Murdoch's father died News Limited was about the only asset of any value he left. It has not been possible to establish Murdoch's precise holding in Cruden at the time of his father's death but his stake was shared between his sisters and mother. Even as late as 1974 his share of Cruden was less than 30 per cent – so his effective share of News Corporation was around 13 per cent.[2] From early on, it must have been obvious that to create anything of value for himself, it was important not to dilute the family's shareholding in the company.

The Murdoch family holding has effectively protected the company from takeover and insulated the board from criticism. Murdoch has claimed that this has made it possible for News Corporation to take risks – such as the takeover of the *News of the World* in 1969 and the launch into television in America and Britain – that would not have been possible with powerful outside shareholders. This is almost certainly true, but the tight control has suited Murdoch's personality well.

A former executive of Murdoch's has said that what he likes most of all is 'order'.[3] And many have testified to his distaste for the conventions of corporate life. He told one executive to whom he had promised a board seat: 'You don't want to bother with board meetings. They are boring. You have to listen to the production director going on about the price of newsprint.'[4] He often irritated his partners in joint ventures by not turning up to board meetings or not having any papers prepared for them. And he hates the annual general meeting of News Corporation – this is one reason why he has never become chairman, leaving the task of handling the meeting to someone else.

So all the instincts in Murdoch's personality as well as his own financial interest militated against giving up any control of News Corporation. But any company which wants to expand by takeovers and does not have large amounts of money in the bank has only two alternatives. It either has to issue more shares to raise cash to pay for the takeovers, or borrow. When Murdoch decided on his first major takeover in Australia, the takeover of the *Sunday Times* in Perth in 1956, he found banks willing to lend against the security of his Adelaide papers. It was a time of rapid growth in the Australian economy and banks were eager to find customers. He quickly became a valued customer of the Commonwealth Bank – a relationship which has lasted until today.

The experience of his early takeovers showed Murdoch that expansion by borrowing was possible. His strategy became, in the words of one of his previous senior executives, 'Borrow and Buy'. For forty years he rarely repaid the debts: any money which was repaid was just replaced by new borrowings, any cash received from selling assets was used to buy others.

This has been a high-risk strategy, made still riskier by the fact that Murdoch often borrowed short-term money from the banks. In effect, he used the cash flow from News Corporation's profitable businesses to pay the interest on the loans which financed the purchase and development of the other businesses. The risk in this strategy is that eventually the lenders start to worry about the security of their loans. Unlike shareholders, banks can ask for their money back. Over forty years Murdoch did face a series of financial crises, which were rarely publicised, when profits fell unexpectedly. There are many reasons why he survived – the mystique which he wove around himself was as alluring to bankers as it was to advertisers, politicians and journalists. Certainly during the 1980s News Corporation was unusual in banking circles because it rarely argued over fees. Nils Ollquist, once a director of Security Pacific Australia, one of the largest lenders to News Corporation, says of Richard Sarazen, then News Corporation's chief financial officer: 'He doesn't screw you to the wall on fees. He won't say, "I won't take the loan unless you give it to me at x minus the world." He's not going to give you what you ask for, but he's a lot more reasonable than other CFOs to deal with.'[5]

But however reasonable and inspiring a man is, in the end the banks do look at the balance sheet and the bottom line. The business they are lending to has to be making money and there has to be some security for their loans. For years Murdoch seemed to be making money and for years there seemed to be plenty of security. But for years the reality was much more prosaic: News Corporation perfected a number of accounting tricks which repeatedly put an attractive gloss on its figures – a gloss which disguised what was really going on. It was made possible by a characteristic trait of Murdoch's. He frequently expanded his newspaper and television empire by disregarding or manipulating regulations

231

and regulators. He refused to be bound by national boundaries in his vision for his television empire. A similar attitude is evident in his approach to the less glamorous but critically important area of financial accounting. News Corporation has used the fact that it is an Australian company like a Liberian flag of convenience to escape the rules and regulations which govern financial reporting in two of the countries in which it is most active: the United States and the United Kingdom.[6]

In all advanced capitalist economies businesses are required to produce an annual report and accounts. The basic purpose of this document is to provide a financial record of the company's performance and condition. Many people have an interest in this document. Shareholders want to see how well the company of which they own a part is performing. Creditors – those who have lent money to the company or are trading with it – want to see how safe their money is. The majority of people who see these accounts – and many who don't, but know of their existence – assume that they provide an unchallengeable and factual account of what is going on. Columns of neatly laid-out figures of a company's profits have a tempting certainty to their appearance. But as Susan Dev, Professor of Accounting at the London School of Economics, once said: 'Profits are not facts; they are just opinions.'

This is one of the great truths of accounting – privately admitted but frequently denied in public by accountants, and usually a revelation to non-accountants. When a company draws up its accounts it needs to make a lot of assumptions. This is mainly because at the end of any year there is a lot of unfinished business, which creates uncertainties. For example there are some unpaid debts, and a judgement has to be made about whether these will be paid. There are lots of assets and a judgement has to be made about how long these will last. All of these are subjective judgements: one company may decide that all the debts will be paid; another that none will be. The second company will then write the debt off and declare less profit that year. Profit is then a matter of opinion.

Accountants are, of course, attuned to the possibility differing opinions, and over the years accounting bodies throughout the world have produced accounting standards. The aim of these is to reduce the scope for subjectivity and increase the amount of information which is disclosed so that those who read accounts can get a good idea of what is going on. But accounting standards around the world differ and some accounting bodies are slower to respond than others. One of the slowest has been in Australia – a weakness which Murdoch has exploited ruthlessly.

When shareholders in News Corporation received the accounts for the year to June 1989, things looked good. After-tax profits were at a record A$496,496,000, US$403,055,000 or £234,892,000 – almost four times the level five years previously. Scratch the surface, and things looked rather different.

First, there was Sky Television. Murdoch's chief executive's review spoke of its successful launch and its higher-than-expected costs but also said, 'We were successful in marshalling the Company's resources to absorb significant investments for acquisitions and new business start-ups . . .' The conclusion which could be drawn from this carefully worded remark was that News Corporation's impressive profits were made after the substantial investment in Sky. Such a conclusion would have been misplaced. Hardly any of the costs of getting Sky airborne passed through the profit and loss account.

It had cost £75 million to get Sky going: wages, salaries, marketing costs, office overheads, programme fees, bank interest and so on.[7] By the time the channel was launched all this money had been spent, effectively lent by the banks. News Corporation did not, however, charge these losses against its profit. It treated them as 'deferred costs', which it would spread over a five-year period when the 'implementation process has been fully completed'. It was impossible to tell from the News Corporation accounts that these costs amounted to £75 million as this was only revealed in the accounts of the UK subsidiary, News International. In the News Corporation accounts these 'deferred costs' were subsumed as an asset in the balance sheet, an investment in a new venture.

This device is known as capitalising costs – treating them as a capital asset of the business instead of a cost of running it. The justification for the accounting policy is that start-up costs such as these are effectively an investment which – unlike the electricity bill – will provide a return in future. The best that can be said of this argument is that not everyone agrees. Among the leading opponents is the American accounting profession.

American accounting regulations (General Accepted Accounting Practices – GAAP) have a very strict attitude to the capitalisation of development costs. They allow certain specific spending, which will clearly benefit future years, to be capitalised. They do not allow start-up losses such as Sky's to be capitalised. News Corporation could only get away with this because it is registered in Australia – where accounting policies are much laxer. In other words, under American accounting rules News Corporation's profits would have been lower.

The treatment of the Sky development costs was by no means an isolated incident. In 1988 News Corporation increased profits by a further A$43 million by capitalising interest on 'certain investments and . . . major projects'[8] – a practice forbidden by American accounting standards.[9] And the costs of starting up Fox were also given special treatment.

234

Fox Broadcasting – the division of Fox that supplied the network of 118 independent affiliated TV stations with programmes – started its national service in October 1986. In its first two years it lost $197.7 million.[10] These losses did not reduce News Corporation's pre-tax profits as News Corporation treated them as 'extraordinary items', which were taken from *after*-tax profits.[11] Again, this would not have been permitted under American accounting rules.

Why did this matter? First, because after its takeover of Triangle in August 1988, News Corporation had a majority of its assets and made a significant proportion of its profits in America. It was controlled by an American citizen and largely run from America. In practice, it was really an American company. In these circumstances it would clearly be more appropriate for it to use American accounting policies. But the price of doing so would have been high. News Corporation's profits would not rise impressively from year to year – reinforcing the Murdoch myth. They would zig-zag up and down. Table 1 compares the profits which News Corporation disclosed in its accounts and what those profits would have been if American accounting policies had been followed.

	After-tax profits as reported in accounts (A$000)	After-tax profits vnder US GAAP (A$000)
1985	80,439	42,213
1986	242,256	221,238
1987	366,366	957,378
1988	464,464	420,565
1989	1,163,626	987,666
1990	343,305	64,637

Source: News Corporation SEC 20-F filings.

As this table shows, 1988 was by no means an exceptional

year for News Corporation – in previous years as subsequently the accounts would have looked very different if drawn up using American accounting standards. There are a number of ways in which the American accounts differ from the Australian. In 1989 the main reason why American-style profits increased was the inclusion of the profits News Corporation made when it sold several of its businesses, including the travel publications which went for US$825 million.

These figures reveal a critical weakness in News Corporation's finances – a weakness which was to bring it to its knees in 1990 and still haunts it today. With very high levels of debt and therefore large interest payments, News Corporation needs a steady and reliable flow of profits. It did not have that. It relied heavily on selling assets and businesses to keep going. Furthermore, its pre-tax profits were boosted by two items which were not by any means a reliable source of income.

Back in 1984 News Corporation had lost a packet speculating on the foreign exchange market. Murdoch had assured his shareholders that in future News Corporation would not be taking risks of this sort. However, in the mid-1980s he changed his mind. Under Murdoch's personal control[12] News Corporation started trading in currencies. In principle it was simple: if you spend £100 million buying dollars when the exchange rate is $2 to £1, you can make a fortune if the pound falls to $1.60. Suddenly, the $200 million dollars you bought for £100 million are worth £125 million.

In 1986 News Corporation made profits of A$85 million – more than a fifth of total profits – from foreign exchange trading. In 1988 it made A$86 million – 15 per cent of its pre-tax profits – from foreign exchange trading. In 1989 it made a further A$33 million; in 1990 A$45 million and in 1991 it made A$42 million. Murdoch's success in producing profits of this size three years in a row is remarkable: few professional foreign exchange dealers could hope for such a hit rate. It was a high-risk strategy to rely on such profits to pay the interest on the company's borrowings.

But at least these profits were actually received by News Corporation – which is more than can be said for some of the other figures which were thrown into the profit and loss account. As well as its own business, News Corporation owned large shareholdings in several other companies – shareholdings large enough to have an impact on the News Corporation profits but not large enough to make them a subsidiary.[13] News Corporation followed the normal accounting convention of including in its profit and loss account the attributable share of these companies' profits. In other words, if News Corporation owned 40 per cent of the shares in a company making £10 million a year profit, then it included £4 million in its profits.

In some years the contribution from these associate companies was very large. In 1988 it accounted for 25 per cent of News Corporation's profit; in 1989, 13 per cent. The problem for News Corporation was that although it included its share of the associate's profits, it didn't receive anything like as much as this as income. Like most companies, the associates did not pay out all their profits in dividends. So in 1988, although News Corporation boosted its profits by including A$144 million from its associates, it only received dividends of A$40 million.

But there was a further problem. Some of the associates should never have been included in the profit and loss account at all. One of News Corporation's major investments was a shareholding in the UK communications group Pearson plc – owners of a wide range of assets, including the *Financial Times*, which Murdoch used to regard as the best quality paper in Britain.[14] Murdoch bought a 20 per cent shareholding in Pearson on the London stock market during the late 1980s. The Pearson board did not welcome this unsolicited interest in their company. The prospect of Murdoch making a bid for the company and controlling the *Financial Times* provoked senior members of that paper's editorial staff to make clear their opposition to his possible ownership. The Pearson board would not contemplate having Murdoch on their board. So there was no way in which News Corporation could really influence what went on in Pearson.

However, the News Corporation accounts say that they include the share of associated companies' profits 'where there is a capacity to significantly influence financial and operating policies'. Despite the fact that News Corporation clearly couldn't significantly influence the policies of the Pearson board, its proportionate share of Pearson profits was included in the 1988, 1989 and 1990 results. Under American and British accounting rules such treatment would not have been allowed. Again the Australian 'Liberian flag of convenience' had been hoisted.

In February 1990, Gary Schieneman, the Wall Street analyst who had coined the Liberian flag metaphor, did some sums. It was obvious why News Corporation favoured all these exotic accounting practices: it made the profit record look better and, crucially, it disguised the deterioration in its 'interest cover'. (Interest cover is simply the number of times pre-interest profits cover the interest charge. A company making profits of £2 million, with an interest bill of £1 million, has an interest cover of 2.) Schieneman found that News Corporation's interest cover had fallen from 2.63 in 1987 to 1.85 in 1989.[15] Given Murdoch's appetite for buying companies on borrowed money and the heavy reliance on those hard-to-repeat foreign exchange profits, this was a warning sign for bankers. It is, perhaps, a warning they should have spotted earlier, but those who lent to Murdoch believed that they had him under control. But here again, News Corporation's convenient Australian residence made it possible for it to window-dress its accounts.

One form of lending on which News Corporation relied heavily was a 'revolving credit' – a loan which didn't have a particular repayment date, which the banks were willing to go on renewing. One of the conditions which was imposed on Murdoch by the terms of these loans was that News Corporation's borrowings on 30 June must never exceed 110 per cent of the business's net assets. For example, if News Corporation's net assets were worth $1,000 million, its borrowings were limited to $1,100 million. It was, therefore, extremely important for News Corporation to keep up the value of its assets. Australia's accounting practices rushed to the rescue again.

Like all businesses, News Corporation owns many tangible assets – factories, equipment, stocks and so on. But most of its assets are intangible – the titles to its magazines and newspapers and television licences. Some of these are clearly worth much more than Murdoch paid for them. For example, by the 1980s, the *Sun* was making tens of millions of pounds of profit every year, compared with the £800,000 it had cost him in 1969. Titles such as this clearly have a value greater than the tangible assets used in producing them. The problem is that putting a value on intangible assets is one of the minefields of accounting. It is, for example, relatively easy to value a stock of cars, as there is a price list and a regular turnover in those particular cars in showrooms throughout the country. It is much harder to put a value on a newspaper title. For this reason American accounting regulations do not allow companies to revalue intangibles and also require any which are bought to be written-off over a period of not longer than forty years. In Australia, however, it is different. There companies are not required to write off the intangible assets and can revalue them as much as they want to.

Every three years News Corporation revalues its titles and television licences. It takes the advice of its merchant bank, Hambros, and told us[16] that it valued its assets at 70 per cent of this assessment. However, valuing intangible assets is a highly subjective matter and this provides great flexibility in keeping to the borrowing ratios imposed by the banks. Quite simply, without Australian registration and accounting policies Murdoch would have found it much harder to borrow the money for his takeovers. In the view of one expert observer 'the goal of the write-up of the intangibles has been to reduce News Corporation's gearing ratio and presumably appease its bankers. The incredible thing to me is that this works.'[17]

There are several interlocking reasons why this worked. The bankers believed in Murdoch. He bought assets of which they had heard and apparently produced the results. He also dealt with literally dozens of them so that detailed knowledge of his company was dispersed. But Murdoch was even bolder than this. He perfected a variety of ways of borrowing even more money to finance his business, without the debts even appearing on his balance sheet.

The condition which the banks imposed on News Corporation's borrowing had one curious feature: it limited borrowings to 110 per cent of net assets *on 30 June*. In effect this meant that Murdoch could run up his debts during the year so long as he got them under control by the year-end in June. As a result, the last few months of the year were often characterised by a desperate scramble to sell some assets. If these could be sold at a profit, so much the better, as the profit would go to boost the asset position. So in June 1989 News Corporation sold its American travel magazines for US$892 million; in June 1990 it sold the *Star* for just under US$400 million.

This was not a good way to sell assets – if a buyer got a whiff that News Corporation was a forced seller, the price would fall and there was always a temptation to sell the most marketable assets which would show a substantial profit. Sometimes a sale was not always possible and News Corporation had to resort to more esoteric ways of getting debt down. A dramatic example of this was the changing ownership of Harper and Collins, its book publishing business.

In the early 1980s Murdoch made a hostile bid for the British publisher, William Collins. Although it failed, News Corporation hung on to a 19 per cent shareholding which – because of Collins's unusual voting structure – gave it more than 40 per cent of the votes. The 1986 accounts of News Corporation gave a glowing account of Collins's progress, as though it was an integral part of the group.

Next year, Murdoch had the chance to use the Collins stake to help build another bit of the integrated world-wide media empire of which he dreamed. The American publisher Harper and Row came on offer. Harper and Row was one of America's leading publishers with a successful specialist medical publisher, J.B. Lippincott. It had been a potential takeover target for years and in the spring of 1987 decided to try and introduce a two-tier share structure as a defence against an unwelcome takeover. Some of its shareholders – notably the arbitrageur Theodore Cross – had different ideas, and quickly an auction developed for the company. The winner – paying an extremely high price of US$300 million – was Murdoch. This price was three times the value of Harper's assets and over fifty times its annual profits. New York publishing had never seen anything like it.

Murdoch's plan was outlined at a small dinner for a group of suspicious leading New York publishers shortly after the takeover was agreed. Murdoch assured them that he was interested in quality and sketched his plan. He believed that a large media group should be able to control every format for an author's work: books, newspaper and magazine seriali- sation, mini-series on TV, feature films. In this way it can secure the best authors by offering a 'one stop' service. It also gave economies of scale and strengthened one's hand with agents.[18]

It didn't take long for the management of Harper and Row to see what Murdoch meant. He was soon complaining about 'preachy' books, and when approving an advance for a book by Gorbachev said, 'I hope that it is not going to be too serious.' By now Murdoch had made his peace with the people at Collins, whose chairman Ian Chapman believed that he had a special relationship with Murdoch. Murdoch's plan was to put Collins in charge of the running of Harper and Row – they were given a management contract to do so and they started chopping away at Harper's costs. In September 1987 the two companies linked up further when News Corporation sold Collins half of its shares in Harper and Row. The theory was that Collins would be able to improve the marketing and distribution of Harper and Row's titles outside the United States, and Harper and Row would handle Collins titles in the USA. A promising and profitable partnership seemed assured.

Except that this was not Murdoch's style. He couldn't really exert much influence over the book publishing operation and in November 1988 launched another bid for Collins. Chapman – who felt he had been double-crossed – fought it, but lost, and early in 1989 the two companies were merged. By now News Corporation had a substantial book publishing operation – boosted by a few other acquisitions. But 1988–89 had not been a quiet year for News Corporation: it included the Triangle takeover as well as an ambitious investment programme in the newspapers. So in

June 1989 – just before the year-end and the day when the banks did their sums on his borrowings – Murdoch sold HarperCollins. It was a most remarkable deal.

The price paid was $1,300 million – part was paid in cash and part was paid in shares, so that News Corporation ended up with a 50 per cent stake in the new company. This was a pretty big deal that would normally attract quite a bit of attention, but it went by unremarked. Because the really interesting thing was the other shareholder. This was not some other media group or book publisher. It was the bank Credit Suisse First Boston. The bank had not taken leave of its senses – by buying a shareholding in HarperCollins, Credit Suisse was playing a part in helping Murdoch get millions of dollars off his balance sheet.

By owning just half of the shares in HarperCollins, News Corporation could treat it as an associate company – take in its share of the profits but leave out its share of the debts. Murdoch remained in control just as before. When shareholders received the 1989 accounts only an obscure note on page 85 gave any indication of what had gone on. In the lengthy review of operations, HarperCollins was treated just as though it was fully owned by News Corporation – with columns of print and pictures of its successful titles. The effect on News Corporation's balance sheet was dramatic – something like US$1 billion dollars' worth of debt had disappeared.[19]

The HarperCollins deal was only part of a bigger plan Murdoch had to keep control of a heavily debt-laden empire stretching across the world. At the beginning of March 1989 he had announced plans to set up a new company, Media Partners International (MPI). The aim was to make US$5 billion available for investment in the media business throughout the world. The deadline for raising at least $1 billion was the end of June,[20] the day the banks looked at his borrowing ratios.

The plan was for News Corporation to hold 20 per cent of

the shares in MPI. There would be total share capital of $1 billion and probably $4 billion of debt. News Corporation would run MPI, in return for a management fee. The whole appeal of the project lay in the Murdoch mystique – this was a way of backing his genius. 'Mr Murdoch's ... total managerial control ... is likely to be put forward as a virtue and a reason for investing in the company ... ', reported the *Financial Times*.[21] One of the first investments was to be the purchase of HarperCollins. The bankers to MPI were Credit Suisse First Boston.

Explaining this venture, Murdoch said, 'The main purpose is not to be stopped from expanding,' but some Wall Street analysts saw it simply as his way of getting rid of News Corporation debt.[22] Others shared their view. Within two months the sales team from Credit Suisse First Boston were reporting that investors were not exactly falling over themselves at the idea of giving Murdoch some of their money to punt around the world's media industries. MPI would have to be delayed. The story broke in the *Wall Street Journal* on 5 June 1989.

Murdoch put a brave face on it – $450 million has been raised so far, his London spokesperson said. Japanese investors were expected to come in soon. The project would go ahead in 'a month or two', assured finance director Richard Sarazen.[23] But it put Murdoch in a quandary – what to do with all the debt which News Corporation had hoped to unload on to MPI? The answer was obvious: he set up the joint venture with Credit Suisse First Boston to buy the HarperCollins book business.

The delay in the MPI deal was not good news for News Corporation shareholders. As the *Financial Times'* influential Lex column remarked: 'MPI remains the key to any restructuring of News Corporation and is one of the reasons why News Corporation's shares have performed so strongly recently.'[24] One shareholder quick to see the significance of the delay was Kayarem, Murdoch's investment-dealing company which had been so quick to buy options in News Corporation the year before when the Triangle deal was in the offing (see pp. 203-6). On 7 June Kayarem sold 300,000 shares in News Corporation at A$14.70. A further 1.15 million were sold on 8 June and 9 June. The total proceeds were A$22.3 million.[25] The optimism which the Murdoch camp voiced subsequently proved to be unfounded.

On 19 September the 'temporary postponement' became permanent and MPI was abandoned. Soon after this, Kayarem sold some more shares in News Corporation. On 5 and 6 October a total of half a million shares were sold at just over A$16 a share. And again price-sensitive news was not far behind. On 10 October, at News Corporation's annual general meeting, Murdoch warned shareholders that 1990 profits would not show 'their customary increase'. This news itself knocked 55 cents of the News Corporation share price. Within a week of the statement News Corporation shares had fallen by more than a fifth and Kayarem was more than £800,000 richer than if it had hung on to the shares (see Appendix VI).

Again, it is hard to believe that Murdoch did not know what he was going to say at the AGM when Kayarem sold part of its News Corporation holding, but Murdoch told us: 'I do not believe that those responsible for the decisions made in relation to the transactions had any price-sensitive insider information.'[26]

The abandoning of MPI and the profits warning in October 1989 were clear signals that the party was over: the years of free spending of other people's money were at an end. With hindsight it is easy to see that there were other warnings in 1989 that the world was turning against companies like News Corporation. More attention should, perhaps, have been paid to a report of the Australian House of Representatives' Standing Committee on Finance and Public Administration, *Tax Payers or Tax Players*. Chaired by MP Stephen Martin, this committee had been studying the Australian tax system for several years. It had turned its attention to the use that Australian companies made of tax havens – countries which have very low rates of tax and which have consciously developed their economies to provide little more than postboxes for foreign companies. Martin's committee reported that in 1988 News Corporation made profits of A$387.4 million in tax havens – 110 per cent of its total profits.[27] News Corporation's tax haven companies were in the Cayman Islands, the Netherlands Antilles and Bermuda. News Corporation had no newspapers or television stations in these places – it had companies there merely to ensure that it paid as little tax as possible. Again, Murdoch was able to use the Australian registration of News Corporation to pull off an audacious financial coup.

Over the years News Corporation has pulled off many tax-dodging tricks, but two essential features lie at the centre of most of them: the company's Australian registration and the construction of a web of inter-company debt within News Corporation. Under Australian tax law, an Australian company is not taxed on the profits it makes outside Australia so long as those profits are not sent back to Australia. This provides a large international group like News Corporation with a great opportunity: to borrow money in one country and lend it to a News Corporation subsidiary in another country. The interest on the loan reduces the profits of the subsidiary in the high-tax area, and passes the money to a subsidiary in the low tax area. In practice, arranging this is a complex affair, but in essence that is what News Corporation has successfully done over the years. It could not have managed it if it had been an American company as the American Inland

Revenue Service taxes companies on their world-wide profits. The net effect in 1990 was that on world-wide profits of A$429 million News Corporation paid only 3 per cent tax – less than A$12 million.

News Corporation has been the bane of the US Inland Revenue Service for years. When Murdoch took over the Metromedia television stations in 1986 he issued US$1.15 billion worth of convertible preference shares. He had not been keen to do this as the shares were eventually convertible into News Corporation shares and would thus dilute his control of the company. However, he had little choice as the bondholders in the Metromedia company would not otherwise give the sale of the television stations the go-ahead and the proceeds of the share sale would pay them off.

The key point about the share issue, however, was the tax treatment. Under Australian and British accounting conventions, preference shares count as equity or share capital rather than debt. This was very attractive to Murdoch as it meant that over US$1 billion which would otherwise have been debt and therefore would have increased the level of his borrowings, was transformed into equity capital. However, the dividends on preference shares are not a tax-deductible expense and paying the hefty 13 per cent interest on them would eat heavily into News Corporation's profits.

Murdoch found a way round this. He decided to treat the Fox preferred stock as debt – and charge the interest as a tax deduction. He took the best legal advice, which informed him that there was a 'split in judicial authority on the issue'.[28] However, News Corporation's finance director, Richard Sarazen, later admitted that the treatment was 'a little aggressive'[29] and that it saved 46 per cent on News Corporation's taxes.[30] And even today News Corporation may not be in the clear as the IRS has not given its final approval.

In Australia, for News Corporation the significance of the

Martin Report – whose investigation had been attacked by Murdoch's *The Australian* as being 'McCarthyist' – was that another gravy train was in danger of being derailed. There is no cause more popular than that of championing the ordinary taxpayer on the grounds that what Martin calls 'the corporate cowboys' are escaping paying tax. And News Corporation's record around the world showed there was plenty of material.

In March 1987 News Corporation bought Hong Kong's *South China Morning Post*, the largest English language paper in the colony, for HK$230 million. The ownership of the paper was entrusted to a News Corporation subsidiary in Bermuda. In June 1987 a complex set of transactions were set up under which News Corporation exploited a loophole in Hong Kong tax law and ended up with a paper tax loss of over HK$2 billion – almost US$300 million. Under Hong Kong tax law the income received from the sale of patents and designs is tax-free if the company selling the design has devised the patents or designs itself. However, any money spent buying a design is a tax deduction. So if a company pays HK$100 million for a design, its taxable profits are reduced by that amount; if someone receives that amount, it comes tax-free.

The purpose of these regulations was to encourage companies in Hong Kong to acquire patents and suchlike so that the colony could develop a manufacturing base. When the law was passed no one could have guessed at the inventiveness of News Corporation and its tax lawyers, who in 1987 decided to sell a design they owned. The 'design' was the masthead of the *South China Morning Post* and the price it was sold for was HK$2 billion. The buyer was a company called SCMP Publishers. In this deal the seller and the buyer had one thing in common – they were both controlled by News Corporation. A further loophole in Hong Kong law was unearthed. There was no provision that said that such transactions had to be between companies which were members of different groups. So News had engineered a situation where the *South China Morning Post* could make profits of HK$2 billion before paying any tax.

The *South China Morning Post* scheme used a number of companies in tax havens like the Netherlands Antilles. These were familiar places for News Corporation as they featured in one complex transaction which was set up to help avoid paying any tax on the massive windfall profits News Corporation stood to make on its shares in the news agency Reuters.

By the end of 1983 it was clear that Reuters was going to be a very valuable company and that one way or another the means would be discovered to float it off as a public company. Although it appeared to be protected by a Trust, the commercial attractiveness in selling off a company making tens of millions of pounds of profit a year was irresistible. In the end, the Reuters board were given the go-ahead by a legal opinion which said that there wasn't a trust after all, just a shareholders' agreement. And what the shareholders have made, they can unmake.

Murdoch, who was one of the first to spot the potential of Reuters, was a big holder of shares – he had some as a result of his takeover of both the *News of the World* and *The Times* newspapers. Reuters was floated in 1984 and soon the 25 million shares owned by the UK business, News International, were worth £77 million, compared with a cost of literally only £1,000. The immediate problem for News Corporation's tax planners was how to avoid paying any capital gains tax when – if ever – these shares were sold. Normally such a gain would be taxed at 30 per cent. So over the next few years these shares were passed round a series of companies in Britain and the tax haven of the Netherlands Antilles, ensuring that no tax was paid on the gain. The key trick in this process was to ensure that any gain arose either in a company which had tax losses or in a company registered in a low-tax country.

The first move came on 28 June 1985. At that stage the Reuters shares were owned by two News International subsidiaries – News Group Newspapers, the owners of the *News of the World* and the *Sun*, and Times Newspapers, the owners of *The Times* and the *Sunday Times* – the papers which had originally owned the Reuters shares. On that day the Reuters shares were sold to another company, News Offset, which was not a News International subsidiary. This meant that News International faced a tax bill of £23,227,000. However, it did not pay it. Instead it simply lent News Offset the money and, as its accounts state 'treated [the gain] as unrealised until the loans due . . . are paid'.

The immediate effect of this deal was to lock a £23.2 million tax liability into the two News International companies but give it the freedom to decide when to realise the gain. The disadvantage appears to be that News International loses a valuable asset, without any cash in return. However, this was not the case. News Offset used the shares as security to borrow £50 million. It then spent this money buying some shares in another company – Newscorp Company, a UK offshoot of Murdoch's Australian master company News Corporation. The small UK Newscorp Company then lent the money back to News International.

Clearly, News Offset was a very obliging company, yet it was not a subsidiary of News International – indeed if it had been a subsidiary it is most unlikely that the sale of the Reuters shares would have been regarded as a disposal for tax purposes. News International defined News Offset as an 'associated company' – one in which it had a shareholding but didn't control. Its relationship with News International was, however, very close. Half the shares were owned by News International, it was run from News International's head office and all its directors were employees of News International. Furthermore, the half of shares owned by News International were the ones which carried the power and the rights to the profits. Nothing was going to go on at News Offset without News International knowing about it and benefiting from it.

There was a further finesse to this game of pass-the-money-parcel. News Offset bought redeemable preference shares in Newscorp Company. This was part of another tax wheeze. At this time, under British tax law, capital gains were index-linked. In other words, the taxable profit was adjusted for inflation. Less well known, there was also a provision for indexing losses. Under this, if an investment was sold after a period of inflation for the same amount for which it was bought, the investor established a loss. The justification for this was that £10 today buys much less than £10 several years ago.

There was a loophole here just waiting to be exploited and News Offset set off to exploit it. The preference shares were redeemable and would be redeemed at their face value of £50 million. The chances were that this would provide an index-linked loss – to be offset against any profits made on a subsequent sale of any Reuters shares. And a sale was not long in coming.

On 9 June 1986 the Reuters shares, by now worth £109 million, were sold. There was clearly a substantial capital gain here but, again, no tax was payable. This was because News Offset was an investment company and so long as the proceeds of its sales were reinvested in the business – i.e. in shares – no tax would be payable. The money was reinvested in shares of book publisher William Collins, bought from News International.

And who bought the Reuters shares? Two companies called Lyntress and Salcombe, subsidiaries of News

251

International. The shares were back in the News International fold, but not for long. On the same day that they bought the shares, News International sold an option over them to another subsidiary of News Corporation – Newscorp Finance NV, registered in the Netherlands Antilles, a place where tax rates are so low as to be imperceptible. The option gave the tax haven company the right to buy the Reuters shares at £4.45p each – the market value – at any time until 2001. From now on, any profit on the sale would arise in the tax-free zone of the Netherlands Antilles (see Appendix VII). And the gains were to prove considerable.

At this time Murdoch was in the middle of his takeover of the Metromedia television stations in America and found an ingenious way to do this using the Reuters shares. In May 1986 he issued US$200 million worth of preference shares on the Eurodollar market. These new preference shares gave shareholders the right to convert into News Corporation's Reuters shares at any time until 2001, but at a price fixed in 1986 only 5 per cent higher than the £4.50 market price. However, for the first seven years they could not convert unless the price rose to more than £6.66.[31]

From Murdoch's point of view this was a smart deal. It gave him US$200 million of cheap money that did not count as debt. For the investors it looked good because it gave them a cheap way into Reuters if the company kept on growing. This right to convert did, in fact, become very valuable as the Reuters shares rose spectacularly in 1987 and 1988. In these years more than 20 million Reuters shares were bought by the holders of the preference shares.

As a result of these complex manoeuvres, the Reuters shares brought News Corporation almost £150 million. The amount of capital gains tax paid was less than £2 million. In 1988 the News Corporation accounts show an extraordinary item of A$99,821,000. Although the accounts do not say so, most of this is profit on the Reuters sale.[32] The total amount of tax paid in that year was less than A$3 million. And this was almost certainly the total amount of tax paid on the Reuters investment. In June 1989 News Offset had still not collected the money owed to it for the Reuters shares sold to Lyntress and Salcombe and reported that 'the surplus arising on the disposal of [Reuters' shares] will not be treated as realised until the company has collected the amounts due . . .' Tax totalling £9,424,489 remained unpaid. And the accounts of News Group Newspapers tell a similar story. 'No current tax charge has arisen as subsequent disposal of the [Reuters shares] by the group companies due to . . . tax losses.'[33]

None of this of course is illegal, though it does question the strength of claims by Murdoch's defenders that his enterprise brings wealth to the countries in which he operates. But for News Corporation the issue is more fundamental. Murdoch has exploited loopholes in international tax law in the same way as he has exploited the loopholes in international accounting regulations. This is fine so long as he is allowed to do it, but the risks are that one day he will be found out. Then the reality of business is exposed for all to see. As the 1980s came to an end, this reality began to dawn on people. For Murdoch the magician, the sun began to set.

12

The Party's Over

A prudent analysis suggests that since late 1988 News Corporation has been living on borrowed time. After Murdoch's long-time finance adviser, Merv Rich, retired in late 1987, Murdoch began to spend, spend, spend. His Fox television station in America was still draining money, he cranked up the Fox Film studio from five movies a year to twenty, he committed News Corporation to spend A$1 billion on printing machinery in Britain, and the same in Australia, he launched Sky Television in Britain knowing it would be years before he got a return, and in October 1988 he bought Triangle Publications for just under US$3 billion.

Unfortunately for Murdoch and the bankers who indulged him, the world economy was about to tilt into recession. Throughout the world, News Corporation is heavily dependent on advertising for its income. But advertising is always one of the first casualties of recession. Just as Murdoch committed News Corporation to the greatest media expansion the world had ever seen, the advertising income he needed to pay for it began to dry up. The heady days were over. Survival rather than expansion was now the main item on the agenda, not only for News Corporation but for many of its customers and its bankers around the world.

The failure to launch Media Partners International in the autumn of 1989 should have been an early warning to Murdoch that the wind was changing. But he got a clear and unambiguous message that News Corporation was in financial trouble in April 1990 – a good five months before the world's financial press latched on to the story. Like many of the causes of the financial crisis which now gripped News Corporation, the roots went back to a small, apparently insignificant deal which the company had made in the mid-1980s.

During 1987, News International plc, the British arm of News Corporation which owns the British newspapers and Sky Television, formed a joint venture with the American convenience store chain, Circle K Inc. The new company, Circle K (UK) Holdings Limited (CKHL) was 50 per cent owned by the two partners. By the beginning of 1990 it operated a total of 200 owned and franchised late-night stores throughout Britain.[1] The venture was partly financed by a £20-million loan from Continental Bank. When CKHL borrowed this money in 1987 the banks were falling over themselves to lend. Back in the boom times of 1987 both News International and Circle K were happy to guarantee to repay the loan in April 1990.

Neither of them expected anything to go wrong. It did. CKHL got into serious financial difficulties and filed for protection under Chapter 11 of the American Bankruptcy Code to reorganise its affairs. The essential feature of this is that all debts are frozen and the company continues to trade while a rescue package is arranged.

This worried Continental Bank, which in April 1990

decided that they would like News International to pay back their share of CKHL's £20-million loan. Although this was perfectly in accordance with the terms of the original agreement, News International had other ideas. They wanted Continental to extend the loan. News Corporation was so strapped for cash it did not want to use up £10 million in honouring this minor obligation if it could possibly avoid it.[2] Continental agreed to roll over the debt (that is, not ask for repayment) whilst negotiations continued. But this was a shock for News Corporation, which had grown accustomed to being courted by the international banks.[3]

In public, however, News Corporation maintained a confident face. On 11 April Murdoch was telling the *Wall Street Journal* that although there would be no more major acquisitions, there would only be 'selective' sales of assets and the company would 'grow organically'.[4]

But within two months News Corporation received another body blow. Back in December 1989 it had borrowed US$750 million from a consortium of banks led by Samuel Montagu, a subsidiary of the British high street clearing bank Midland. This was due for repayment in June 1990. Rather than repay, News Corporation wanted to refinance it with a three-year loan. When it tried, it failed. The most the banks would agree to was a US$500 million loan for three months.[5] News Corporation, which was already baulking at repaying the £10 million (just under US$20 million) to Continental Bank had suddenly to find more than twenty times this.

At the same time, the general economic climate was turning much colder, all over the world. The Japanese banks were pulling out of the short-term money market in Australia, where News Corporation was a heavy borrower. The availability of leasing finance was drying up and banks everywhere were losing their enthusiasm to lend. All this was very bad news for heavily indebted companies like News Corporation.

But to the world outside, Murdoch and News Corporation were presenting an optimistic face. On 24 August the company announced its results for the year to June. Profits were down 45 per cent at A$282.3 million (£120.6m). These results provoked media analysts in the United States, Australia and Britain to reassess News Corporation's prospects. They did not like what they saw. News Corporation was a company heavily reliant on the United States at a time when the American economy was going into recession. Worse, it was heavily reliant on advertising when spending on advertising was being cut.

The American credit-rating agency, Standard and Poor, gave some of News Corporation's debt a rating of Triple C plus. This was the equivalent of a junk-bond rating. 'It reflects a very high level of financial risk,' explained the company's media analyst, Heather Goodchild; 'Although his cash flow of combined operations is very large, the cash flow coverage of his interest charges is extremely thin. It does cover interest charges but it doesn't allow an enormous margin for weakness within magazines or newspapers, or endless room for money-losing start-up operations.'

Shortly after the 1990 results, News Corporation produced its Annual Report and Accounts. As always, Rupert Murdoch was upbeat, telling his shareholders that News Corporation was 'well on the way to becoming the most versatile and skilled media company in the world'. The accounts told a different story. They showed just how thin the operating margins were. News Corporation's total borrowings at the end of June 1990 were over A$10.5 billion. There were two particular sources of concern in this. First, almost A$3 billion of these loans were short-term. Most of these loans (A$2.45 billion) had been run up during the course of 1989–90, and the single most important reason was the takeover of Triangle, publishers of *TV Guide* in America. Although the precise terms of the loans varied, in practice all of this money could be called in by the banks within the next twelve months. It was clear from the accounts that News Corporation did not have the cash to cope with this. The only way in which it could hope to repay the banks was by selling some assets. This was the second worry.

Every three years News Corporation revalues it assets. By and large these assets are not plant and machinery but newspaper and magazine titles and television licences – *in*tangible assets. In 1990 the News Corporation directors put a value of A$13.34 billion on these. News Corporation's capacity to repay its short-term debt clearly depended on being able to sell some of these assets at these values. By September 1990, most analysts thought it highly unlikely that any of the publications in the Triangle group could be sold at the prices Murdoch had paid only a year before. In other words, the accounts made it clear that News Corporation was both desperately short of cash and of the means of generating it.

In fact the situation was much worse even than these accounts revealed. The problems with the loans from Continental Bank and the Samuel Montagu consortium were not mentioned. The accounts, signed by the directors on 23 August 1991, confidently claimed: 'The directors are not aware of any matter or circumstance that has arisen since the end of the financial year that has significantly affected or may significantly affect the operations of the group.' But News Corporation's own internal forecasts showed that it would not make enough money in 1990–91 to repay loans which fell due, unless the banks were willing to renegotiate terms.[6]

On top of this, the valuations of some of the titles were considerably more optimistic than in previous years. In 1987 the UK titles were valued at £385 million.[7] By 1990 this had risen to £1,068,000.[8] Although the profits had increased sharply in this period, the circulations and advertising of Murdoch's papers were now falling. Despite this, the valuation basis in 1990 took a more optimistic view of the future than that in 1987.

A common way of valuing a business is to express the value as a multiple of its profits. The better the prospects for a company, the higher the multiple. For example, a company making profits of £20 million, valued at £100 million, would be on a multiple of five. If the general prospects improved, the multiple might rise to 7, valuing the company at £140 million. In the case of News Corporation's British newspaper titles, the 1990 valuation placed them on a multiple of 7, compared with one of only 3.5 three years earlier. It is hard to see how it could be argued that Murdoch's UK titles were now worth twice as much as they had been three years earlier. The financial position of these papers had improved. But this was as a result of the move to Wapping, and much of the improvement due to Wapping had come through by 1987. Since then the day-to-day performance of the newspapers in the market-place had actually been deteriorating. In the six months to June 1990 all the major British newspaper titles had circulations lower than in June 1989 and June 1988, and two of them had circulations lower than in 1987. In most cases advertising income was higher than in 1987 but the volume of advertising was falling as an advertising recession began.[9]

In other words, the value placed on the British titles in June 1990 was optimistic. The valuation was made by the News Corporation directors, based on advice from the merchant bank Hambros (for Britain and Australia) and R. Gary Gomm and Associates (for the United States). Murdoch has never explained how such a high valuation was reached.

He has told us that it represents only 70 per cent of the value given to the titles by Hambros. The valuation was critical to News Corporation's ability to continue to trade. Under the terms of some of its bank arrangements, News Corporation's borrowings were limited to 110 per cent of its net assets. So for every £1,100 of debt, News Corporation had to have £1,000 worth of net assets. At the end of June total debts were A$10,533 million, compared with net assets of A$9,597 million. Debts were 109.75 per cent of assets. News Corporation was right on the edge. If any of News Corporation's titles were worth less than the balance sheet valuation of A$13,340 million, then the company would very quickly be in breach of its loan agreements.[10]

However, none of this was known by or revealed to the public in the late summer and autumn of 1990. Indeed, it seems that the ever-optimistic Murdoch thought that there was a way of avoiding the financial calamity which events should have told him was now almost inevitable. In the summer of 1990 he had struck on an idea which he thought could help get News Corporation out of its hole. For a company in News Corporation's position there was only one place it could go for money other than the banks – its shareholders. Of course, this posed Murdoch with a particular problem. He and his family owned almost 45 per cent of the News Corporation shares, and he liked it that way. It meant that he could run the company as he wanted without any real interference from shareholders. If he wanted more money from shareholders he was in a dilemma. By issuing more shares he would reduce his family's holding and therefore votes in the company, unless he bought 45 per cent of the new shares on offer. The Murdoch family was rich, but not that rich.

Murdoch's way out of this problem would be to issue non-voting shares. His own share of the profits would fall after such an issue, but his control of the company would be unaffected. So in August, although saying he had no immediate intention of raising new capital, Murdoch asked the Australian Stock Exchange for permission to issue non-voting shares.[11] There was one problem. The Australian Stock Exchange did not allow the listing of non-voting shares. Murdoch simply threatened to stop the listing of News Corporation shares in Australia unless he got his way. Once this tactic would have worked, but in the nervous times of mid-1990, it only added to concerns caused by the publication of the accounts and fuelled fears for the future.[12] By the end of September 1990, News Corporation's shares had fallen by a quarter since the results were announced. At A$7.80 they were only half of their high for the year. Murdoch was forced to make an unplanned appearance at an investment seminar in New York to reassure investors.[13] He admitted that News Corporation's short-term debt was too high, but said that profits would recover in 1990–91. But this was not enough. Investors did not readily believe that, with world economies going into recession, Murdoch could make enough money both to repay debt and pay for the major reinvestment programme in his printing and newspaper operations.[14] (In part, this was one of the ghosts of Wapping coming back to haunt Murdoch. As explained in Chapter 3 the printing machinery at Wapping was in fact quite old. At the time of the move to Wapping this did not matter as the main financial benefit came from the cuts in the labour force. But by 1990 Murdoch's competitors, notably Robert Maxwell, the owner of the *Sun*'s main competitor, the *Daily Mirror*, had a substantial lead over Murdoch in being able to produce full-colour newspapers. Murdoch's British business was suffering from the competition.)

At the end of September Murdoch's (anonymous) colleagues were still assuring the financial press that

Murdoch 'retained the confidence of his bankers',[15] but rumours that he was in difficulties continued. Things were not improved when the story leaked out that Richard Sarazen, Murdoch's financial supremo, had been moved to an obscurely titled job as 'Senior Executive Vice President and Member of the Office of Chief Executive'. Sarazen had held the News Corporation purse strings since Merv Rich's departure. He was liked by the banks and this was widely seen as a demotion.[16] The mere fact that Murdoch visited Melbourne at the beginning of October was enough to start the story that he was thinking of selling many of his Australian papers to keep his bankers at bay.[17]

Early in October, News Corporation finally faced the inevitable and called in its bankers at Citicorp to help it out of its troubles.[18] The rescue was under way and News Corporation was given the code name of 'Dolphin'. The choice of Citicorp was a smart move. Like many other international banks, it had expanded aggressively. One of Citicorp's largest corporate customers was News Corporation. In total the bank had lent Murdoch's company more than US$700 million, almost 10 per cent of News Corporation's total debt and the largest amount lent by any single bank. Bluntly, Citicorp had a powerful incentive to make the News Corporation rescue work. It could not afford another multi-million-dollar write-off. As one of the bankers involved in the lengthy negotiations that followed put it: 'From the beginning it was clear that Citicorp were pushing the company [i.e. News Corporation] line with a big stick.'[19] The presence of the British bank, Midland, as the second largest lender, and of their merchant banking subsidiary, Samuel Montagu, as joint advisers, also helped. Midland was the weakest of the four British clearing banks and had serious problems of its own. Like Citicorp, Midland too needed to avoid making bad debt provisions if it possibly could.

To start with, Citicorp and Samuel Montagu were very keen to get an agreement before 31 December 1990, the day on which the banks' financial year ended and the day on which bonuses would be calculated. With total fees of £25 million, there was a great deal of money to be made.

Citicorp had two main aims: to get the other 145 banks to agree not to press for the immediate repayment to which they were entitled, and to raise some extra money to finance News Corporation through to better times. To succeed it had to play a delicate game of poker with both the other banks and the company.

Theoretically the banks could push News Corporation to repay its debts. But in practice if they pushed too hard they would force the company to collapse. And that would make it even harder to get their money back. Privately some of them discounted this possibility right from the start. They liked and respected Murdoch and saw him as a 'winner'. If they pulled the plug on him, they did not believe that anyone else could run the business as well as he could – in which case, they could wave goodbye to their money. Others took a much tougher line. If News Corporation was allowed to exploit the weakness of the banks' position too much, others who were less supportive of Rupert Murdoch might easily lose patience.

There was a further delicate balancing act to be achieved between the banks. Nine banks were big lenders to News Corporation. In addition to Citicorp there was Westpac (US$582 million); Commonwealth Bank of Australia (US$545 million); Midland Bank (US$407 million); National Australia Bank (US$333 million); Barclays (US$226 million); Manufacturers Hanover (US$218 million); Lloyds Bank (£210 million); Crédit Lyonnais (US$175 million); and Deutsche Bank (US$173 million).[20] These banks (known as the Tier One banks) and some of the other large lenders realised that they would all have to stick together if they were find a successful solution, even though some were entitled to repayment earlier than others. Their major problem was going to be persuading the smaller banks to co-operate with the rescue scheme. This proved harder than they expected.

Citicorp's main task was to discover the precise scope of News Corporation's crisis. 'We had to answer the question of "where are we?", before we could figure out what to do,' said Ann Lane, the Citicorp executive in charge of the operation.[21] Citicorp had to establish whether News Corporation's assets were worth more than its debts and the precise nature of these debts. Valuing the assets, as has been said, is a highly subjective activity – never more so than when the market is crashing and profits are falling. By the autumn of 1990 it was clear that there was no one in the world willing to pay the prices which Murdoch had paid for some of his more recent acquisitions, such as Triangle. It was also clear that the profits of many of his businesses were under pressure. In the three months to the end of September 1990 News Corporation's profits fell by almost a third to A$25.9 million.

In making its assessment Citicorp was helped by the British merchant bank Hambros, the long-serving advisers to News Corporation who had helped in the increased valuation of the UK newspaper titles back in June 1990. As a result of the review made by Hambros and the American company, Wertheim Schroder, Citicorp convinced itself that News Corporation's assets were worth more than its debts. This was, perhaps, the last achievement of the Murdoch mystique. Unlike some other media moguls Murdoch had been around for a long time, the record was seen as a tribute to his skill as a manager and deal-maker and, for many bankers, newspapers, magazines and TV stations were better quality assets than empty office blocks. All these factors encouraged bankers to be generous in their assessment of News Corporation's chances of survival.

The Murdoch magic gave them comfort. In reality, they had little choice. If they decided that the Hambros and Gomm revaluation was seriously out of line, the whole house of cards would collapse and Citicorp and the other lead banks would never get the deal they all so desperately needed.

When Citicorp turned their attention to News Corporation's debts it discovered a web of incredible complexity. In a simply constructed company, bank loans are often made to one company in a group, secured against that company's assets, with a guarantee from the parent company. But News Corporation was not a simple company. Citicorp discovered that there were all sorts of cross-guarantees so that it was not clear which bank had what security.[22] This quickly led Citicorp to decide against any attempt to restructure News Corporation's debts as it would lead to interminable wrangles with the other lending banks. Instead they decided they would suggest an 'Override Agreement' in which all the existing terms of the loans would be overridden by some new terms. The most important of these were the date of repayment and the interest charged on the loans. In other words, Citicorp's plan was to propose that all banks hold off demanding repayment for a period of three years in return for a higher rate of interest on their loans. If News Corporation were to come into any funds, these would be distributed *pro rata* among the banks.

Throughout October there were recurrent rumours that News Corporation was negotiating with its bankers. The rumours were true but News Corporation managed to keep a straight face when denying that there was a financial crisis. On 19 October the *Wall Street Journal* reported that Murdoch and his bankers were in 'intensive talks', but Murdoch spoke confidently of News Corporation 'trading its way through', with the outlook for United States 'great', and of *TV Guide* and the film business being recession-proof.[23]

Murdoch even managed to survive the annual general meeting of shareholders at the end of October without giving a hint of what was going on, merely saying that the company planned to turn its short-term debt into long-term borrowings.[24]

At that stage Murdoch had no grounds for believing that this was possible. As he well knew, the package of proposals which Citicorp had just about finalised fell a long way short of this ambitious and desirable objective. However, the Tier One banks were pleased with the progress which their talks with News Corporation were making. They were particularly impressed by the Sky-BSB merger (see Chapter 8) announced at the beginning of November, which helped convince them that Murdoch was serious about his plan to sell assets and reduce News Corporation's cash drain. They were reassured that, under the deal, the maximum new money they believed that News Corporation would have to put into Sky–BSB was £30 million.[25]

This deal was a promising background against which Citicorp could tell the other banks about the proposed rescue package. Over the next two weeks, Murdoch went to New York, Sydney and London talking to bankers and outlining his plans. It was an unusual experience for him to be grilled on News Corporation's figures. In the past, the banks had sold themselves and their services to News Corporation. Now the roles were reversed and Murdoch was having to sell himself and convince them that he was a long-term survivor. Originally Murdoch hoped that he could persuade them to provide a seven-year loan to repay the short-term debt. He had to lower his sights to five years and then to three.[26] By 16 November the major lenders and a majority of the Second Tier lenders had agreed to these terms, so long as there was an asset disposal programme as well. In return they would get an extra 1 per cent interest on their loans as well as a 1 per cent arrangement fee in advance.[27]

However, the battle for the hearts and minds of the bankers was far from won. For the scheme to work, all 146 banks, no matter how small their exposure to News Corporation, had to agree to the plan. And Citicorp had made two tactical errors. First, it decided that some of the big lenders around the world would be put in charge of organising the other banks in their region. This was a good idea in principle, but unfortunately in Australia Citibank chose the Commonwealth Bank of Australia and Westpac. This was taken as a corporate affront by two other Australasian banks, National Australia Bank and Australian and New Zealand Bank who had lent US$333 million and US$64 million respectively.[28] At various stages in the negotiations which were to follow, these banks created difficulties for the Citicorp-led group. Some of those involved attributed this to their initial pique at being excluded.

Citicorp also made a second error of etiquette. In its first world tour of lenders it missed out Hong Kong and Japan. As Citicorp pushed to achieve its tight timetable, the Hong Kong banks dragged their feet, innocently saying: 'Oh, we didn't realise that our part was that important.' It was also a mistake to miss out Japan. Many of the Japanese banks were not keen to co-operate in the rescue or to roll over their debts whilst the negotiations were under way.

In December Citicorp decided to bring in William Rhodes. Rhodes was brought in because he had considerable experience of renegotiating the debts of Third World countries in Latin America, the very countries which Murdoch and his papers despise so much. His job during December and January was to bring the difficult banks into line and keep the central bankers on three continents informed.[29] There seems little doubt that some central bankers felt that if the rescue failed the whole of the financial system was at risk.

During November a number of News Corporation's debts had fallen due for repayment. It was able to repay these by selling some assets and using a special A$100 million facility provided by the Commonwealth Bank of Australia. But it needed a further £142.5 million in December and January. Six of the major lenders agreed to provide a facility of this size. Their security was the mastheads of the *Sun* and *News of the World* and 'the Page Three trademark'. So for a short period of time the whole financial future of News Corporation in part depended on its daily publication of a picture of a topless woman in the *Sun*.[30] The banks were as exposed as the women who boosted the circulation of Murdoch's British papers.

This was a relatively minor problem to solve compared with the more intractable one of Queensland Press. The problem here went back to Murdoch's purchase of the Herald and Weekly Times in 1987 (see Chapter 5). Murdoch had made a serious tactical error in not recognising that he needed control of Queensland to get control of HWT. When he did realise this it was almost too late: the banks would not lend any more money to News Corporation to buy Queensland, and if News Corporation paid for Queensland with shares, it would dilute Murdoch's control of News Corporation. Murdoch's only option was to use Cruden, the family investment company, to bid for Queensland. As Cruden had no cash of its own, it had to borrow the money, using its shareholding in News Corporation as security. But the loan which Commonwealth Bank made to Cruden was repaid when Cruden (which Murdoch controlled) sold a 16 per cent shareholding in News Corporation (which Murdoch controlled) to Queensland Press (which Murdoch controlled).

So that it could make this investment, Queensland Press

had to borrow A$500 million. Commonwealth Bank arranged a syndicated loan for this purpose and at the same time arranged a A$500-million loan for News Corporation. Both loans were repayable on 7 December 1990. When Citicorp tackled this aspect of Murdoch's finances they soon hit trouble.

Citicorp took the view that Queensland Press was effectively part of News Corporation and that the A$500 million should be part of the Override Agreement – in other words the lenders would have to stand in line with the lenders to News Corporation to get their money back. In practice Queensland Press *was* part of News Corporation – its presses were used to produce News Corporation's newspaper *The Australian*. However, in law Queensland Press was not part of News Corporation. It was only an associate, and 54 per cent of the shares were owned by Cruden. The banks who had lent to Queensland Press, many of whom were also lenders to News Corporation, immediately saw the chance of getting some of their money back as the Queensland loan was due for repayment.

For Citicorp this would have been a disaster. Queensland Press could not afford to repay the loan so the banks would have ended up controlling Queensland's assets – the largest of which was a 16 per cent stake in News Corporation and a holding of convertible notes, convertible into News Corporation shares. Together these would give the banks control of 21 per cent of News Corporation's share capital. If they sold these shares, the price would collapse further, undermining confidence in the rescue negotiations: disaster all round. Murdoch was also opposed to this happening, and Citicorp was keen to keep Murdoch on its side. Along with many of the other banks it considered his involvement critical to the rescue's success.

But some of the banks involved in the Queensland Press

loan dug their heels in. They saw no reason to co-operate in shoring up the Australian banking system. One small American bank was particularly obstructive. In desperation Murdoch himself tried to ring the chief executive, but he refused to take the call, saying he didn't know a Mr Murdoch. Once again the American regulators stepped in to help Murdoch at a difficult time. The American Federal Reserve contacted the banker and told him to talk to Murdoch.

By Christmas a compromise was reached over the Queensland Press affair. The Queensland loan was included in the Override Agreement but, in the event of any Queensland assets being sold, they would not go into the pot. They would be used to repay Queensland lenders. In addition, a A$170 million loan from News Corporation to Queensland Press would not be repaid before bank lenders to Queensland Press and News Corporation guaranteed the interest on the Queensland loans.[31]

However, the argument over the Queensland loan had caused serious delays in getting the rescue package agreed. Citicorp's first deadline of 21 December passed without a signature to the first draft of the eighty-page document detailing the Override Agreement. A new deadline of 31 December was set and although this was later extended to 31 January 1991 it still involved many Christmas and New Year holiday telephone conference calls. Frequently the American bankers and lawyers were surprised to discover that their Australian counterparts were not to be found in their offices, but at home by the barbecue.

Given the size of the task, it was a very tight timetable. Citicorp were keen for an early agreement for a number of reasons. First, President Bush had set 16 January as the deadline for Iraq to withdraw from Kuwait. Many of the bankers feared that if a land war got under way, Murdoch's problems – and the banks' willingness to help solve them –

would be eclipsed by bigger concerns. Second, a larger number of the loans to News Corporation were now in arrears, and a further great chunk fell for repayment on 31 January. It was stretching the patience of the banks to keep asking them to roll over these loans. Already some of them were being difficult. Ann Lane, the Citicorp executive in charge of the negotiations, described the situation:

> Banks would tell you of their intention to get out of the facility. They would push you to the edge. In the end no bank was willing to play chicken to the point where they would pull the plug on the company, but that's not to say that at every point there wasn't someone willing to play chicken.[32]

There were two particularly intransigent banks which, ironically, were owed comparatively small amounts of money. The Bank of Singapore was owed just $7.68 million dollars and Swiss Bank Corporation was owed $58 million. Both favoured exercising their rights to foreclose on their loans. If they had done so the effect would have been disastrous. The whole of News Corporation would have been put into liquidation. In the end Citicorp and the Tier One banks had a winning argument. If any bank foreclosed they would get very little money. With the exception of a small amount of money in Australia none of the loans were secured on individual assets. If a bank foreclosed, they would only get their proportionate share of what was left. And in forced sales, who could tell how much that would be? Given that News Corporation's assets were producing good cash flow, it always made sense for lenders to hang on until the undoubted value of the assets could be realised.

Citicorp's third anxiety about delay was closely connected to this: as time went by the rumours increased, undermining confidence in News Corporation's ability to survive. As the New Year started the financial press was reporting that banks accounting for 20 per cent of the loans had yet to give their agreement.[33] And fears that the negotiations might fail meant that for a brief period the publicly quoted bonds of some News Corporation subsidiaries were selling on yields of almost 50 per cent. In other words, for every £1 invested in News Corporation bonds, an investor would receive an annual income of 50p. This is only appropriate for a company about to go bust.[34]

Murdoch, skiing at his home in Aspen, appeared confident of success. But he spent some time in early January on the phone to the chief executives of some of the major banks to nudge them into signing. Even at this late stage the News Corporation executive negotiating the deal tried to wring a few more concessions. Part of the rescue package provided News Corporation with a new US$600 million facility to help finance its business. Some executives wanted News Corporation to be able to draw down money from the US$600 million facility at any time during the three years of the facility's life. Under the terms of the facility this effectively gave News Corporation an extra 180-day credit. Unfortunately for News Corporation, one sharp-eyed Australian banker spotted the loophole and closed it.

By 10 January a final draft agreement, which with all its schedules ran to more than 300 pages, was ready. The most important 27 banks had agreed the terms. Their job was now to ensure that the other 120 banks signed by the deadline of 31 January. The deadline was met, but as one banker said 'it was a very close thing'. Some banks waited until the very last minute. A serious setback for the Americans in the Gulf War or another corporate collapse could easily have killed the deal.

The package which was eventually agreed has two main

elements: the Override Agreement and the US$600-million bridging loan. Under the Override Agreement the banks effectively agreed that they would not expect their money back for three years – whatever the terms of the original loan. There was, of course, a price for this. They received a fee up-front of 1 per cent of the total loans outstanding and will receive another 1 per cent of the amount outstanding in three years' time. The interest rate charged on the loans was increased by 1 percentage point. So in the first year the deal was likely to cost News Corporation an extra US$150 million, compared with after-tax trading profits of just over US$200 million in 1990. The US$600-million bridge facility was a one-year loan at 2¼ per cent over the average rate in the money markets. The purpose of this was to provide News Corporation with the working capital it needed whilst it set about a programme of disposals. These sales targets were the conditions on the deal which really bit into News Corporation.

News Corporation was committed to reducing its debts by at least US$800 million by 1 February 1992 and then by a further US$400 million on three successive dates: 30 June 1992, 31 December 1992 and 30 June 1993.[35] Given News Corporation's own demands for cash, this meant that in effect US$900 million of assets had to be sold in a year.[36] News Corporation's room for manoeuvre is negligible. A series of special bank accounts has been established to hold the proceeds of any sales and to ensure that lenders get the benefit, and a series of ratios control capital spending and cash management.[37] These ratios are reviewed every quarter and, if the target is not achieved, holders of 75 per cent of the debt can claim that News Corporation is in default of the Override Agreement. This is a powerful sanction on Murdoch to keep his promises to the banks. The net effect, in the words of the explanatory memorandum, is that 'very little headroom has been permitted'. The days of spend, spend, spend are over.

Murdoch himself is tied into the deal. The whole rescue is off if Murdoch ceases to be News Corporation's chief executive or if the Murdoch family shareholding in the company falls below 20 per cent of the voting rights. But at the same time the Murdoch family cannot receive any dividends from News Corporation. It has to take more shares instead.[38]

There was only one conclusion for Murdoch to draw from this: the next three years would be a hard slog as he tried to sell businesses at good prices in hard markets. At the same time he had two other tasks: to increase the profits of his remaining businesses and to renegotiate his loans with the lenders. The terms of the Override Agreement are strict. At the end of three years all the debts which were overdue have to be repaid. These total $5.6 billion.

Murdoch set about this task in the spring of 1991. It proved hard going. He had already sold Townsend Hook, the UK paper manufacturing company, and had told the bankers that he was already well along the road to selling a 50 per cent share in his Australian commercial printing operations for a good price. Indeed news of this was one of the things that encouraged them to sign the deal. A memo to News Corporation lenders said:

> The company [News Corp] perceives the target investor as being among a limited group of strategic partners for this asset. Further, the investor's preference for a 50% interest and its willingness to pay an attractive price for such a stake, is derivative of its belief that [News Corporation] will provide significant intangible value through ongoing management interactions.[39]

Translated into English, this banker's gobbledegook means that the deal is very good for News Corporation because it proves there is confidence in the company's ability to survive.

Unfortunately, News Corporation's confidence appeared misplaced. Six months later the Australian printing businesses remain unsold. As the refinancing deal was being signed it was reported that News Corporation was about to sell its 50 per cent stake in the Eurosport satellite for an undisclosed amount. By July 1991, the deal was still not done. Murdoch's UK finance director, Peter Stehrenberg, had said in January that Eurosport would be the last significant sale of UK assets.[40] But here, too, things did not go as expected. In May 1981, News Corporation announced that it was open to offers for most of its UK magazine titles: *New Woman, Car, Supercar* and *Classics* – the loss-making *Mirabella* had been closed. In August 1991 the three remaining titles were sold for a mere £10 million.

The difficulty in selling assets put extra pressure on the everyday business of News Corporation. Across the globe, Murdoch's papers faced an advertising recession; he needed to cut costs if he was to achieve the cash flow targets which the banks had approved. But he faced an immediate problem: cutting costs was a Murdoch speciality which he had already indulged to the full. The scope for cost-cutting was very limited and the unions, which he had thought so pliant, were not keen to co-operate.

In London the quality newspapers, *The Times* and the *Sunday Times*, were given a target of cutting 10 per cent off their costs by June. The annual *Sunday Times* Fun Run was cancelled. In the middle of January 1991, a small number of staff at the *Sunday Times* were offered voluntary redundancy[41] and a more draconian 30 per cent of the staff were sacked from the *Today* newspaper. Here, circulation was down by a fifth since the previous summer. For *Today*, the rushed move to Wapping has been disastrous.[42]

But worse was to come. At the beginning of April reports of an interview in Australia with the recently appointed chief operating officer of News Corporation, Gus Fischer, suggested that perhaps 1,000 jobs would have to go in Britain.[43] News International officials were coy about denying the story absolutely. The reason became clear at the end of the month when News International announced redundancies of 185 in its newspaper printing operations, mainly at Wapping. Those not sacked were told they would now have to work a five- instead of four-day week.

A series of events rich in irony followed. Printing machines mysteriously started to break down, costing the company tens of thousands of pounds. Workers at Wapping suddenly joined the union and demanded that their national officials call a ballot on whether there should be a strike. Unofficial industrial action disrupted production of the newspapers. All this had been familiar in the 'bad old days' of Fleet Street, from which Murdoch had escaped in 1986. But the workers responsible at Wapping were those Murdoch had employed to replace the traditional print unions. And the union they joined was the Electrical Electronic Telecommunication and Plumbing Union (EETPU), which had secretly conspired with News International to recruit workers for the Wapping plant back in 1985.

The EETPU was in a difficult position, however. News International did not recognise the union and it was hard to see how its members could hang on to their jobs if they went on strike. But in the end, in late May, the EEPTU members in Wapping voted by an overwhelming majority in favour of industrial action just short of a strike.

At the same time, there was some good news for Murdoch, as News Corporation made its first significant sale. The company got $650 million for all its American magazines except for *Mirabella* and *TV Guide*. Although the cash put Murdoch well on the way to his $800 million target, the total amount represented a substantial loss on the costs of the titles. Two of the titles, *Seventeen* and *Racing Form*, had been part of Triangle Publications, owners of *TV Guide*, which he had bought for nearly $3 billion in 1988. In effect, this meant that he had paid more than US$2.5 billion for *TV Guide* alone.

Murdoch's third major problem in 1991 was hanging onto his stake in BSkyB. The promise to refinance it with a £400-million loan, a promise which he had made to his bankers, was not easy to keep. By the middle of March it was clear that there was little enthusiasm among banks to lend this money without some form of guarantee from the BSkyB shareholders. But the terms of the News Corporation rescue prevented the company from doing this. BSkyB was going to have to return to its shareholders for finance, but News Corporation could not provide any of that either. Eventually it was agreed that News Corporation would buy its new shares in kind – by providing Fox films and television programmes for free. This, of course, does nothing for News Corporation's overall finances. Fox's profits will just be lower than they otherwise would be, as Fox is effectively swapping some of its income for shares in BSkyB.

By July 1991, the future of 'the most versatile and skilled media company in the world' was still not assured.

13

The Future

The days of the ever-expanding world-wide empire may be over for Rupert Murdoch. There may be no great acquisitions for several years to come – only disposals. Murdoch's agenda used to be dominated by one item: global expansion. Now the plan is simpler: survival. By 1994, when he next reaches crunch time with the banks, News Corporation will be a much smaller company than it is in 1991.

When Murdoch signed the Override Agreement with the banks at the beginning of 1991, it looked as if the future of News Corporation was assured. This agreement basically gave him three years to sort out News Corporation, though at a high price. He now has to pay more for News Corporation's debt, and in 1994 he has to meet News Corporation's outstanding obligations to the banks. To meet these obligations he is trying to improve his profitability, cut costs and sell off parts of his empire.

But so far not everything is going to plan. Although the sale of his American magazines in early 1991 will help to meet the $900-million target for sales this year, other disposal plans have not gone so well. The Australian printing business, which the bankers thought was on the verge of sale, remained unsold by the summer of 1991. Eurosport, which was left over from the Sky-BSB merger, is also still unsold. On top of that, several new problems have emerged. Together these could mean that Murdoch will be back at the bankers' table sooner than he – or they – expects. In the United Kingdom, the merger of Sky and BSB is going well. The financing is not. And for Murdoch financing is the key.

Before he merged his Sky satellite television station with BSB, Murdoch told the *Sunday Times* editor and former Sky chairman, Andrew Neil: 'This had better work. I've bet the company on Sky.' This was the second time he had bet the company since 1985. The first time was when he gambled on being able to move his British newspapers to Wapping. This move effectively gave him another £100-million-a-year profit on his UK newspaper operations. Before he made the move, he had already used the future profits from his British newspapers as his stake money to help buy and finance Fox Television in the United States. If Wapping had failed, News Corporation would not have been able to meet its commitments to its bankers and the financial crisis which engulfed him in 1990 would have arrived five years earlier.

Fox is now established and making money, so the gamble has paid off. But Sky has always been different. Starting a fourth network channel in America meant breaking into an established market and holding on until the viewers and the advertisers arrived. Starting a new satellite station was a gamble of a different order. The technology was new and untested. The television and video market in Britain is as sophisticated as any in the world. To establish satellite as a medium of choice meant changing British television consumption patterns, which had matured over the previous thirty years.

By the time of the BSkyB merger, Sky had cost News Corporation something of the order of £350 million. Though News Corporation is providing the day-to-day management and has kept its 48 per cent shareholding, it is holding onto control by a slender thread. The days of believing there was a market for the product and backing his hunches are over. It is now all about cash flow. After the merger, BSkyB was looking for a project loan of £380 million from the banks. It did not get it. The banks regarded the venture as highly speculative. They asked the major shareholders to give guarantees of £200 million before they would lend them £380 million. These terms were so unattractive that the shareholders of BSkyB lowered their sights and raised £200 million from their own pockets, though Reed International did not take up its rights at this stage. News Corporation found half this sum. But, because of the harsh terms of the rescue package that Murdoch has signed with the banks, he could not put this in as cash. Instead he has had to make up much of News Corporation's half in kind. This has come from rental on the Astra transponders, rights to films from his Hollywood film studios and programmes from Fox Television. It does not cover the full £100 million required and News Corporation will still have to find some cash during 1992. Given the tight restrictions imposed on him by the banks, it is hard to see where it will come from.

But this is not the only bad news for Rupert Murdoch. BSkyB may well need to go back to its shareholders for more money. The agreement which covers the £200-million capital-raising in 1991 also allows BSkyB to raise more capital from the shareholders if it requires. The 1991 News Corporation annual accounts suggest that the May agreement may just be the first in a 'series of rights issues' to 'secure future funding'. If this happens, then News Corporation will have to find the cash or equivalent value. If it does not, it will see its stake in BSkyB diluted. Persuading the bankers to allow him to put yet more money in just to stay in the game will be difficult, even for a consummate communicator like Murdoch. As far as many of them were concerned when they signed the agreement, News International's obligation to BSkyB was limited to finding £30 million of loan stock.[1]

For Murdoch the prospect of any return on his Sky investment remains as enticing as ever. The BSkyB management believes that break-even on operating costs is likely to be reached sometime in 1993. Much of the financing so far has been put in as loans. Even if BSkyB moves into operating profit, the repayments on the loan capital will probably not start until 1994 or 1995. The original terms of the Sky-BSB merger were very favourable to News Corporation. It received 80 per cent of the first £400 million of dividends, split the next £400 million 50:50 and then got 20 per cent of the final £400 million. Under the refinancing, the distribution of dividends on the new money, which equals 65 per cent of the equity, is split 50:50. In other words, News Corporation will only receive about 60 per cent of the first flow of dividends, not 80 per cent.

The other surprise problem is Ansett Airlines. News Corporation have held a large stake in Ansett since 1979 – at first 41 per cent, later increased to 49 per cent. The other half of the company is owned by the Australian transport company TNT, run by Murdoch's old crony Sir Peter Abeles. Ansett is a huge company. In the mid-1980s it employed 12,000 people and made very large profits by operating in a highly regulated market, free from serious competition. That is now changing and changing fast.

Throughout the 1980s, the internal airline business in Australia was controlled by the Airlines Agreement, which restricted the number of operators to two: Ansett and a sleepy Government-owned company called Australian Airlines. Airfares, routes and even equipment were all controlled by the Government which ensured that fares were set at a level which guaranteed the airlines a profit. It was a great business to be in. In many years News Corporation's share of Ansett's profits was substantial. In 1988 – a peak year – it accounted for 20 per cent of News Corporation's after-tax profits. But since then it has been subjected to something very unpleasant: competition.

The Australian Government decided in 1987 to bring the Airline Agreement to an end. As the law provided, it gave three years' notice but immediately started to gee up the performance of Australian Airlines. Under a new chief executive, James Strong, Australian Airlines took a high-profile marketing approach. Staff were retrained, line managers given more responsibility and costs were cut. Although it was not allowed to compete on price, Australian Airlines started to take market share from Ansett. But worse was to come for Ansett.

The end of the two-airline policy encouraged a former Ansett executive and personal assistant to Murdoch and Abeles to start up a third airline. Brian Grey was living in retirement on his sheep farm when his wife died and he was at a loss what to do. Going back into the airline business seemed a good idea and he started a new airline company called Compass.

But although the Government had decided to bring the Agreement to an end, it also made a secret pact at the end of 1986 to give thirty-year leases covering all the airport facilities to Ansett and Australian Airlines. This was a wonderful boost for Abeles and Murdoch. Without anywhere to fly from, Grey could not establish Compass as serious competition. However the Australian Government had not bargained for an opponent as intrepid as Brian Grey. He used the Australian Freedom of Information Act to get the details of the deal and the Government was forced to make a concession: at each airport Ansett and Australian Airlines had to provide a competitor with access to their boarding and landing gates.

This was still not much of a concession in Grey's view. He quickly calculated that he could not make money on this basis. Half of all Australia's flights go between Sydney and Melbourne and a further quarter go through just five airports. But with only two gates allocated, it was not possible for Compass to operate more than six planes a day. Given the capacity of the narrow-bodied planes, that meant there would not be enough passengers for Grey to produce a decent return.

Grey is convinced that Ansett had done the same sums as he did and so knew that the two-gate concession was worthless. What they had not bargained for was Grey's solution – use widebodied craft. Grey's Compass Airlines flew just as Ansett was trying to recover from a costly strike which cost it an estimated A$100 million.[2] Compass is a success. It has persistently taken market share from the competition: so much so that by June 1990 Ansett had to warn News Corporation that demand had fallen.

By June 1991, News Corporation's share of Ansett's operating losses was A$25 million, which the company attributed to 'deregulation and the ongoing recession'. News Corporation's Report added: 'While air travel has increased recently, deep price cutting by competition has forced Ansett to match these rates, which has eroded margins.' Hard words for the champion of deregulation to have to deliver to his shareholders.

In 1991 things have gone from bad to worse for Ansett. At the end of June its American offshoot, America West, had to file for protection under Chapter 11 of the US Bankruptcy Code – the American equivalent of calling in the receiver. It was the fifth American airline to do so in the face of a collapse in business. Ansett owned 20 per cent of American West Airlines. According to News Corporation's financial results for the year to June 1991, News Corporation has had to write off A$75 million as a result of Ansett's problems including Ansett's 20 per cent holding in American West Airlines. But there was worse news for Murdoch. A joint News Corporation and TNT aircraft-leasing venture was a major supplier to America West.

Ansett Worldwide Aviation Services (AWAS) is the world's third largest aircraft-leasing group. Because of the high costs of manufacturing planes, many of the world's airlines do not buy all their own planes. Instead, they rent – or lease – them from specialist firms such as AWAS. Typically AWAS will commit itself to leasing planes from the owner for twenty years and then find sublessees for shorter periods of time. This would usually be for five to ten years. The risk in the business comes when the sub-leases come to an end and AWAS has to find a new lessee. If there is no one to lease the aircraft, then the leasing company (AWAS) takes the hit.

Aircraft leasing is a typical Murdoch business: it is run on debt. At the end of June 1990 AWAS had outstanding commitments to aircraft owners of A$1,156 million more than it expected to get from lessees. Half of this was News Corporation's responsibility. In fact virtually all this liability was on leases that had more than five years to run. So everything is all right – so long as the lessees pay up. But by May 1991 America West could not afford to pay its monthly lease fee of A$2.35 million.

Unfortunately for AWAS – and News Corporation – America West is typical of the quality of AWAS customers. The names of the world's great airlines – British Airways,

United, Qantas – are not numbered among AWAS clients.
AWAS deals with second-tier airlines. Some of these are
heavily reliant on the charter market, which is very sensitive
to the recession. The pressure is now on AWAS. The market
in leases is softening while it still has to honour its
commitments, which are substantial. By the end of 1990 the
company had contracts to buy a further US$3.136 million
worth of aircraft.

When the rescuing banks looked at AWAS they decided
that, on balance, it was not too much of a risk for News
Corporation. But they did not anticipate such a collapse in
the market. Nor, it seems, did they realise just how deep the
recession was going to be in one of News Corporation's other
core businesses – Australian newspapers. This is one of the
prime areas where Murdoch might consider selling some
assets. Like many other parts of the empire, this too is beset
with problems. In the twelve months to June 1991 News
Corporation's Australian profits dropped by 22 per cent. In
addition Murdoch has continued to pay the price for the
HWT deal. During 1990-91 he had to write off A$35 million
on the loans to the proprietors of the *Sun* (Brisbane) and the
News (Adelaide).

In October 1990 Murdoch started to batten down the
hatches ready to face the coming recessionary storm. He
merged the Sydney papers, the *Daily Telegraph* and the *Daily
Mirror*, and in Melbourne the *Herald* and the *Sun
News-Pictorial*. The Melbourne closure cost A$15 million.
The papers, renamed the *Daily Telegraph-Mirror* and the
Herald-Sun, became 24-hour papers. As always, News
Corporation tried to put a brave face on this cost-saving
exercise by claiming that the new papers were meeting
readership demands and that the company was carrying out
'the biggest single initiative in Australian publishing since the
launch of our national daily *The Australian*, 26 years ago'. But

285

while this may have cut costs, it has left Murdoch with fewer papers to sell off to pay off his massive debts. More seriously, he is fast running out of potential buyers for his Australian papers, either international or domestic.

Australian companies are governed by rules which limit foreign ownership. Despite allowing the American citizen Rupert Murdoch to take over Australia's largest media group HWT in 1987, other 'foreigners' like the British Robert Maxwell have so far been kept out of Australian media. If Murdoch is to find an overseas buyer for any of his Australian papers, he will need to persuade the Australian Government to relax its rules on foreign ownership. Given his track record for changing the rules, this may not present him with a serious problem. If he cannot pull off this trick, he will have to find a domestic buyer for his papers.

This will not be easy. Many Australian media companies have gone bankrupt in the last couple of years after paying enormous sums for television stations. This has left few, if any, domestic buyers for Murdoch's papers. After the recent track record of Australia's entrepreneurs, many banks will now be leery of any other Australian companies wishing to burden themselves with debt through major acquisitions.

Even if he could find a buyer, the market for Australian media assets is soft. By the summer of 1991 there were too many media assets on the market. John Fairfax Group Pty Limited, Murdoch's only big competitor, went into receivership in 1990. The Fairfax papers, the *Sydney Morning Herald* and the *Age* in Melbourne, are the 'better' papers in the cities when compared to Murdoch's. Because they are more prestigious they attract the vast bulk of the classified advertising. This makes them much more financially viable. Murdoch himself has always wanted to get his hands on them, describing the papers as 'rivers of gold'. When Fairfax was first put into receivership there was a great deal of concern that Murdoch might make a move for them. This was before people realised Murdoch was in the market to sell titles, not buy them. His position was only slightly better than the young Fairfax chairman, Warwick Fairfax, who could not cover the interest payments on his debts.

Through the last forty years Murdoch has run his sprawling media empire as a personal fiefdom, answerable to no one. But now the rules have changed. Murdoch is no longer working for the shareholders, of which his family is the most significant. He is now working for the banks and will be doing so for the next few years.

Surviving until 1994 will require all Murdoch's legendary charm to soothe his bankers' jangled nerves. The process began in June 1991 when he addressed the world's leading bankers at the International Monetary Conference in Osaka. His theme was scarce capital and credit allocations. With debts of US$8 billion it was a theme on which he was uniquely qualified to speak. He charmed them, admitting to past mistakes of over-ambitious expansion based on short-term borrowing. He stressed the virtues of relationship banking, sticking with your regular bankers, rather than shopping around.

Surviving in the 1990s is a wholly different proposition from prospering in the 1980s. The rapid expansion of News Corporation and the shrill tone of Murdoch's tabloid newspapers fitted the years of right-wing populism under Mrs Thatcher and President Reagan. But the world has now changed dramatically. Murdoch's two closest allies have gone, only to be replaced by governments for whom getting things done is more important than any form of ideological commitment. It will be a testing time for Murdoch. His uncanny ability to read the public pulse appears to be weakening. The circulations of his tabloid newspapers are in decline.

Murdoch's problem is encapsulated in the *Sun*, the paper which has always been closest to his heart. Few papers have ever suited the age the way the *Sun* fitted the years of Mrs Thatcher. It matched her raucous right-wing idealism with its own unique blend of streetwise wit and popular prejudice. But as the decade finished, the *Sun* began to misjudge the popular mood. It launched a ludicrous attack on Liverpool football fans after the Hillsborough tragedy when 95 football fans were killed. Liverpool is a city with long memories. The *Sun*'s circulation collapsed and has never recovered. The *Sun* also launched a series of vituperative attacks on Elton John, without understanding just how popular he is with the paper's readers. In the end the *Sun* had to apologise and pay him £1 million libel damages.

The malaise is now deeper. The desire to shock and amaze on every page has meant that many stories are oversold. Throughout the 1980s, the *Sun* sensationalised and trivialised. It devalued the basic need of newspapers to tell stories which at least resemble the truth. But it is now becoming increasingly difficult for the paper to meet the public's appetite for the bizarre which it helped to create. Much to Murdoch's surprise he has suddenly discovered that the gutter has become a crowded place. The *Sun* now faces competition from the *Sunday Sport*, a mildly pornographic tabloid. Where the *Sun* has one pair of naked female breasts per issue, the *Sport* has several – and in colour. Where the *Sun* now launches attacks on the French and the Germans, the *Sport* has captured the market in the truly extraordinary, with headlines like 'WORLD WAR TWO BOMBER FOUND ON MOON – SCIENTISTS BAFFLED' and 'HITLER WAS A WOMAN'.

The first indication of how News Corporation was coping with the new world order came in August 1991 when it published its results for the year which ended in June. The press release was able to speak of an increase in operating profit before abnormal items of almost A$40 million to A$321.3 million. But both a cursory and more detailed examination show that recovery is still a long way off. News Corporation's own trading profits were unchanged, and if drawn up on a basis strictly comparable with the year before would have fallen. And the forced sales of assets meant that some were going at knock-down prices.

The costs of the rescue and the survival strategy amounted to over A$714 million – fees to banks, losses on the sale of investments and businesses and redundancy payments. These were all treated as 'abnormal items' and deducted from the after-tax profit. The pre-tax profit – which was not depressed by any of these costs – was 4.5 per cent lower at A$410 million, and around 10 per cent of this was (as in the previous year) gains made on trading in the foreign exchange market.

The 'pre-tax profit' is higher than the 'profit before abnormal items' largely because it is struck before paying dividends on preference shares. The increase in the profit before abnormal items to which the press release refers relies heavily on this reduction. Although useful it clearly does not reflect any change in the underlying trading position of the company. The profit before abnormal items also benefits from another very low tax charge – just 4.5 per cent. This subnormal tax charge is very similar to the level of recent years but is rather surprising as News Corporation were telling analysts in 1990 that they expected to start paying a more normal tax charge in future. News Corporation refuse to say whether they still expect this to happen, but a more normal tax charge of 30 per cent would cut A$100 million from profits. The results show a tax charge of A$99 million as an abnormal item. Again News Corporation refuse to explain this, but it may be the result of some previous year's tax ingenuity – which has succeeded only in deferring taxes not removing them completely.

Further close examination of the figures shows that operating profits were deteriorating sharply as the year went on – whilst total operating profits for the year were 14.3 per cent higher than in 1990, in the three months to the end of June they were down 5 per cent. ('Operating profits' are the profits before paying interest – which was still absorbing three quarters of the operating profits.)

More significant results included a full year's contribution from the book publisher HarperCollins. As explained in Chapter 11, the ownership of this company moved in and out of News Corporation – whilst remaining under Murdoch's control – to help reduce the apparent level of the company's debt. HarperCollins became a wholly owned subsidiary of News Corporation just before its year ended in June 1990 – so that year's results included only part of HarperCollins's profits. The 1991 results included a complete year for the book publisher and according to News Corporation this 'largely accounted for' the 25 per cent increase in the company's total income. In other words, the increase was not because of an improvement in the underlying trading position of HarperCollins but simply because of the changed accounting treatment. News Corporation refused to quantify the effect of this on their figures but the indications are that the underlying trading position at HarperCollins is deteriorating. News Corporation said that trade and general books sales were affected by the recession (that is, profits were down) and that the results from the religious books and school and college books were 'strong and performed ahead of expectations'. Translated, that probably means that profits were down, but not as much as feared.

In the UK the position was serious. News International lost £215.3 million before tax and exceptional items, which is equivalent to a loss of almost A$470 million. One reason for this loss is clearly Sky Television, though it is not easy to say precisely how much. This is because, once again, the accounting policies have come to Murdoch's rescue.

Until 3 November 1991 Sky was a subsidiary of News International and all its losses came into News International's profit and loss account. Then it was merged with BSB and the plan was that in future new finance would come in the form of loans from banks. Eventually it was impossible to arrange this and the shareholders agreed to put in more money themselves through a series of rights issues – though News Corporation will have to pay for their new shares in kind (cut-price films and so on) as the rescue agreement prevents the company investing more in BSkyB.

In the period between November 1990 and May 1991 when BSkyB was trying to raise its loan, News Corporation decided upon a controversial accounting treatment of their investment. They decided to treat the investment in BSkyB as a loan. The effect of this was that none of the losses went into the News Corporation profit and loss account. In fact, rather the opposite. News Corporation say: 'Under the terms of the merger agreement, the Group's investment in BSkyB was represented by a loan *on which interest would be paid on a current basis*' (our emphasis). From this it would seem as though for the six months from November to May BSkyB stopped being a drain on News Corporation's profit and loss account and actually contributed income in the form of interest. When we asked News Corporation to explain this, they refused. (They refused to answer all eight questions we asked about the results – a curious attitude for a communciations company, some of whose papers have financial pages which comment regularly on companies' financial results. A complete text of our letter is given in Appendix III.)

After the money-raising talks broke down in May 1991, News International had to treat BSkyB as an associate company and take in their share of its losses – a further £5 million at the operating level. If, in the intervening period, as seems likely, BSkyB actually contributed to profits, then it is quite possible that it did not make a pre-tax loss so far as the News International accounts are concerned. Quite an achievement as it was losing almost £2 million a week at the time.

But if this is so, which part of the UK operations were losing so much money? There is only one answer: the newspapers. Indeed, it is clear that the operating profits fell by over a quarter to £115 million but interest charges were likely to be up sharply as a result of the big investment in colour printing plants. News International themselves say that profits of the *Sun* and *News of the World* were higher than in 1990, so there is only one conclusion: *Today* and the quality papers are losing money on a handsome scale.

But if the UK is losing A$470 million and News Corporation as a whole is making A$447 million, including these losses, where are the profits being made? They are clearly not being made in Australia – where Murdoch has been forced to merge some of his papers, close one down and retrench as fast as possible – profits fell by more than a fifth. The big money is being made in America – in Fox Film and Television. Fox Television doubled its profits – and Fox Films hit the jackpot with three box-office hits – *Home Alone, Sleeping with the Enemy* and *Edward Scissorhands*. The irony is that this is one area of News Corporation about which Murdoch knows least and can interfere least – the contract of Fox's boss Barry Diller specifically confines Murdoch to an advisory role. Although the profits of Fox Television may be secure, repeating the trick of three box-office hits a year is a hard task in Hollywood.

The Future

America is now producing two thirds of operating profits and in view of the losses in the UK, probably over 100 per cent of group total profits. But it is a rather different story on the assets side. During last year Murdoch sold virtually all his US magazines except *TV Guide* for a total of US$650 million, taking a loss of around US$175 million on the deal. This is clear evidence that the titles which Murdoch still owns are valued in the News Corporation balance sheet at well above their current market value.

The nine magazines which News Corporation sold include some which they have owned for some years and two which were bought as part of the Triangle deal – *Daily Racing Form* and *Seventeen*. This means that the only title left from the Triangle deal is *TV Guide*. If one assumes that the US$650 million is largely accounted for by *Daily Racing Form* and *Seventeen*, then that means that *TV Guide* is now in the News Corporation at around US$2.3 billion. In the current market there is no way that it can be worth anything remotely approaching this amount. As the US$650 sale proceeds included various other titles, it is possible that *TV Guide* remains in the books at an even higher figure. We asked News Corporation to explain how the loss on this deal of US$175 million was arrived at but they refused to reply. In addition, they would not say whether, in view of these deals, the remaining titles would be written down to nearer their market value. But to be able to make a realistic assessment of the company's chances of meeting its asset disposal targets and of its financial condition, these questions have to be addressed.

News Corporation has to make further debt repayments of US$400 million by June 1992, December 1992 and June 1993. The problem for Murdoch is that everyone knows he is a forced seller. The question now is whether he will have to sell more assets at a loss to keep his bankers happy.

One of Murdoch's bankers told us that it has stuck with him because it has always seen him as a survivor. For its sake he needs to be. And they might be encouraged by a story told by an old friend of Murdoch's about going swimming with him at Shark Bay, along with a group of journalists. As they were splashing about and having fun a shark's fin appeared. It got closer and closer. There was a lot of screaming and everyone fled in panic. The last one out of the water was Rupert Murdoch.

Appendix I

Letter to Rupert Murdoch from Fulcrum Productions requesting information for the Channel 4 programme Empire (*transmitted 20 December 1990*).

Rupert Murdoch
Chief Executive
News Corporation
PO Box 495
Virginia Street
London E1 9XY

PRIVATE AND CONFIDENTIAL

26 November 1990

Dear Mr Murdoch,

As you are aware we are currently preparing a television programme for Channel 4 about News Corporation. I know that you feel unable to appear in the programme because of your other commitments, but there are several factual matters on which I believe either you or one of your staff may be able to help me. They are:

1. The valuation of UK newspaper titles and magazines

At 30 June 1990 the directors of News International placed a value of £1,068,000,000 on these assets. This represented a multiple of 7.52 times the pre-tax profits of the printing and publishing activities, compared with a multiple of 3.91 when they were last valued in 1987.

Please could you tell me the grounds on which the directors decided to use such a multiple, or what other considerations lead to the recent valuation.

2. Ownership of shares in Reuters plc

In June 1985 News International sold 24,739,190 B shares in Reuters to an associate company – News Offset; a year later these shares were repurchased by two News International subsidiaries, who granted an option over them to a News Corporation subsidiary incorporated in the Netherlands Antilles.

Please could you tell me:

a) the purpose of these transactions;

b) the amount of capital gains tax paid by News International plc, or subsidiary companies, on any disposal of these Reuters shares.

Appendix I

3. Dealings in shares of News Corporation Limited

Documents filed with the Sydney Stock Exchange show the following share dealings by yourself and Kayarem Pty Limited:

i) Between 21 July and 5 August 1988, the purchase by yourself of 2,394,000 call options in News Corporation.

ii) On 7, 8, 9 June 1989, the sale of 1.45 million shares in News Corporation by Kayarem.

iii) On 5 and 6 October 1989, the sale of 500,000 shares in News Corporation by Kayarem.

Please could you tell me why you decided on these transactions and whether in your view they comply with the provisions of Section 128 of the Securities Industry Act 1980.

4. Queensland Press

The 1988 accounts of the News Corporation associate Queensland Press disclose that in 1987-88 this company acquired a 16% stake in News Corporation from Cruden Investments. The same accounts reveal an increase from $12,000 to $670 million in Queensland's long term debt. It therefore appears as though Queensland has borrowed money to buy the shares in News Corporation and that Cruden has benefitted accordingly.

Please can you confirm the details of this transaction and explain why it was thought in the interests of News Corporation shareholders for its associate company to undertake this investment? Please could you tell me whether Cruden has made either a capital distribution or paid a dividend as a result of this transaction?

5. Dexenne Pty Limited

This company, which appears to be under the control of News Corporation and Cruden, has an investment in News Corporation convertible notes.

Please can you tell the circumstances in which this investment was made and what the purpose of Dexenne is?

I look forward to hearing from you,

Your sincerely

Christopher Hird

Appendix II

Rupert Murdoch's reply to Fulcrum Productions' letter

1. The valuation of UK newspaper titles and magazines

UK newspapers and magazine titles are revalued every third year. The first valuation was in June 1984, the second in June 1987 and the third in June 1990. Valuations are done by an independent outside company, Hambros Securities Limited. We do not contribute to the valuations other than by supplying information to Hambros which they then use to arrive at their independent valuation. The figure appearing in our accounts represents 70% of the value placed on the titles by Hambros.

2. Ownership of shares in Reuters plc

As a result of the Reuters' flotation in 1984, News Group Newspapers (12,503,368) and Times Newspapers Limited (12,232,822) had a total of 24,736,190 'B' shares. In 1985, these shares were sold to a company called News Offset Limited for £3.13 each.

News Offset was owned 50% by News International plc

and 50% by a company called Newsett Limited which was owned 50% by News International plc and 50% by Ansett Transport Industries.

News Offset used the shares as collateral for a loan arranged through Swiss Bank Corporation of £50m.

Both Newsett Limited and News Offset Limited were treated as associate companies of News International plc for Companies Act purposes and not as subsidiaries.

In 1986 the shares were repurchased by two News International plc subsidiaries, Lyntress Limited and Salcombe Securities Limited (50% each) for £108,836,236.

At the same time Newscorp Finance N.V., a Netherlands Antilles-based Newscorp subsidiary company, issued 200,000 Exchangeable Guaranteed Redeemable Preference Shares exchangeable into Reuters' shares at the option of the shareholders. To date, a vast majority of these shares have been exchanged and only 810,969 remain of which Lyntress Limited holds 405, 484 and Salcombe Securities 405,485.

The taxable capital gain was not incurred until the Reuters' shares were exchanged for the Preference Shares as all prior transfers had been tax free intra-group transfers. These exchanges took place mostly in 1989 and 1990. Due to uncertainties on the 1982 value of the Reuters' shares and the correspondence on tax losses available to certain companies within the News International group, no computation of the capital gains tax has yet been finalised. But, of course, capital gains tax will be paid on this transaction if required.

3. Dealings in shares of News Corporation Limited

I regard shares in The News Corporation Limited as a good investment and, despite our efforts to provide as much information as possible to the market regarding the company, typically undervalued by the market.

This was my view at the time the call options were acquired. Unfortunately, the market did not agree, at least during the period of the call options, and the options were allowed to lapse as shares could be acquired on the market more cheaply than under the options.

The directors of Kayarem share my views regarding the virtues of News Corporation shares as an investment, and the company invests surplus funds in such shares when it can. You will appreciate, however, that Kayarem has other commitments, and occasionally disposes of News Corporation shares to obtain funds to meet these commitments.

Those responsible for making investment decisions within Kayarem and I are each well aware of our obligations under Section 128 of the Securities Industry Code. I do not see any reason why the transactions to which you refer would not have complied with that section of the Code, since I do not believe that those responsible for the decisions made in relation to the transactions had any price sensitive insider information at the time of any of the transactions.

In any case, the notices to which you refer are made public by being filed with the Australian Stock Exchange, and are the subject of a good deal of media interest in Australia when they are filed. There has never been any suggestion in the media or by relevant Australian authorities of any non-compliance or concern.

301

4. Queensland Press

At the beginning of 1987, Queensland Press Limited was owned as to 46% by The Herald & Weekly Times Limited and as to the remainder by the public. QPL has a history of investment in shares in media companies. For example, it progressively built up a holding of 40% in Provincial Newspapers (Queensland) Limited and took a position of 27% in Brisbane TV Limited, but by far its largest asset at the time was a 27% holding in HWT, which had been progressively built up from a 7% holding in 1959.

In January 1987, a subsidiary of News Corporation made a takeover offer for HWT. Prior to the takeover offer succeeding, QPL's independent board decided to accept the offer, selecting News Corporation convertible notes as QPL's desired consideration. Together with News Corporation's existing holding of HWT shares and other acceptances, this acceptance gave News Corporation compulsory acquisition powers. HWT thereby became a wholly owned subsidiary of News Corporation. In consequence, News Corporation became entitled to a 46% interest in QPL through HWT.

In March 1987, a wholly owned subsidiary of Cruden Investments Pty Limited made a takeover offer for the 54% of the shares in QPL held publicly. Cruden Investments is a private company associated with the Murdoch family, and has for many years directly or indirectly owned the bulk of shares in News Corporation usually attributed to me and my family. The takeover offer was successful and, in the result, QPL became a 54% subsidiary of Cruden Investments and more of a private company also, having ceased to be a public listed company.

Appendix II

In late 1987, QPL was given the opportunity to acquire approximately 42 million News Corporation shares (amounting to approximately 15.6% of News Corporation's present issued capital) from Cruden Investments. Against the background of QPL's history of investment in media company shares, the QPL board took up the opportunity. They apparently took the view that, together with HWT's existing holding of convertible notes in News Corporation, the shares would give QPL a substantial position in probably the most dynamic and successful media company in the world. No member of the Cruden Investments board or member of the Murdoch family participated in the QPL board's decision, or was present when it was made. When the convertible notes convert to shares in 1992, QPL's total holding of News Corporation shares will amount to approximately 21% of News Corporation's then issued share capital.

The QPL board has recently indicated that, having regard to the future prospects of News Corporation and its present asset backing, QPL is completely satisfied with its investment in News Corporation, which it regards as long term. The interest cost of the purchase is covered by internal cash flow, and the company's long term cash flow forecasts indicate that it will be able to handle its debt obligations and capital projects.

Cruden Investments has made no capital distribution nor paid any special dividend as a result of QPL's acquisition of News Corporation shares from Cruden Investments. The only dividends paid by Cruden Investments have been of monies representing dividends paid by News Corporation on News shares held by the Cruden Investment group.

303

5. Dexenne Pty Limited

Dexenne was inherited with the takeovers of HWT and QPL mentioned above. It was established prior to News Corporation's takeover of HWT as, and still is, an investment company owned as to 50% by HWT and as to the other 50% by QPL.

Each of Advertiser Newspapers Limited (publisher of the Adelaide Advertiser) and Davies Bros Limited (publisher of the Hobart Mercury) had significant holdings of HWT shares at the time of News Corporation's takeover offer for HWT, and in turn HWT had significant holdings in each of Advertiser and Davies Bros. In common with QPL's board, the then independent boards of Advertiser and Davies Bros decided to accept News Corporation's offer, and selected the convertible notes consideration. As a result, each company became a holder of an appreciable number of News Corporation convertible notes, and through its acquisition of HWT, News Corporation became entitled to substantial interests in each of Advertiser and Davies Bros.

At the beginning of 1988 News Corporation, through HWT, made what turned out to be successful takeover offers for the outstanding shares in Advertiser and Davies Bros, and they became wholly owned subsidiaries.

Later in 1988, the News Corporation convertible notes held by Advertiser and Davies Bros were transferred to Dexenne, consistently with applicable Australian legal requirements and accounting principles. The requirements were to the effect that the notes should not be retained by a News group, at least after conversion, if not before, and accounting principles supported this approach. Retention by a company such as Dexenne, however, was permissible and was a procedure similar to that which had been adopted by some other notable Australian companies (such as BHP) in respect of shares in themselves. The price for the notes was marginally above the then market price and had been advised by well regarded independent valuers as being fair.

Appendix III

The cross-shareholding structure between Herald and Weekly Times and its affiliates Queensland Press and Advertiser Newspapers before News Corporation's takeover bid in December 1986.

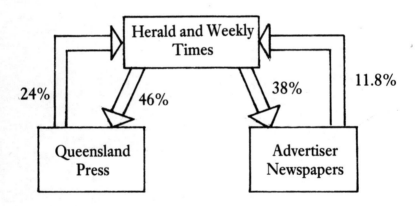

Appendix IV

Letter from Fulcrum Productions to News Corporation regarding their 1991 Financial Results

Jane Reed
News International plc
PO Box 405
Virginia Street
London E1

6 September 1991

Dear Jane,

Following our telephone conversation today, here are my questions about the News International and News Corporation results.

1. Among the abnormal items in News Corp's figures is a A$35 million write-off in relation to loans to the proprietors of the Brisbane Sun and the Adelaide News. I have four questions about this:

i) How has this write-off arisen? In particular, has it arisen as a result of loans made by Citibank to either Northern Star Holdings or the existing proprietors of these papers?

ii) I believe at the time of the refinancing Citibank agreed not to seek to collect the money due under these arrangements. Have they now decided to demand payment?

iii) Does News Corp have any claim against any other company or person in relation to these loans?

iv) As this appears to be a contingent liability, where in the 1990 News Corp accounts was this liability disclosed?

Tax. I have three questions in this area.

i). The News Corp tax charge is shown at 4.5%. Last year several analysts' reports said that News Corp expected to pay nearer a normal tax charge in future. Is this the case and when is it expected to be so?

ii) Note B says that the Income Tax charge is A$146 million higher than the prima facie expense. How does this reconcile with the A$18.63 million expense shown in the figures?

iii) What are the A$549.1 million of losses not tax effected?

iv) How did the A$98.977 million income tax expense on abnormal items arise?

308

3. At least one of the American magazine titles which was sold at a loss was purchased as part of a group of magazines – some of which remain in the company's ownership. How were such losses calculated and allocated to individual titles?

4. As it is clear that there has been a fall in the values of the company's titles, will the 1991 accounts include a revaluation of those titles retained?

5. What impact has the consolidation of HarperCollins for a full year had on the trading profits before interest and abnormal items?

6. There is a substantial reduction in the minority interest charge. I assume that this is because of the redemption of various preference shares. Please can you confirm that this is the case?

7. Please can you explain how the losses on the Reuters and Pearson shares has arisen? Does this mean that the shares were transferred from News International to (I assume) the companies in the Cayman Islands and the Netherlands Antilles, at less than their cost to News International?

8. Sky/BSB. I am not sure that I have understood the accounting treatment of this properly. Was it as follows: to 3.11.90 Sky's operating losses were included; from November to May interest on the loan to BSkyB is included; from May equity accounted losses of £5 million have been included?

I look forward to hearing from you as soon as possible,

Yours sincerely

Christopher Hird

Appendix V

Kayarem Filing with the Australian Stock Exchange, 19 August 1988

From 21 July to 29 July, 1988 and on 3 and 5 August, 1988, 2,394,000 call options over shares in The News Corporation Limited were acquired on the Stock Exchange as follows, in consequence of which Mr. Murdoch obtained a relevant interest in the shares the subject of such options.

100,000 call options at $0.65 per option
225,000 call options at $0.85 per option
375,000 call options at $1.00 per option
 80,000 call options at $1.10 per option
344,000 call options at $1.25 per option
370,000 call options at $1.30 per option
900,000 call options at $1.35 per option

Appendix VI

Kayarem Filing with the Australian Stock Exchange, 16 October 1989

B. Particulars relating to change:

(a) The dates of change in relevant interest were:

1. 7th June, 1989
2. 8th June, 1989
3. 9th June, 1989
4. 5th October, 1989
5. 6th October, 1989

(b) Particulars of the valuable consideration given in relation to the change, including nature of that part that did not consist of money, are as follows (and as set out in (c) below):

1.   300,000 shares at $14.70 per share
2. 1,000,000 shares at $15.41 per share
3.   150,000 shares at $16.57 per share
4.   232,200 shares at $16.45 per share
5.   267,800 shares at $16.62 per share

Appendix VII

(i) Ownership structure of the companies involved in the Reuters'
share transactions

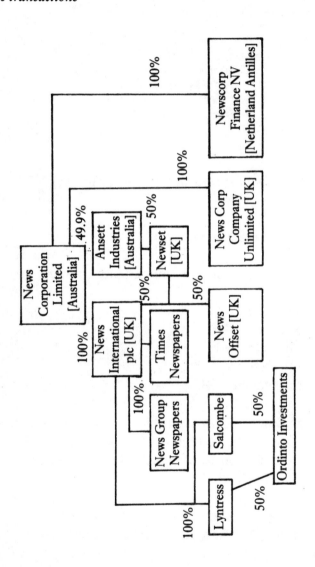

Appendix VIII

(ii) Flowchart of News Corporation's ownership of Reuters' shares

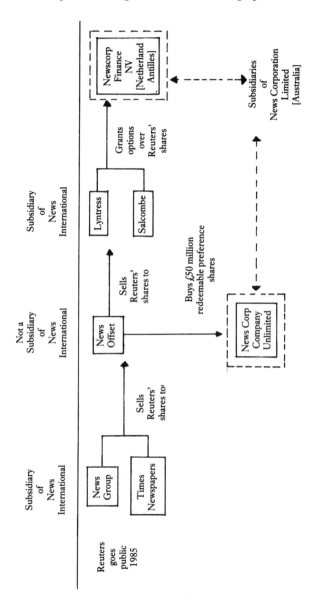

Notes

Introduction

1. *New York Times, Financial Review*, 16 November 1990.
2. News Corporation, 20-F Filing with the Securities and Exchange Commission, Washington DC, USA, 1990.
3. Ibid., pp. 58, 59.
4. Thomas Kiernan, *Citizen Murdoch* (New York, Dodd, Mead & Co., 1986), p. 23.
5. Off-the-record conversation with the authors.
6. Off-the-record conversation with the authors.
7. *Times on Sunday*, 15 February 1987, as quoted in John Pilger, *A Secret Country* (Vintage, London 1989).
8. Quoted in the *Sydney Morning Herald*, 2 February 1991.

Chapter 1   Chronology

1. George Munster, *Paper Prince* (Australia, Viking, 1985), p. 34.
2. Ibid., pp. 70–1.
3. Ibid., p. 73.
4. Thomas Kiernan, *Citizen Murdoch*.
5. Australian Senate Debates 1976, vol. S67, p. 359.

6. Michael Leapman, *Barefaced Cheek* (London, Hodder and Stoughton, 1983), p. 101.
7. Ibid., p. 243.
8. Ibid., p. 251.
9. Jerome Tuccille, *Murdoch: A Biography* (New York, Piatkus, 1989), p. 106.
10. Ibid., p. 114.
11. Ibid., pp. 119–24 and News International, Report and Accounts, 1984 and 1985.

Chapter 2   Manipulation: Murdoch Learns his Trade

1. Munster, *Paper Prince*, p. 35.
2. Kiernan, *Citizen Murdoch*, p. 259.
3. Off-the-record conversation with the authors.
4. Frank Giles, *Sunday Times* (London, John Murray, 1986), p. 249.
5. Ibid., p. 229.
6. Paul Chadwick, *Media Mates* (Macmillan Australia, 1989), p. xxxiii.
7. Munster, *Paper Prince*, p. 87.
8. Ibid., p. 136.
9. Ibid., p. 141.
10. Chadwick, *Media Mates*, p. xxxv.
11. Munster, *Paper Prince*, p. 101.
12. Ibid., pp. 100–2.
13. Conversation with a journalist present at the time.
14. Chadwick, *Media Mates*, p.xxxv.
15. Ibid.
16. Interview for *Empire*, a Channel 4 television programme made by Fulcrum Productions Limited, London, 20 December 1990.
17. Kiernan, *Citizen Murdoch*, p. 168.
18. Ibid., p. 171.
19. Ibid.

20. Kym Bergmann, *The Press as King-Maker* (Canberra, Australian National University, 1980), p. 72.
21. Munster, *Paper Prince*, p. 108.
22. Ibid., pp. 106–7.
23. Letter quoted in Bergmann, *The Press as King-Maker*, pp. 60–1.
24. Ibid.
25. *The Australian*, 14 November 1975, as quoted in Munster, *Paper Prince*, p. 110.
26. Ibid., p. 111.
27. *The Australian*, 6 December 1975.
28. Munster, *Paper Prince*, p. 112.
29. Ibid., p.114.
30. *The Australian*, 5 March 1976, as quoted in Munster, *Paper Prince*, p. 114.
31. Gough Whitlam, *The Whitlam Government 1972–75* (Australia, Viking, 1985), p. 581.
32. Munster, *Paper Prince*, p. 102.
33. Ibid., p. 103.
34. In conversation with the authors.
35. In conversation with the authors.
36. Munster, *Paper Prince*, p. 186.
37. Transcripts A, p. 223 as published in Munster, *Paper Prince*, p. 188.
38. Munster, *Paper Prince*, pp. 186–9.
39. Ibid., p. 189.
40. Ibid., p. 191.
41. ABT Inquiry (Canberra, Australian Government Publishing Service, 1980), p. 29.
42. Ibid., p. 28.
43. Off-the-record conversation with the authors.
44. ABT Inquiry, p. 31.
45. Ibid., p. 36.
46. Ibid.
47. Ibid.
48. Ibid, p. 37.
49. *Sydney Morning Herald*, 15 December 1979.

50. Ibid.
51. Munster, *Paper Prince*, p. 197.
52. For a full account of the ABT hearings see Munster, *Paper Prince*, pp. 185–203.
53. Ibid., p. 198.
54. ABT Inquiry, p. 64.
55. Munster, *Paper Prince*, p. 199.
56. Munster, *Paper Prince*, p. 200
57. In conversation with the authors.
58. *The Australian*, 18 July 1981, quoted in Munster, *Paper Prince*, p. 203.
59. Munster, *Paper Prince*, p. 203.
60. In conversation with the authors.

Chapter 3   *The Times*

1. Peter Chippendale and Chris Horrie, *Stick it up your Punter* (London, William Heinemann, 1990), p. 24.
2. Harold Evans, *Good Times, Bad Times* (London, Weidenfeld and Nicolson, 1983), ch. 9.
3. Leapman, *Barefaced Cheek*, p. 150.
4. Munster, *Paper Prince*, p.226.
5. Ibid., p. 227.
6. He bought out the remaining Special Dividend Shares in 1983.
7. *Sunday Times*, 15 February 1981.
8. Ibid.
9. Ibid.
10. Ibid.
11. Evans, *Good Times, Bad Times*, p. 218.
12. Lawrenson and Barber, *The Price of Truth: Story of the Reuters Millions* (London, Mainstream, 1985).
13. *Panorama*, BBC television programme, 1981.
14. *Sunday Times*, 15 February 1981.
15. *Sunday Times*, 15 February 1981.
16. Munster, *Paper Prince*, p. 228.

17. Evans, *Good Times, Bad Times*, p. 191.
18. *Sunday Times*, 15 February 1981.
19. Ibid.
20. In conversation with the authors, December 1990.
21. Kiernan, *Citizen Murdoch*, p. 311.
22. Vic Giles in an interview for *Empire*.
23. News Corporation, Annual Report, 1982.
24. News Corporation, Annual Report, 1981.
25. Evans, *Good Times, Bad Times*, p. 18.
26. Ibid., p. 24.
27. *The Clarion*, 8 December 1986 (printed by the Australian Journalists' Association, Sydney).
28. Giles, *Sundry Times*, p. 202.
29. Ibid., p. 203.
30. Ibid.
31. Evans, *Good Times, Bad Times*, p. 19.
32. Interview with Mike Royko.
33. Hugo Young, *Rupert Murdoch and The Sunday Times: A Lamp Goes Out*, Political Quarterly, vol 55, Issue No. 4, Oct-Dec 1984, pp. 382–90.
34. *The Clarion*, December 1986.
35. Evans, *Good Times, Bad Times*, p. 18.
36. Ibid.
37. News Corporation, Annual Report, 1982.

Chapter 4   Wapping

1. For a wonderful account of this story read *Selling Hitler* by Robert Harris (London, Faber, 1987), which was made into a television series by Thames Television in 1991.
2. Giles, *Sundry Times*.
3. Dimity Torbett, 'Rupert Murdoch in his own and others' words' (Sydney, News Unlimited Conference, February 1989).
4. Bert Hardy, in conversation with the authors.

5. Linda Melvern, *The End of the Street* (London, Methuen, 1986), pp. 121–5.
6. His advice was leaked and published in the *Journalist*, October 1980.
7. Melvern, *The End of the Street*, p. 131.
8. *The Times*, 30 December 1985.
9. Melvern, *The End of the Street*, p. 8.
10. Ibid., p. 14.
11. Ibid., p. 17.
12. Ibid., p. 18.
13. Ibid., p. 19.
14. Ibid., p. 21.
15. Letter from Geoffrey Richards to Bruce Matthews, 20 December 1985.
16. Torbett, 'Rupert Murdoch in his own and others' words'.
17. Melvern, *The End of the Street*, p. 125.
18. Chippendale and Horrie, *Stick it up your Punter*, p. 196.
19. Magnus Linklater and David Leigh, *Not With Honour*, (London, Sphere Books, 1986).
20. Torbett, 'Rupert Murdoch in his own and others' words'.

Chapter 5 Fox

1. Rupert Murdoch's speech to United Cerebral Palsy dinner, New York, 10 January 1991.
2. Kiernan, *Citizen Murdoch*, p. 272.
3. Ibid., pp. 273–4.
4. In conversation with the authors, October 1990.
5. Alex Ben Block, *Outfoxed*, (New York, St Martin's Press, 1990).
6. Ibid., pp. 61–2.
7. Within months of this deal Davis had sold his remaining share in 20th Century-Fox, and News Corporation was able to announce its plans for the fourth network.
8. News Corporation, Annual Report, 1986.
9. Block, *Outfoxed*, p. 103.

10. Kiernan, *Citizen Murdoch*, p. 260.
11. Tuccille, *Murdoch: A Biography*, p. 127.
12. Mark Fowler in conversation with the authors, October 1990.
13. In conversation with the authors, October 1990.
14. Letter from Federal Communications Commission to Efren Palacios, 7 October 1982.
15. *New York Times*, 5 September 1985.
16. Australian Broadcasting Tribunal, *Report*, 1979, and *Sydney Morning Herald*, 7 May 1985.
17. Federal Communications Commission, *Second Report and Order*, paras 1079–80, 1975.
18. Media Access Project, Petition to deny submission to the FCC, 5 August 1985.
19. Associated Press report from memo to staff, 10 May 1985.
20. News America Television Inc., Submission to FCC, 20 August 1985, p. 7.
21. *Washington Post*, 9 May 1985.
22. *New York Times*, 10 May 1985.
23. *Chicago Tribune*, 10 May 1985.
24. *New York Times*, 9 May 1985.
25. Media Access Project, Petition to deny submission to FCC, 5 August 1985.
26. Affidavit of Stanley Shuman, filed with News America Television, Submission to FCC, 16 August 1985.
27. Ibid.
28. FCC 85–606 36249, *in re* Application of Metromedia Radio and Television, November 1985.
29. Ibid.
30. Interviews for *Empire*.
31. Media Access Project, Submission to FCC, 5 August 1985.
32. Ibid.
33. News America Television Inc., Submission to FCC, 20 August 1985.
34. Ibid.
35. *New York Times*, 23 August 1985.
36. News America Television Inc., Application to FCC 314, 22 June 1985.

37. Block, *Outfoxed*, p. 106.
38. Statement by Mark S. Fowler, chairman of FCC, November 1985.
39. *Australian Bulletin*, 28 May 1985, quoted in Media Access Project, Submission to FCC.
40. David Johnson, interview for *Empire*.
41. In conversation with the authors, October 1990.
42. Block, *Outfoxed*, p. 156.
43. In conversation with the authors, October 1990.
44. David Johnson, in conversation with the authors, November 1990.
45. Block, *Outfoxed*, p. 227.
46. Television Network Broadcasting, CL Global Partners, July 1989.
47. David Johnson in conversation with the authors, November 1990.
48. Annual accounts of Times Newspapers Holdings Limited and News Group Newspapers Limited.
49. Block, *Outfoxed*, p. 248.
50. Ibid., p. 226.

Chapter 6   HWT and Queensland Press

1. *More* magazine, November 1977.
2. Munster, *Paper Prince*, p. 181.
3. V. J. Carroll, *The Man Who Couldn't Wait* (William Heinemann Australia, 1991), p. 94.
4. Interview with the authors, March 1991.
5. News Corporation, Annual Report, 1986.
6. Kiernan, *Citizen Murdoch*, p. 229.
7. Ibid., pp. 228, 229.
8. Carroll, *The Man Who Couldn't Wait*, p. 97.
9. Interview with the authors, 1991.
10. In conversation with the authors.
11. *The Age*, 26 December 1986.
12. *The Age*, 3 January 1987.

13. Chadwick, *Media Mates*, p. 57. *Media Mates* provides an excellent account of the HWT takeover.
14. *Independent Monthly*, March 1991, based on an interview with Keating by Max Suich.
15. Chadwick, *Media Mates*, p. 58
16. Ibid.
17. Ibid.
18. Ibid.
19. *Sydney Morning Herald*, 6 March 1991.
20. *Independent Monthly*, March 1991.
21. Interview with the authors, March 1991.
22. Chadwick, *Media Mates*, pp. 61, 62.
23. Ibid., pp. 61–4.
24. Ibid., pp. 63–4.
25. Chadwick, *Media Mates*, p. 65.
26. Ibid.
27. Ibid., pp. 62–3.
28. Ibid., p. 66.
29. Off-the-record conversation.
30. In an interview with the authors, March 1991.
31. *Sydney Morning Herald*, 30 July 1988.
32. Interview with the authors, March 1991.
33. Chadwick, *Media Mates*, pp. 70–1.
34. Ibid., pp. 71–2.
35. *The Age*, 22 January 1987.
36. Chadwick, *Media Mates*, pp. 78, 79.
37. Ibid.
38. Ibid., p. 81.
39. Chadwick, *Media Mates*, p. 83.
40. John D'Arcy in an interview with the authors, March 1991.
41. Interview with the authors, March 1991.
42. Offer document for HWT, 7 January 1987.
43. Cruden Investments Pty, Part A Filing with Queensland Commission for Corporate Affairs.
44. Off-the-record conversation with the authors.
45. *Sydney Morning Herald*, 1 August 1988.
46. *Sydney Morning Herald*, 1 August 1988.

47. The News Corporation, County NatWest Securities, Sydney, March 1990.
48. Memorandum from Citibank and Samuel Montagu & Co. to 'Dolphin Lenders', 19 December 1990.
49. Ibid.
50. Off-the-record conversation.
51. Citicorp memo, see note 42.

Chapter 7   Sky: The European Dream

1. News Corporation, Annual Report, 1983.
2. News Corporation, Annual Report, 1984.
3. News Corporation, Annual Report, 1984.
4. News Corporation, Annual Report, 1984.
5. News Corporation, Annual Report, 1983.
6. News Corporation, Annual Report, 1983.
7. News Corporation, Annual Report, 1984.
8. News Corporation, Annual Report, 1984.
9. News Corporation, Annual Report, 1985.
10. News International plc, Annual Report, 1986.
11. News Corporation, Annual Report, 1986.
12. MTV is an American pop video programme.
13. News Corporation, Annual Report, 1987.
14. Sky Television, Annual Report and Accounts.
15. *Sunday Times Business World*, 23 June 1991.

Chapter 8   Pie in the Sky

1. News Corporation, Annual Report, 1988, p. 39.
2. *New York Times, Financial Review*, 16 November 1990.
3. *The Times*, 11 October 1986.
4. *Sun*, 11 October 1986.
5. News Corporation, 20-F Filing with the Securities and Exchange Commission, Washington DC, USA, 1989, p. 36.
6. *The Times*, 4 February 1989.
7. *News of the World*, 5 February 1989.

8. Sky Television, Report and Accounts, 1989, p. 13.
9. News Corporation, Annual Report, 1989, p. 69.
10. *The Independent*, 7 November 1990.
11. *The Independent*, 4 November 1990.
12. *The Independent*, 10 November 1990.
13. In May 1991 W.H. Smith sold its satellite and cable interests to a consortium which included the existing management, Canal+, the French television company, Capital Cities/ABC, the American communications group, and Compagnie des Eaux, the ambitious and expansive French water company, for £65 million. A more modest venture than Sky, it had already absorbed £80 million, required further capital and is still two years away from break-even.

Chapter 9   The Purchase of *TV Guide*

1. Rupert Murdoch in an interview with David Frost on London Weekend Television, 1973, quoted in Leapman, *Barefaced Cheek*, p. 50.
2. News Corporation, Annual Report, 1987.
3. *Newsday*, 9 August, 1988.
4. UK Press *Gazette*, 15 August 1988.
5. Quoted in *Financial Review*, 10 August 1988.
6. *Los Angeles Times*, 19 August 1988.
7. *Newsday*, 8 August 1988.
8. *NewsWeek*, 22 August 1988.
9. *Financial Review*, 10 August 1988.
10. *NewsWeek*, 22 August 1988.
11. *San Francisco Chronicle*, 8 August 1988.
12. Private conversation with former *TV Guide* executive.
13. Rupert Murdoch, quoted in the *Sydney Morning Herald*, 2 February 1991.
14. Statement from Rupert Murdoch to Fulcrum Productions Limited for *Empire*.
15. Lex column, *Financial Times*, 9 August 1988.

16. Andrew Schwartzman, quoted extensively in newspapers at the time including the *Guardian*, 8 August 1988.
17. See Chapter 8 for examples.
18. *Newsday*, 8 August 1988.

Chapter 10   The Trashing of *TV Guide*

1. *Los Angeles Times*, 30 November 1988.
2. For a fuller account of this story see Leapman, *Barefaced Cheek*, pp. 91–2.
3. Rupert Murdoch in a speech to the Newspaper Publishers' Association, 1977, quoted in Leapman, *Barefaced Cheek*, pp. 106–7.
4. News Corporation, Annual Report, 1989, p. 26.
5. Interview with Mike Royko for *Empire*.
6. Ibid.
7. *NewsWeek*, 22 August 1988.
8. Interview with *NewsWeek*, 22 August 1988.
9. Quoted in the *Sydney Morning Herald*, 2 February 1991.
10. *Sydney Morning Herald*, 2 February 1991.
11. *Sunday Telegraph*, 30 September 1990.
12. *Wall Street Journal*, 19 October 1990.
13. Interview with Heather Goodchild.
14. *Los Angeles Times*, 8 August 1988.
15. Private conversation with former *TV Guide* writer, relayed to the authors.

Chapter 11   The Debt Machine

1. Quoted in Tuccille, *Murdoch: A Biography*.
2. Cruden Investments' document filed with the Melbourne Corporate Affairs' Commission.
3. In conversation with the authors.
4. In conversation with the authors.
5. Quoted in *Institutional Investor*, November 1989.

6. The News Corporation Ltd., *A Cloud Called Australian GAAP*, Prudential Bache Securities, 6 January 1989.
7. News International, Accounts, 1989.
8. News Corporation, Accounts, 1988, note 1(i).
9. News Corporation, 20-F Filing with Securities and Exchange Commission, Washington DC, USA, 1988, note 21(i).
10. Gary S. Schieneman, 'The News Corporation Revisited', *International Strategy Weekly*, Prudential Bache Securities, 12 February 1990.
11. Gary S. Schieneman, *International Accounting Perspectives*, Prudential Bache Securities, 6 January 1989.
12. Block, *Outfoxed*, p. 94.
13. That is, the shareholding is 50 per cent or less.
14. Cecil King, *The Cecil King Diary, 1970–1974* (London, Jonathan Cape, 1975), p. 111.
15. Schieneman, 'The News Corporation Revisited'.
16. Letter from Rupert Murdoch to authors, December 1990.
17. Gary Schieneman, in an interview with the authors, November 1990.
18. Conversation with a former Harper executive.
19. *News Corporation Limited* (Australia, County NatWest Securities, March 1990).
20. *Independent*, 9 June 1989.
21. *Financial Times*, 8 March 1989.
22. *Wall Street Journal*, 3 March 1989.
23. *Independent*, 9 June 1989.
24. Letter to authors.
25. *Financial Times*, 5 June 1989.
26. Filings with Sydney Stock Exchange.
27. Australian House of Representatives' Standing Committee on Finance and Public Administration, *Tax Payers or Tax Players* (The Martin Report), p. 63.
28. News Corporation, 20-F Filing with Securities and Exchange Commission, Washington DC, 1986, pp. F1–28.
29. *Institutional Investor*, November 1989.
30. Block, *Outfoxed*, p. 107.
31. *Wall Street Journal*, 16 May 1986.

32. News Corporation, 20-F Filing with the Securities and Exchange Commission, Washington DC, USA, 1988, p. F22.
32. News Group Newspapers Limited, Accounts, 1987.

Chapter 12   The Party's Over

1. Memorandum from Citicorp and Samuel Montagu & Co. to 'Dolphin Lenders', 19 December 1990.
2. Ibid.
3. The eventual outcome was that Continental agreed at the end of September to lend News International US$10 million to satisfy the Circle K loan. This loan was only for a period of 30 days and was eventually repaid out of the restructuring of News Corporation's debt in 1991. In 1991 News Corporation wrote off the whole of its investment in CKHL at a cost of US$25 million.
4. *Wall Street Journal*, 12 April 1990.
5. *Financial Times*, 4 April 1991.
6. 20-F Filing with the Securities and Exchange Commission, Washington DC, USA, January 1991.
7. News International, Accounts, 1987, p. 18.
8. News International, Report and Accounts, 1990, p. 19.
9. Circulation of News Corporation national titles. Averages for 6 months ending:

	June 1987	June 1988	June 1989	June 1990
The Times	442,375	450,626	441,342	432,453
Sunday Times	1,220,021	1,362,743	1,317,865	1,186,667
Sun	3,993,031	4,146,644	4,137,267	3,936,692
News of World	4,941,966	5,213,901	5,294,317	5,036,019
*Today**	307,356	408,078	548,362	581,240

Advertising volume of UK titles for 12-month period ending:

	June 1987	June 1988	June 1989	June 1990
The Times	34,931	38,369	41,346	38,317
Sunday Times	23,198	26,577	30,428	26,961
Sun	20,575	22,906	25,839	24,405
News of World	7,183	8,057	8,267	7,146
Today*	25,475	24,927	29,054	27,618

* News International took over *Today* in July 1987.

Source: News Corporation's 20-F filings to SEC, 1988 and 1990. Circulation figures as published by the Audit Bureau of Circulations; advertising volumes expressed as columns based on News International figures.

10. There are other indications that News Corporation was putting the best gloss possible on its figures in 1990. For example, in June 1987 it was owed A$1,156 million by its customers for goods and services. As in any business, it was prudent to make some provision for the possibility that all these bills would not be paid. News Corporation provided for A$31 million. Three years later when the amount owed was two-fifths higher, at A$1,660 million, News Corporation provided only fractionally more, A$34 million (source: SEC 20-F filings).

11. *Financial Times*, 28 September 1990.

12. By the summer of 1991 News Corporation had still not issued any non-voting shares.

13. *Financial Times*, 28 September 1990.

14. Ibid.

15. *Financial Times*, 28 September 1991.

16. *Sydney Morning Herald*, 2 February 1991.

17. *Independent*, 3 October 1990.

18. *Financial Times*, 4 April 1991.

19. In conversation with the authors, February 1991.

20. Override Agreement, appendix.
21. *Financial Times*, 4 April 1991.
22. *Financial Times*, 4 April 1991.
23. *Wall Street Journal*, 19 October 1990.
24. *Financial Times*, 24 October 1990.
25. Memorandum to 'Dolphin Lenders', 19 December 1990.
26. *Financial Times*, 4 February 1991.
27. *Sydney Morning Herald*, 14 November 1990; *Independent*, 16 November 1990.
28. Conversation with Australian banker, February 1991.
29. *Financial Times*, 4 February 1991.
30. Memorandum to 'Dolphin Lenders', 19 December 1990.
31. Ibid.
32. *Financial Times*, 4 January 1991.
33. *Financial Times*, 31 December 1990.
34. *Financial Times*, 8 January 1991.
35. Override Agreement, clause 8.2(B).
36. Explanatory Memorandum relating to Override Agreement, 13 December 1990.
37. Ibid., clause 8.1.
38. Override Agreement, clause 22.1.
39. Memorandum to 'Dolphin Lenders', 3 January 1991.
40. *Financial Review*, 31 January 1991.
41. *Financial Times*, 19 February 1991.
42. *Marketing Week*, 5 April 1991; *Guardian*, 25 March 1991.
43. *Independent*, 3 April 1991.

Chapter 13   The Future

1. Memorandum to 'Dolphin Lenders', 19 December 1990.
2. 20-F Filing with the Securities and Exchange Commission, Washington DC, USA, 1988, p. 49.

Index

Index

Index

Kerr, Sir John 43-4
Khemlani, Tirath 43
Kiernan, Thomas 35, 80
Kinnock, Neil 99, 182
Kluge, John 90, 101, 105, 114
Knight, Andrew 187
Knightley, Philip 79, 82
Koch, Edward 24, 46

Lamb, Larry 21, 75
Lambton, Lord 195
Lamont, Norman 83
Lane, Ann 264, 271
Late Show 119
Lex column 207, 244
Lippincott, J.B. 241
Lloyd, Peter 187
Lloyds Bank 263
'loans affair' 42-3
London Post 88-9, 90-1, 92
London School of Economics 232
London Weekend Television (LWT) 22,
    25, 38-9, 100
Long, Gerald 61, 68-9
Lowy, Frank 142
Luxembourg 162
Lyntress 251-3

McDonald, Keith 138, 142
Mackenzie, Kelvin 97
MacPhee, Ian 136, 141
Mandarin Chinese Restaurant 176
Manufacturers Hanover 263
Marco Polo satellite 170-1
Marenzi, Gary 191
Margerison, Tom 38
Marks & Spencer 228
Married . . . with Children 121
Martin, Stephen 246-7
Matthews, Bruce 88, 93-4
Matthews, Victor 69
Maxwell, Robert 20, 38, 87, 110, 261
McCabe, Gibson 216
McComas, Bob 132
McEwen, John 19, 37
McKay, Muriel 195
McMahon, William 20-1, 37-8, 39-40
Media Access Project 111, 112-13, 208
Media Partners International (MPI)
    243-5, 255
Melbourne Channel Ten (ATV-10) 25,
    48-58, 126, 140, 143, 144
  warehousing of shares 55-7
Menzies, Robert 18, 19
Mercedes advertising 167
Metromedia 29-30, 90, 105-6, 113-14
MGM Studios 190
Midland Bank 255, 258, 262, 263

Milken, Michael 105, 114
Mirabella 224, 275, 276
Mirror Newspapers Limited 17
Mitchell, Austin *see under* Sky Television
Monopolies and Mergers Commission 26,
    31, 62, 73-4
Moore, Frank 151-2
More 217
Morgan Grenfell 20, 48-9, 50
Morling, Mr Justice Trevor Reese 57-8
Morris, Stuart 54-6
Ms 216
MTV 164
Muir, Sir Laurence 140
'Murdoch amendments' 25, 58
Murdoch, Anna (née Torv) 18, 19, 95,
    194-5
Murdoch, Dame Elizabeth 18, 71
Murdoch, Patricia (née Booker) 17
Murdoch, Rupert
  American citizenship 29, 106, 108-9,
    114, 126-7, 144, 146
  American satellite 155
  Australian Labour Party 19-20, 40
  bankers 32-3, 120, 294
  corporate culture 6-11
  Daily Mirror (UK) 4-5, 21
  debt 20, 32
  editorial interference 4
  editors 6-7
  family fears of kidnap 195
  family stake in News Corporation 260,
    274
  father 16, 199
  Geelong Grammar 15
  hands-on manager 19
  inheritance 1, 16
  left-wing 34
  monopoly 5
  nickname the 'Dirty Digger' 60, 61, 195
  objections to 'preachy editorial' 213,
    242
  Oxford University 3, 15-16, 34-5
  personal share dealings 203-6, 245
  polite English society 194-5
  politics 3-4, 23, 35
  press conferences 177
  Ronald Reagan 77, 78
  sackings 214
  tied into Override Agreement 274
Murdoch, Sir Keith 1, 15-16, 25, 228, 229
  effect of his death on his son 229
  Herald and Weekly Times 16
  will 16, 199
Myerson, Beth, 46

National Australia Bank 263
National Enquirer 23

333

Index